"Thanks in large part to the lessons in this book, the success of United Way Women's Leadership Councils is beyond our expectations. Yours could be, too. Start by reading this book!"

—Linda Paulson, director of strategic markets,
United Way Worldwide, New York, New York

"Anyone involved with donor education will benefit from this wise, clear, story-filled book. *Women and Philanthropy* shows step-by-step how to design programs that will nurture women from their first tentative gifts into their full philanthropic leadership."

—Anne and Christopher Ellinger, founders, Bolder Giving
in Extraordinary Times and *More Than Money Journal*,
Boston, Massachusetts

"A great resource for the women's funding movement, this book demystifies women's giving."

—Jacki Zehner, former Goldman Sachs Partner; vice-chair,
The Women's Funding Network, New York, New York

"When it comes to advancing women's philanthropy and giving circles, there are few other leaders who match the passion and knowledge of these authors. I recommend this book to everyone who cares about raising more money while addressing important transformational changes in our society."

—Tracy Gary, philanthropist, nonprofit entrepreneur, and legacy
mentor; and author of *Inspired Philanthropy*, Houston, Texas

"Real experts in the field share their energetic, imaginative look at the force women have become in philanthropy. The authors provide many excellent workshop pages set up for duplication and use with staff, trustees, donors, or students. *Women and Philanthropy* is a book I will use all the time."

—Claire Gaudiani, former president, Connecticut College; author,
*The Greater Good: How Philanthropy Drives the American
Economy and Can Save Capitalism*, New York, New York

"*Women and Philanthropy* provides a thoughtful and comprehensive donor education curriculum that will be a valuable tool for organizations and individual advisors to empower female donors to reach their full philanthropic potential."

—Dune Thorne, principal and client advisor,
Silver Bridge Advisors, Boston, Massachusetts

"For a generation, these authors have been pointing women and men who care about fundraising in the right direction, and this book is important to all those who care about the future of philanthropy."
—Bruce W. Flessner, founder and principal,
Bentz Whaley Flessner, Minneapolis, Minnesota

"Warning: This book, written by the modern founders of their field, outlines practical and new tools to unleash women's philanthropy. Are you ready?"
—Lisa Witter, chief strategy officer, Fenton Communications; and coauthor with Lisa Chen of *The She Spot: Why Women Are the Market for Changing the World and How to Reach Them*, Brooklyn, New York

"*Women and Philanthropy* illustrates how and why younger, diverse generations of women feel compelled to create their own philanthropic journey and be role models for their peers."
—Beverley Francis, president and CEO, The Columbia Foundation, Howard County, Maryland's Community Foundation, Columbia, Maryland

"This book does a wonderful job tracing the evolution and deepening impact of women's philanthropy through the generations. This accessible volume captures how women's philanthropic identities are distinct from those of men, informed by the myriad roles they have to balance as well as the life stages that continue to render those roles poignant over time."
—Sharna Goldseker, director of 21/64, a consulting division of the Andrea and Charles Bronfman Philanthropies, New York, New York

"I was introduced to the exciting world of women's philanthropy by Martha Taylor and it changed my life. This book will impact the lives of all women who already are philanthropists, large or small, or want to become one. The guidebook we have all been waiting for, *Women and Philanthropy* provides the tools women need to use the power of their wealth to transform institutions and our lives."
—Joy Picus, philanthropist, former member of the Los Angeles City Council, Los Angeles, California

"The founders of the women's philanthropy movement have done it again! After catalyzing the explosion of interest in women's philanthropy over 15 years ago with *Reinventing Fundraising*, Shaw-Hardy and Taylor bring us the must-have guide to helping women shape the future of our world through philanthropy."

—Ellen Remmer, president and CEO,
The Philanthropic Initiative, Boston, Massachusetts

"This new book from the authors of the seminal book on women's philanthropy celebrates the impact of their work and that of many others to help women break the 'philanthropy glass ceiling.' The ceiling may be shattered, but much work is left to be done. This book will motivate women to 'be bold!'"

—Cheryl L. Altinkemer, associate vice president for
advancement, Purdue University, Lafayette, Indiana

"While Shaw-Hardy and Taylor are rightly recognized as pioneers in the field of women's philanthropy, their foremothers like Mary Lyon, Sophia Smith and Ellen Browning Scripps—all who founded colleges for women using either their own funds or those they had raised—would also extol the virtues of Sondra's and Martha's groundbreaking work, and would each want to have a copy of *Women and Philanthropy*."

—Trish Jackson, vice president for development,
Smith College, Northampton, Massachusetts

"In the world of philanthropy, these authors once again raise the critical role that women continue to play in its evolution. It's a must-read for all boards, organizational and institutional leaders and staff who are engaged in raising support with and from women. As the title suggests, it's bold!"

—Cynthia Woolbright, founder and principal,
The Woolbright Group, Webster, New York

"Board members and nonprofits alike will benefit from this winning combination of the nuts and bolts and inspirational stories."

—Diane Thornton, director of planned giving, University of
St. Thomas; board member, Planned Giving Council
of Houston, Houston, Texas

"This is the definitive book on women and their historical quest toward philanthropic significance."

—Margaret May Damen, president and CEO, the Institute for Women and Wealth, Inc.; and coauthor of *Women, Wealth, and Giving*, Palm City, Florida

"*Women and Philanthropy* is an exciting read not only for the development professional, but also for the emerging women philanthropist. It affirms many of her innate instincts about wanting to change and improve the world, as well as provides inspiring role models and practical advice on how to do so."

—Christine Lodewick, community volunteer and philanthropist; University of Wisconsin Foundation and Women's Philanthropy Council board member

"This book is a wake-up call for fundraisers and boards who have yet to recognize the important role women of all ages play in today's philanthropy."

—Wanda Gottschalk, chief development officer, Child Saving Institute, Omaha, Nebraska

"*Women and Philanthropy* offers guidance to all nonprofits on how to engage and support the charitable dreams of women, who now more than ever before have the powerful assets, empathic visions, and dynamic diversity to contribute to social change."

—Jessica Chao, principal, Lotus & Grain LLC, and former executive, Rockefeller Philanthropy Advisors, New York, New York

"This book shines a lantern on common mistakes, misperceptions, and bad practices of fund development operations that have resulted in the under-involvement of female supporters. Best of all, the book provides hundreds of practical tips and strategies that could help organizations connect with the needs, values, and aspirations of women philanthropists and inspire increased and sustained support from them."

—Lorraine F. del Prado, senior director of development, Seattle Children's Hospital Foundation, Seattle, Washington

WOMEN AND PHILANTHROPY

Boldly Shaping a Better World

SONDRA SHAW-HARDY

AND

MARTHA A. TAYLOR

WITH

BUFFY BEAUDOIN-SCHWARTZ

Foreword by Debra Mesch and Andrea Pactor

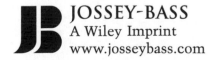

JOSSEY-BASS
A Wiley Imprint
www.josseybass.com

Published by Jossey-Bass
A Wiley Imprint
989 Market Street, San Francisco, CA 94103-1741—www.josseybass.com

Library of Congress Cataloging-in-Publication Data

Shaw-Hardy, Sondra.
    Women and philanthropy: boldly shaping a better world / Sondra Shaw-Hardy and Martha A. Taylor, with Buffy Beaudoin-Schwartz; foreword by Debra Mesch and Andrea Pactor. —1st ed.
        p.   cm.
    Includes bibliographical references and index.
    ISBN 978-0-470-46066-5 (hardback)
        1. Women philanthropists—United States.   2. Fund raising—United States.
I. Taylor, Martha A.   II. Beaudoin-Schwartz, Buffy.   III. Title.
HV27.S533   2010
361.7'40820973—dc22

                                                                        2010027002

Printed in the United States of America
FIRST EDITION
HB Printing   10 9 8 7 6 5 4 3 2 1

Contents

Web Contents

FREE
Premium Content
▼

JOSSEY-BASS™
An Imprint of
🕭WILEY

This book includes premium content that can be accessed from our Web site when you register at **www.josseybass.com/go/shaw-hardy** using the password *professional*.

Worksheet 2.1: Women's Philanthropic Potential

Worksheet 7.1: Active Listening Skills by Dr. Alma Baron

Sample Focus Group Questions

Higher Education Case Studies

Planning and Carrying Out Your Own Successful Power of the Purse Event:

> Planning a Successful Power of the Purse Event

> "Women's Philanthropy: Empowerment, Passion & Impact"—A Sample Email Campaign

Giving Circles and the Nine Cs of Women's Giving

Organization Case Studies

Suggested Donor Panel Topics

Inspired Legacies Youth Giving Circle PowerPoint Presentation

Benchmarks and Resources

The Importance of Research to Women's Giving Circles

Bread Upon the Waters: Women Philanthropists' Impact on America—Keynote by Martha Taylor at Eau Claire, Wisconsin, and UW Madison

Book Discussion Questions

Whys and Hows of Starting a Women's Giving Circle—PowerPoint Presentation by Sondra Shaw-Hardy for Inspired Legacies

Survey of the Relationship Between Women's Generation and Their Philanthropy

To the bold and brave women of the past and present who have made women's philanthropy a movement that stands for equality, justice, peace, and a sustainable world for all. And particularly to those who in the future will lead women's philanthropy to even greater heights. Through their efforts, inspiring all those who will follow, the world will be a better place, not only for women and girls, but for all humankind.

Foreword

THIS BOOK SHOULD BE REQUIRED READING FOR EVERYONE WHO cares about bringing as many individuals and resources as possible to the table to advance the public good, whether they are fundraisers or donors, men or women. The truth, plain and simple, is that stereotypes linger when one uses the words *women* and *philanthropy* in the same sentence. This book offers solid evidence that women's philanthropy is not a trend or a passing fancy, but that it has become, in rich and varied ways, an important component of the philanthropic landscape.

Women's philanthropy emerged as a field over the past forty years to bring attention to and raise the profile of what women have been doing for hundreds of years in the United States: investing their intellectual, financial, social, and cultural capital in improving the world around them. The goal has been to change the way people think about women and philanthropy, to see women as partners at the philanthropic table. The world underrates women's philanthropic capacity and impact. When Shaw-Hardy and Taylor published their first book on women's philanthropy in 1995, *Reinventing Fundraising: Realizing the Potential of Women's Philanthropy*, the notion of women's philanthropy was a novelty. Although women had made significant gains in business and professions, philanthropy was still perceived as a man's world. In some corner offices, that perception remains.

What is different about the contemporary women's philanthropy movement is women's increasing access to the financial resources to make serious change. In the past forty years, American women have enjoyed more access to education and income than ever before. Benefiting from the momentum of the women's movement of the 1960s and 1970s, women began to approach philanthropy intentionally and strategically. They created new models of engagement. In 1972, the first women's fund, the Ms. Foundation for Women, was created and began a trajectory that continues unabated. Women's funds are generally founded and led by women and allocate grants to support programs for women and girls. Giving circles were another new model that attracted scores of women in large and small communities around the country. Women's philanthropic initiatives grew on campuses as well, encouraged by Taylor's initial efforts at the University of Wisconsin in 1988. Women leveraged their capital outside and inside the mainstream.

At the same time, researchers began to explore gender differences in philanthropy. Historians documented the rise of women's benevolent associations in the nineteenth century and told of wealthy women philanthropists who contributed significantly to the growth of higher education and arts institutions. Economists began to ask about gender differences in altruism and generosity and the influence of women in making charitable decisions in households. Sociologists and psychologists examined leadership issues and charitable inclinations. Those in the field of religious studies examined the impact of religiosity on overall charitable giving.

This interdisciplinary perspective toward research in this field has shown that men and women do indeed differ in their approaches to philanthropy. Much of the conventional wisdom, which holds that women do not have the capacity, interest, or resolve for philanthropy, is simply inaccurate today. A different perspective is needed, one that recognizes that just as men and women have different communication and leadership styles, their motivations for and patterns of giving differ as well. Shaw-Hardy, Taylor, and Beaudoin-Schwartz, through their stories, discourse, and interviews, demonstrate that what works for men often does not work for women.

Is what is good for politics and business good for philanthropy? In *Women Lead the Way*, author Linda Tarr-Whelan affirms that moving beyond tokenism to balanced leadership moves the conversation beyond gender to focus on issues. She writes that since the

Fourth UN conference on Women in Beijing in 1995, 23 countries around the globe have met or exceeded the goal for one-third of their legislature to be women and 101 countries are working to reach that goal. As early as 1977, Harvard Business School professor and prolific author Rosabeth Moss Kanter argued that a critical mass of one-third of women in corporate decision-making roles positively affects outcomes. Research by Catalyst shows that Fortune 500 companies that have more women on boards make more money than those with fewer women. These are only a few examples of what happens when women fully contribute in society.

What distinctive traits do women bring to the philanthropic table? The list closely resembles leadership styles that are more and more in demand in today's workplace: collaboration, communication, consensus, building relationships, imagination, inspiration, ingenuity, and networking. With these assets in hand and the rich capital that women can leverage, what hinders the full blossoming of women in philanthropy?

Two key stakeholder groups resist fully accepting and integrating women at the philanthropic table. One group is fundraisers. Not all, but some fundraisers are reluctant to change the status quo, and may perceive that women are irrational, take too long to make a decision, or give small gifts. The other group is women. Yes, some women, often well-meaning and with the best of intentions, enervate the field with reluctance to think of themselves as philanthropists and an unwillingness to seek and receive public recognition for their gifts. Although such public recognition goes against the grain of how women are socialized, this barrier impedes recognition of the capacity, influence, and power of women to contribute substantial wealth for the public good.

Women and Philanthropy shatters those perceptions. Readers will learn to see with new eyes the philanthropic landscape and the potential for women's involvement. With a broad overview of the field and stories that demonstrate time and again women's philanthropic capacity, commitment, and leadership, this book presents a compelling case for increased attention to women in philanthropy.

What is the goal of women's philanthropy? Ask five people and you will likely receive five different answers to this question. For some the goal is parity, ensuring that women are at the philanthropic table as often as men. For others, the goal is equality: women are asked for gifts as often as men, and they are treated equally with men. For some the goal is increased visibility for women's roles in philanthropy as donors, fundraisers, volunteers, leaders, and mentors. And for others, the goal is diversity, because with diversity, different perspectives are represented, contributing to a richer understanding of the issues at hand. For still others, the goal is inclusivity, that philanthropy includes *all* people from across the world, rich and poor, white and black, men and women of all faiths and cultures, because we are stronger when all participate in finding solutions to challenging issues.

At the Center on Philanthropy's 2008 symposium, *Moving Women's Philanthropy Forward*, center staff announced the creation of a new award, the Shaw-Hardy Taylor Achievement Award for extraordinary contributions to advancing women's philanthropy. It was fitting that Sondra Shaw-Hardy and Martha Taylor receive the first award. They saw the potential for women's involvement in philanthropy long before it became a trend or a strategy to enrich the philanthropic table. They created an organization to advance women's philanthropy that evolved into the Women's Philanthropy Institute, now housed at the Center on Philanthropy at Indiana University. Their vision, commitment, and pioneering spirit have never wavered. This book is a testament to them, as well as to the field of women's philanthropy.

Debra Mesch, Director
Andrea Pactor, Associate Director
Women's Philanthropy Institute at the
Center on Philanthropy at Indiana University
June 2010

Preface

WOMEN AND PHILANTHROPY, WOMEN'S PHILANTHROPY: HOW THE meaning of those words has changed. When one of us, Martha Taylor, began talking about the subject in 1988, people often looked confused. Some even said that "women and philanthropy" was an oxymoron. Many others believed philanthropy was strictly associated with men because it was men who had the money. If women gave at all, it was to the causes to which their husbands or their families gave. So they said. But Martha knew, from both her academic and practical perspectives, that something was wrong with this philanthropic picture. Were women not giving? If so, why was that?

She began asking questions: Why weren't women giving to their universities in the same numbers they were represented as students and alumna? Why were so many more men than women in positions of leadership within advancement? Why were so few buildings, programs, and scholarships named after women? Why were schools of liberal arts, education, human ecology, social services, and nursing not being funded to the same degree as business, engineering, and athletics? Martha asked coauthor Sondra Shaw-Hardy, a fundraising colleague in Madison, Wisconsin, to help her learn more. Together we set out to find answers.

We interviewed hundreds of women philanthropists and development officers throughout the country, conducted numerous focus groups, and presented to scores of community and national organizations and institutions. The result—at the urging of Martha's mother,

Esther Hougen Taylor—was our first book, *Reinventing Fundraising: Realizing the Potential of Women's Philanthropy*, published in 1995 by Jossey-Bass.

THE BOLD NEW PHILANTHROPY

Philanthropy has changed a great deal in the last two decades. Even a few years ago, scarcely anyone was talking about passion, values, vision, and responsibility. Now those terms and usage are commonplace. Now they mean women's philanthropy. In effect, women's philanthropy has led the way and "reinvented" fundraising.

But some still don't understand that "women's philanthropy" is no contradiction in terms. Too often women still are not taken seriously as philanthropists, and when they are, the ways in which women are approached to give don't take into account how women give and what they care about.

We felt called on to address these continuing issues, to spread an understanding that women are perhaps the largest of their donor constituencies. We feel there's a need to update the concepts of fundraising that best appeal to women and will lead to the creation of more women philanthropic leaders.

Add to this the fact that many nonprofit computer systems are designed to credit only one donor per address record—and generally that's the man, or at best "Mr. and Mrs. John Doe." And finally, *women's philanthropy* has not yet become a mainstream term meaning "shaping a better world."

In our research, we turned up a number of topics that people want explored:

- What is behind the women's philanthropy movement?
- In what ways have women changed philanthropy?
- Has women's philanthropy brought about social change? In what ways?
- How can women donors' loyalty be maintained after a gift has been made?
- What ethnic and cultural differences are important in women's giving? How are younger generations of women giving?

- How can nonprofit institutions develop more women donors and what does that mean to their future?
- Are women accepting the power of their new status as philanthropic leaders?
- How should women be encouraged to become philanthropic leaders and to encourage others to become leaders as well?
- What might the world look like if women's philanthropy was the accepted way for everyone to give?

Once again we set out after answers, approaching colleagues in the field, many of whom were working with women donors, developing different approaches and programs and eager to share their results.

Women philanthropists themselves were also extremely forthcoming. They talked to us about the joy they received from giving and the responsibility they felt to give to their communities, their nation, and the world. They shared stories quite different from ones we heard in the 1990s.

This time around, women were anxious to lead the way in philanthropy and to educate, inspire, and encourage others as well. They were happy to be recognized for their gifts—to be role models for others. They had become bold about their philanthropy, not only in terms of large gifts but also in daring, dauntless, and audacious efforts to make a better world.

Much of what we record in *Women and Philanthropy* will become the norm for all future fundraising. Women's philanthropy has reinvented fundraising and will continue to do so.

A TOUR OF *WOMEN AND PHILANTHROPY*

Many, many topics bear on women's philanthropy—values, passion, compassion, ideals, socialization, generation, gender, and experience among them. Appreciating this is important to understanding how best to engage women as donors. We recommend reading *Women and Philanthropy* in its entirety, starting at the beginning. The chapters group themselves into four general themes: gender differences and potential, how women give and their motivations, reaching women donors, and the impact of women's philanthropy.

Each chapter includes examples of women philanthropists and their giving motivations and ways to apply the knowledge gained from each section and concludes with "Takeaways" summarizing the chapter material.

Acknowledging the Differences: Chapters One and Two—Why women's philanthropy is different and its importance to the future of nonprofits.

Chapter One describes gender differences in women's and men's actions, giving, and communicating. Reasons for these differences are discussed as well as strategies to address and recognize these special traits and their importance and benefit to nonprofits.

Chapter Two documents women's potential for giving and reviews the expansion of women in the workplace, their economic gains, increased career choices, and educational achievements. This chapter describes how women have taken control of their finances and consequently their lives. It identifies the new woman philanthropist, how much she is giving, and where. Chapter Two concludes with how one university invested in women and changed the culture of giving at the institution.

The Hows and Whys of Women's Philanthropy: Chapters Three through Five—How women give, what women want, and their characteristics as donors.

Chapter Three looks at the modern women's philanthropy movement and the media's role in creating and shaping it. Stereotypes of women's giving are detailed with ideas for overcoming any barriers that may still exist.

Chapter Four describes the motivations of women givers using the core six Cs: create, change, commit, connect, collaborate, and celebrate, as well as the three new Cs that have resulted from women's philanthropy: control, confidence, and courage. It also suggests how to incorporate the Cs into development efforts.

Chapter Five features issues that impact women's giving, including life stages and life styles, with a particular emphasis on generation. Through stories and case studies from each generation, readers will learn how to approach women "of a certain age."

Building Bridges to the Other Half: Chapters Six through Nine are strategies to involve more women in philanthropic leadership and build lifelong relationships and loyalties.

Chapter Six contains important information about how to assess an organization's readiness to better engage women donors:

development office strategies; successful methods to reach women through the annual fund, major gifts, planned giving, and other fundraising programs; and prospecting for women donors.

Chapter Seven describes the qualities that women bring to philanthropy and how those qualities can benefit nonprofits. The importance and benefits of including women in nonprofit leadership positions are contained in the chapter as well as suggestions for developing women leaders and philanthropists.

Chapter Eight is all about women's philanthropic program development. The focus is on women's philanthropic initiatives in higher education and giving circles. Explanations are provided of how the philosophies and characteristics of these programs are applicable to all other nonprofits as well.

Chapter Nine examines the five stages of women's philanthropic journey and how women view nonprofits at each stage. A particular focus of the chapter is on donor education. A complete syllabus is provided using "best practices" and showing how best to present this new financial and philanthropic program to women.

The Future of Philanthropy: Chapters Ten and Eleven—the impact and future of the women's philanthropy movement.

Chapter Ten looks at how bold women are elevating philanthropy to new levels. Special attention is on women's funds and increasing diversity in women's philanthropy. New iterations of women's giving are described as well as how they occurred: the women, the cause, and the result.

Chapter Eleven addresses the need to institutionalize women's philanthropy and speculates about how the world might look if women working together and with nonprofits used their particular traits, power, and philanthropy to address the bracing issues of today.

WHO WILL WANT TO READ
WOMEN AND PHILANTHROPY?

Women and Philanthropy is intended for all those wanting to know more about philanthropy. It will appeal to all genders, races, and diverse communities. It will be of particular interest to development officers, philanthropists, volunteer fundraisers, staff and board members of nonprofit organizations, foundations and corporate executives, fundraising consultants, women's organizations, financial advisors, computer software firms, marketers, politicians and government officials, educators, and anyone interested in the status, roles, responsibility, and power of women in American society.

A NEW PARTNER

Much of our research over the past twenty years has focused on the differences in giving styles in different generations. Generations that were merely dots on the horizon in 1995 have since come to the forefront, in particular Gen X (born between roughly 1965 and 1976) and Gen Y (born between roughly 1977 and 1985). To adequately explore and represent them in *Women and Philanthropy*, we brought in Buffy Beaudoin-Schwartz. Apart from her credentials in philanthropy, Buffy is a wife and mother of four children from toddler to teens, which makes her very much aware of the important issues facing women and families today. We are proud to have her on board.

Our vision has always been to help women work as partners with other women and with development professionals to bring about change and help create the kind of world that will become their legacy. Our lives have been dedicated to women and philanthropy, and the results have been extremely gratifying. We know that women's philanthropy can bring about the kind of changes in the world that will better our children's and grandchildren's lives.

Acknowledgments

WOMEN AND PHILANTHROPY IS THE RESULT OF THE COLLABORATIVE and sharing efforts of so many remarkable women, and some men as well. Our book could not have been written without their continuing belief in women and philanthropy, their constant support, their research, and their originality in helping design programs appealing to women donors. Words are our tool to express our heartfelt gratitude for the emotion we so strongly feel for all these wonderful people.

We are also indebted to the Center on Philanthropy at Indiana University and its former executive director, Dr. Eugene R. Tempel, who long ago recognized the importance of women and philanthropy. In 2004 the Women's Philanthropy Institute (WPI), cofounded by Martha and Sondra, became part of the Center's programming through the work of Tempel and of WPI's president, Cheryl Altinkemer. This happy merger between an internationally recognized research institution and an organization dedicated to gender diversity has strengthened both groups, and we are proud to have been a part of that process and to remain involved. Special thanks go to Tempel, now president and CEO of Indiana University Foundation, for his foresight, and to Altinkemer for her commitment and perseverance in helping bring about this joining of important efforts.

The Center has clearly demonstrated, through research, that talking about the differences in the ways women and men are giving is not sexist or stereotypical, but statistical and representative. This quantitative research gives great credence to our previous anecdotal research, and we are happy to feature it prominently in *Women and Philanthropy*. The Center understands the excitement about and value of the subject and has both convened two national symposiums dedicated to the topic[1] and focused its significant publishing efforts, through New Directions for Philanthropic Fundraising and the Center's own resources, on six books whose theme is women and philanthropy, two of which are available online.[2] The Center also has a two-day course on the topic and an online course developed with the *New York Times Knowledge Network*.

Nothing as significant as a social movement can happen without the support of hundreds. We thank the many women, and a number of men as well, who have dedicated their efforts to bringing women's philanthropy to our institutions and organizations. Together, we created a movement.

In particular, we want to thank the scores of women who helped create and carry on the Women's Philanthropy Institute from the time it was the National Network on Women as Philanthropists to its becoming the Women's Philanthropy Institute and now a program of the Center on Philanthropy. The women who were presidents, board members, and executive directors during its infancy and adolescence deserve special recognition: Andrea Kaminski, Debra Engle, Patricia Lewis, Ellen Remmer, Jane Justis, Joy Picus, Meg Hendricks, Kay Ballard, Mary Pat Berry, Kay Sprinkle Grace, and, of course, Cheryl Altinkemer. When writing this book, we once again realized how much Kaminski contributed to the earlier book in all ways, including the often very tedious job of references and endnotes. We are sure to have missed others who were part of this journey; we apologize and hope they understand that their efforts did not go unnoticed and are greatly appreciated.

Women and Philanthropy could not have been completed without the superb editing of Heather Shaw, who also edited *Reinventing Fundraising: Realizing the Potential of Women's Philanthropy*. Our everlasting gratitude to Sondra's daughter, who thoughtfully and professionally made *Women and Philanthropy* possible. Other editors who were a very important part of the process were Alan Venable and Kristi Hein, as well as the extraordinary staff at Jossey-Bass who supported us daily on this incredible journey. We thank them all.

We are most grateful for the everlasting support from Buffy's husband, Howard Schwartz, and Martha's husband, Gary Antoniewicz. Their patience and enthusiasm for our work were incredible.

And finally, a very special thanks to Jack Christensen, Sondra's beau, for sharing the time while she wrote this book and keeping her balanced while "holding her feet to the fire" to be sure it was done on schedule.

About the Authors

SONDRA SHAW-HARDY, J.D., was described by *Town & Country* magazine as "the pioneer" in women's philanthropy. Since 1995 she has authored, coauthored, or coedited five books: *Reinventing Fundraising: Realizing the Potential of Women's Philanthropy*; *Creating a Women's Giving Circle: A Handbook*; *The Transformative Power of Women's Philanthropy*; *Youth Giving Circles: Inspiring Youth to Bring About Change*; and *Women's Giving Circles: Reflections from the Founders*.

An advancement officer for over twenty-five years, her work has been quoted in national and international media. She has founded or cofounded numerous nonprofit groups and, with Martha Taylor, cofounded the Women's Philanthropy Institute, now a program of the Center on Philanthropy at Indiana University.

Visualizing the growth of women's philanthropy, Shaw-Hardy chaired the first national meeting on the subject, *Women and Philanthropy: A National Agenda*, in 1993 at the Johnson Foundation at Wingspread.

After she formed one of the first giving circles in the nation in 1999 in Traverse City, Michigan, Shaw-Hardy's dream was that every city in the United States would have a women's giving circle. Some ten years later these giving circles number in the hundreds, and Shaw-Hardy has helped initiate scores of them. She has been called "the mother of giving circles."

The Center on Philanthropy at Indiana University awarded Shaw-Hardy and Martha Taylor the first Shaw-Hardy Taylor

Achievement Award for Extraordinary Contributions to Moving Women's Philanthropy Forward in 2008.

Shaw-Hardy was an elected official and is a philanthropist and an active community volunteer in Traverse City. She is the mother of three grown children and a proud grandmother.

As a vice president of the University of Wisconsin Foundation, MARTHA A. TAYLOR has been a key player in the growth of one of the most successful institutionally related foundations in the United States. Among public universities, the UW–Madison ranks in the top five for private gifts received. In her more than thirty-year tenure at the Foundation, she has worked in major and principal gifts and philanthropy advising. In 1988 she founded the Foundation's Women's Philanthropy Council, the first women's major gift council at a large coed university.

Envisioning the need to take the women's philanthropy message to a national audience, in 1991 Taylor cofounded, with Sondra Shaw-Hardy, the Women's Philanthropy Institute; again, now at the Center on Philanthropy at Indiana University.

Inspired by the hundreds of women nationally seeking to make change in a different way, in 1995 Shaw-Hardy and Taylor wrote the field's bible, *Reinventing Fundraising: Realizing the Potential of Women's Philanthropy.* In 2006 they coedited *The Transformative Power of Women's Philanthropy.* They have written approximately thirty articles about women's philanthropy and have been widely quoted in most leading newspapers and women's magazines.

Taylor has presented her keynotes and workshops across the United States and abroad. She chaired the first three national conferences on women's philanthropy for the Council for Advancement and Support of Education (CASE) and served as faculty member for others. Her work has been recognized with many awards.

Born in Madison, Taylor grew up in a culturally diverse area in Los Angeles. She is a third-generation graduate of the University of Wisconsin–Madison. She received her master's degree at West Virginia University with her thesis on philanthropy in higher education. Taylor enjoys music and the arts. She is married and has two grown sons.

BUFFY BEAUDOIN-SCHWARTZ is the communications director at the Association of the Baltimore Area Grantmakers, a membership association of 135 foundations and corporate-giving programs. She serves as the national spokesperson on giving circles for the Forum of Regional Associations of Grantmakers and is the coauthor of *A Plan of One's Own: A Woman's Guide to Philanthropy* and *Growing Philanthropy Through Giving Circles* and coauthor of a chapter in *The Transformative Power of Women's Philanthropy*.

Beaudoin-Schwartz was chosen as one of Maryland's Top 100 Women in 2003, 2008, and 2010 by the *Daily Record* newspaper. She was named an "Innovator of the Year" in 2004 by the *Daily Record* for her work with giving circles, and was named one of "40 Under 40" in 2004 by the *Baltimore Business Journal*. Beaudoin-Schwartz is a founder and immediate past chair of the Women's Giving Circle of Howard County and is a founding donor of the B'MORE Fund at the Baltimore Community Foundation. She is an active community volunteer and currently serves as a trustee of the Columbia Foundation. Beaudoin-Schwartz lives in Howard County, Maryland, is married, and has four children.

Women and Philanthropy

PART
ONE

Acknowledging the Differences

1

Women Are Not Little Men

What I find particularly gratifying about the growth of the women's philanthropy movement is not just that more women are participating and at higher giving levels, but that this has caused us to think differently about how we engage women—and men—in philanthropic activity. We are no longer comfortable with "one size fits all." We recognize that people give for different reasons, respond to different messages, and want to be engaged in different ways. And so we conduct research, we test, we ask questions, and we listen. We are more open to exploring new and creative strategies to meet donors on their terms, and in ways that advance their values and the goals of the causes they care about. We have all been enormously enriched by this transformation.[1]

—Edith Falk, chair and CEO,
Campbell & Company, Chicago, Illinois

GENDER DIFFERENCES ARE JUST THAT: DIFFERENCES in the ways women and men think, behave, look, and communicate. (Not to mention our very different reproductive organs and voices.) None of the differences are bad or wrong and, contrary to popular media depictions, it's not a battle of the sexes. That would be defeating for both genders. It's just an understanding that there are differences, and they affect the ways we relate to one another. Male and female complement one another and need one another's differences to improve our world.

Plenty of books, articles, plays, and movies have been written about gender differences, but the book that started a revolution was a small one written in 1982 by Harvard professor Carol Gilligan: *In a Different Voice: Psychological Theory and Women's Development*.[2] In it, Gilligan claims that women had been misunderstood in the past and should be heard in their own voices and with their own sense of integrity. This was a revelation to most people, particularly to many feminists who had claimed there were no differences between males and females.

Gilligan looked at children at play and the sociological messages they received from those around them. From these observations she concluded that women have differing moral and psychological tendencies than men and a different sense of values. Gilligan also said that women think more in terms of relationships, whereas men think in terms of rules. The book rocked the psychological world and continues to do so to this day. We were struck by the book's messages and used them early on in our women's philanthropy work. We could see how these unique differences affected women's motivations for giving as well as the ways women were asked for gifts.

It stood to reason that if women thought in ways different from men, and their values were different, then their philanthropy would be different as well. We concluded that because women thought so much about relationships and caring, they wanted to give to causes that helped solve societal issues. We also took away from Gilligan's book the theory that women needed to find their philanthropic voice and often were interested in doing their philanthropy together, with other women: the philosophy behind women's giving circles and women's philanthropic initiatives.

It is well worth reading *In a Different Voice* today—as women become bigger and better philanthropists—in order to understand, based on the female experience, women's motives and moral commitments as well as their gender's view of what is important in life. Whether or not one agrees with Gilligan's theories, they have inspired new research, educational initiatives, and political debate while helping women and men understand each other in this different light.

This chapter will look at a number of these differences and how they translate into action related to philanthropic work.

NATURE VERSUS NURTURE:
IT ALL STARTS IN THE BRAIN

A number of studies show the vast differences in women's and men's brains and thus their actions. For example, a University of Pennsylvania researcher says men lose their brain tissue three times faster than women, and with it some memory, concentration, and reasoning power. Dr. Ruben C. Gur concludes that's why men's shrinking brains may make them more ill-tempered—hence "grumpy old men."[3]

Then there's the less rigorous conclusion reached by former Harvard president Lawrence Summers that the difference in men's and women's brains could be one explanation for the dearth of women in tenured positions in science and engineering at the country's top universities.[4] This conclusion cost Summers his job and inspired women all over the nation to rise up and claim otherwise. University of Wisconsin's psychology professor Janet Hyde says she was inspired by Summer's remarks to finish her research.[5] In an analysis of about seven million students released in 2006, Hyde concluded that sex differences in math and science are negligible, reinforcing a 1990 analysis she had completed on math.[6]

But it's not about wanting more female brains than male brains, it's about needing all brains. We need all of our brain power to contribute to the intellectual output of this country, including our philanthropy.

Most researchers do agree about two brain facts: men's brains are larger than women's, but women have more neurons[7] and their corpus callosum is larger than men's.[8] This cluster of fibers and tissues connecting the right and left hemispheres of the cerebrum sends information back and forth between the right and left brains. As a consequence of this larger corpus callosum, women can multitask better than men—no doubt necessary when women were caring for children, keeping the home fires going, cooking, making clothing, and working in the fields while the men were out hunting.

A Transfer to Action. Women want to look at all sides of the problem or solution: from both the left side of the brain, or the more practical side, as well as the right side of the brain, the more emotional side. They want to see the big picture, not just one part of it. Give women the whole story—all the links from beginning to end.

COMMUNICATION: SHE SAYS, HE SAYS

Whereas Dr. Gilligan looked at psychological theories in women's and men's development and believed that women's voices hadn't been heard, Deborah Tannen—a linguist, author, and Georgetown professor—wanted to find out whether women's communication was different from men's. Her seminal book, *You Just Don't Understand: Women and Men in Conversation*[9]—in which Tannen said that yes, there were differences in the ways women and men communicate—was a best seller in 1991, and her terms "rapport talk" and "report talk" were tossed around when people discussed those differences: that is, women use conversation as a way to get to know one another, and men converse to impart information.

Tannen wrote about not only the ways women and men talk and the words they use, but their actions as well. To visualize these differences, picture the two men in the 2004 movie *Sideways*. The main characters, Miles and Jack, seemed most comfortable sitting next to one another in a bar or a car. The actors rarely looked one another squarely in the face but rather looked "sideways," invoking an impersonal rather than a personal relationship. Women, on the other hand, are most frequently pictured in films sitting around a table or gathered in a circle, as in the television show *Sex and the City*, where the four women, unless shopping or having sex, are often seated around a table in a restaurant looking one another squarely in the face.

Tannen's theories about women and men communicating, both verbally and through their actions, are as pertinent today as they were when her book was written. Gilligan would add that because women and men are products of different cultures, we have different ways of connecting and communicating with one another.

A Transfer to Action. Read about different styles of gender communications and be aware of them when talking with donors. Recognize women's interest in the personal aspects of your conversation and use it as a discussion before providing a solution.

BELIEFS ABOUT MONEY

Women and men have different feelings and beliefs about money.[10] Many men tend to view increasing their wealth as an end in itself, whereas women often perceive their money in a broader context—

as a means to be independent, care for children, or make philanthropic gifts.

As for how much money is enough, Linda Basch,[11] president of the National Council for Research on Women, says, "For women it's not just the thrill of making money, it's the social purposes that the money can be used for. What we've seen with some women in our research about women in fund management is that they have a sense when they've made enough and they cash out."

Basch points to Jacki Zehner as an example. In 1996 Zehner was the youngest woman and the first female trader to be invited into the partnership of Goldman Sachs. After leaving the firm in 2002 at the age of thirty-five, and having done well financially, she is now committed to doing good through her philanthropy concerning the economic empowerment of women.

Kathryn Hinsch, formerly of Microsoft and founding director and board president of the Seattle think tank Women's Bioethics Project, has her own views about women and money. Hinsch believes that women in their forties and fifties are more likely than men to consider what they want to do for the world rather than the legacy they want to leave for their offspring. "I think of women in my situation as women of means with dreams," Hinsch says.[12]

A Transfer to Action. Consider sponsoring women's donor education programs to help women discover their dreams and discuss money and philanthropy with other women in a controlled and friendly atmosphere. (See Chapter Nine.)

THE DESIRE TO MAKE A DIFFERENCE

Thomas Kavanagh, nonprofit consultant and former vice president for advancement at Northwood University in Midland, Michigan, puts it this way: "Women seem to find satisfaction in knowing that their giving makes a difference in people's lives, whereas men seem to tend more toward supporting institutions that helped them, such as their schools and affiliations from their youth like Scouts, and Boys' and Girls' Clubs."[13]

According to a *Chronicle of Philanthropy* survey, women are more likely than men to contribute to causes they strongly believe in, to carry on their parents' legacy of giving, and to give to a charity linked to an illness. In contrast, Donna Hall, executive director for the Women Donors Network, says that "men are more likely to give to traditional charities, their university, sports clubs, or their churches."[14]

Other significant gender differences in giving have been released by the Center on Philanthropy at Indiana University. The research shows that:

- Women are more likely than men to say they give because those who have more have a responsibility to help those who have less.
- Women are more likely than men to give to meet basic needs and to health issues.[15]

Judith Nichols, a New York–based author and trend analyst, says that although men describe their giving as practical—filling in the gaps that government can't or won't—women describe theirs as emotional, an obligation to help those with less.[16]

A Transfer to Action. Place your organization's or institution's needs in the context of making a difference and changing things for the better. Put a different "spin" on your cause and include the emotional face. Feature programs that help others. Don't be afraid to ask for a cause that is unique and not a mainstream action.

RELATIONSHIP BUILDING

Shaw-Hardy has a Pandora bracelet that other women often comment on, noting its charms and colors. Rather than just saying thank you and moving on, she will generally acknowledge the compliment, then talk a bit about the charms. This usually leads to a discussion in which she and the woman both share something personal.

Deborah Tannen says that personalizing and sharing is a women's thing; that men tend to connect through status, usually through their jobs, whereas women tend to connect through storytelling.[17] All of us remember people or subjects much better if there is a story attached. For one thing, it helps create a connection with the person or the subject. Through storytelling, we find out the details of other people's lives, compare experiences, and discover similarities.

Kay Ballard, former director of major gifts and planned giving for the American Association of University Women Educational

Foundation, puts it this way: "I believe that instead of guiding our potential donors through pages of diagrams, spigots, and flow charts, we should tell interesting stories in an enthusiastic and jargon-free manner. The stories that we tell should give simple examples of financial and family situations that demonstrate how . . . gifts were used to provide beneficial outcomes for the donors involved."[18]

A Transfer to Action. Find similarities between your life and your donor or prospect's life. Find out what experiences have had the greatest impact on her life and share similar happenings that you have had. Tell a personal story or recount a special individual's situation to describe your cause, whether you do this in person or through your communications—tell stories, show people.

ASKING FOR THE GIFT: WHO, WHAT, AND HOW?

How much does the purpose of a gift matter, versus who is asking you to give it? Is there a difference in the ways women and men respond, depending on these factors? Vanderbilt University Dean of Nursing, Colleen Conway-Welch, believes that women and men do respond differently: "Women value the connection with the solicitor and cause while men say that 'who asks' is the most important," she says.[19] In other words, although women will more willingly give when asked by someone they know, the cause must be one that is important to them, one they believe in emotionally, passionately, and compassionately. Men, on the other hand, can often be influenced by their perception of the person doing the asking: Is that person important to their career? Do they owe the asker a gift because he gave to their cause?

Bruce Flessner, founding principal of Bentz Whaley Flessner Consultants in Minneapolis, takes this a step further. "Guys bond through competition," he says. "We can push our close friends for gifts because making it uncomfortable for them is a sign that we are good friends. I don't ever recall hearing a woman say, 'I want to call on my friend Sue and squeeze the last dime out of her.' For men it shows we care."[20]

A Transfer to Action. Review your donor files and find out who is closest to your woman prospect and is also an advocate for the institutional cause. Don't use peer pressure when asking for a gift. However, it's all right to mention others with whom the woman has a relationship to encourage not competition, but *collaboration*.

TIME AND DETAILS

We have found when working with women that they want to hear about all the pieces between the beginning and the end as well as the strategy involved. By way of analogy, men want the executive summary; women want the entire report. Yes, it takes longer to present the entire report; it takes longer to work with women. They often ask more questions and don't jump to a conclusion, even if it seems to be a logical one.

When Shaw-Hardy was raising funds for a political party in Washington, D.C., she worked with political action committees, mostly headed by men. It was pretty easy getting the money because the men just wanted to know what politician the money was for and how much it was going to cost. It was a case of in and out the door or a brief phone call. It surely didn't require much time—but then, it didn't always result in much of a lasting commitment. Of course, the donor expected to have favor with the politician; that was a given. No negotiations even had to take place.

A Transfer to Action. Be prepared to take the time to answer questions and provide more information, with the knowledge that even though a woman may take longer to make a decision, once it's made she will usually stick by it.

RECOGNITION AND ACKNOWLEDGMENT

In research conducted by the National Foundation of Women Business Owners (NFWBO) with corporate women, only 40 percent of these high-powered business women were interested in recognition.[21] According to nonprofit consultant Thomas Kavanagh, that research, completed in 1999, remains true today: "Women donors tend to be very specific in their giving, in that they want to see the results of their giving more than the recognition that accompanies it. Men, on the other hand, seem to like seeing their generosity recognized in more concrete terms, like their name on a building—no pun intended!" Dean Conway-Welch agrees: "Men want recognition and women want involvement when they give."

Philanthropy consultant Robert Sharpe relates it to our earlier point that women want to make a difference. He claims that in his experience, the husband is usually more interested in naming opportunities (he calls it "monument-building"), raising more than the last college class, and advancing his career; women want to make a difference in society and aren't as motivated by a need for recognition.[22]

The issue of recognition wouldn't be complete without talking about anonymity (a generational consideration that we discuss more fully in Chapter Five). Women in the "traditional generation" are more likely to ask for anonymity because it was not considered ladylike in their generation to discuss money and especially not to display it by having their names on buildings. This attitude is changing as women see the necessity of being role models for others; happily, women like Darla Moore (see Chapter Three) and Christine Lodewick enjoy the responses they get from their gift.

Lodewick says she doesn't feel at all uncomfortable being noticed for having given a gift with her husband, Philip, to help build the University of Connecticut Visitor's Center. "People ask if I'm the Lodewick that gave the building, and they do so in a very pleasant way," she says. "I think it's not the name or the money, it's how you act about it. And giving that gift and having my name up there with Philip's name makes me very happy. So others are happy for and with me." Christine credits Philip for encouraging her to put her name on the building as well as his. "He said otherwise no one would ever realize a woman had a part in it."[23]

When cofounding the Three Generations Circle of Women Givers in Traverse City, Michigan, Shaw-Hardy wanted to make sure women would allow their names to be in print. She provided an easy way to do this by asking the women to give their gift in honor or memory of someone in the three generations of their family. Women loved the idea and had no qualms at all about having their thousand-dollar gift mentioned in publications because it was associated with someone very personal to them. We stress this point because there is nothing, absolutely nothing that receives more complaints from women than men being credited for women's gifts. Along that same line, a woman in one of our focus groups complained that she and her spouse gave together to their university, but her husband was the one who always received the invitations to football games. Her husband wasn't interested in going to the games, but she was—although her name wasn't included. One can only wonder how she will feel about the university if and when she becomes a widow.

A Transfer to Action. When a gift is made, ask how the parties would like to be credited. Should it be in her name? In his name? Or in both? Review your nonprofit's record keeping and be sure that it is consistent with the donor's wishes throughout the institution. If a mistake is made and she contacts you, apologize profusely as you change the acknowledgment, and make sure it never happens again. Unless directed not to, always invite both spouses to events.

Encourage women to allow their names be used for their gifts. Be aware that recognition alone is not a motivator for a woman's gift; what counts most to her is the cause itself, how she can be involved, and how her gift will make a difference. Provide opportunities for women to honor and memorialize others through their gifts.

VOLUNTEERING

Women do seem to be more hard-wired than men to be engaged in their communities. According to a *Chronicle of Philanthropy* study, they consider volunteering as part of their lives; by contrast, most men have been socialized to do things and get paid for them. A male volunteer from the same study, Michael Wingfield, who has served alongside both women and men, says, "Men tend to respond to a crisis; they're reactive, and women are proactive. Men sit with their spears waiting for someone to attack the village while the women gather the berries and tend the children and just generally keep everything together."[24]

We have had numerous occasions to serve on boards with men who worked very hard as volunteers. However, until retirement, they seemed less willing to volunteer unless there was a leadership position involved. Women, on the other hand, are usually willing to stuff envelopes and answer the phone, not expecting a reward.

There was a time when women equated giving their time to giving money. But as precious as time is to today's women, most seem to understand the difference now and realize that giving money means being able to have an impact on the organization. This differs from giving time, which is generally more affecting for the person, not the organization.

Women do want to be engaged with the institutions they support. Even in the NFWBO study mentioned earlier, corporate women showed they wanted connection, such as mentoring young women in business schools. Volunteering as a mentor or involvement with students or girls is high on the list of ways women choose their involvement. It is not enough for women to just write a check; they want the personal involvement as well—or at least to be offered the chance.

A Transfer to Action. Debra Mesch, director of the Women's Philanthropy Institute at the Center on Philanthropy at Indiana University, observes that "[t]he likelihood of giving a gift rises with the amount of time volunteered. [In that sense], time definitely is money, and it's well worth the time to develop volunteer activities."[25]

Create a grid for volunteer help and publish this on the organization's Web site or in the media. Inform donors of volunteer opportunities. Include ways for volunteers to work with young people.

Ensure that there is a volunteer coordinator to train and schedule the volunteers. Volunteers understandably get frustrated when they are recruited and then have nothing to do. They become discouraged and disinclined to continue their support with either time or money.

LOYALTY

Investment firms and financial managers have long known that women need more time to make a decision than men do. Lynn M. Schmidt, president of Meritus Financial Group in Elgin, Illinois, says the payoff is a high level of loyalty if women like the service. "Men want less information, but they are less inclined to stick with the plan. They switch around a lot. Women want more education and they take longer to make a decision. But they will stick with the plan and remain loyal to you," Schmidt says.[26]

The same loyalty holds true for women as donors, according to Andrea Pactor, associate director of the Women's Philanthropy Institute. "Women are committed donors who care deeply about the causes they support." Pactor likens this loyalty to that found in the consumer world. "The three main indicators of brand loyalty in the consumer world—trust, commitment, satisfaction—are the same qualities that women donors especially seek in long-term relationships with nonprofits."[27]

A Transfer to Action. Loyalty is deeply associated with stewardship, and both function together. Beyond thanks for the gift also comes the organization's responsibility to retain donors' loyalty by providing accountability and periodic reporting about the impact of their gift. Let donors know that you value their contribution. Their continued interest will sustain their loyalty and belief in you and the organization.

BEQUESTS AND LEGACY GIVING

Bequests have long been popular with women, and a Blackbaud Company study shows that most charitable bequests are given by women. In arranging to give away their money after their death, they don't have to worry about depleting their resources during their lifetime or becoming "bag ladies."[28]

The reasons women give bequests differ significantly from those of men. Women are more likely than men to respond to appeals that focus on the impact a bequest can achieve or on the value of helping those with less, according to research published by the Center on Philanthropy at Indiana University. However, both women and men under forty are more responsive to requests that emphasize basic needs.[29]

Interestingly, in a 2007 survey done by the Association of Healthcare Philanthropy, 54 percent of men over sixty-five with an income of more than $100,000 said they made bequests because charities provide better services than the government.[30] Although the survey doesn't draw any conclusions, many women want to partner with government and think government has a responsibility to be involved.

A Transfer to Action. When working with women donors, emphasize how their bequests will help the organization benefit society and make the world a better place. Encourage women to make a gift during their lifetime so they can enjoy seeing the results.

GLOBAL GIVING

Although many women say they would rather give in their community or to organizations and institutions that directly affect them, more and more women are giving globally. And according to a study conducted by Karen Winterich at Texas A&M Mays Business School, they're more likely than men to support overseas causes.[31]

Why are women more likely than men to give globally? In Shaw-Hardy and Carmen Stevens's 2008 research, many women said they considered themselves "global citizens" or "citizens of the world."[32] These philanthropic women said they give globally because of the extreme need—they see need locally, of course, but also understand the link between local and global issues.

Winterich's study results showed that women are more likely than men to support "out group" causes to which they have no tie, such as international tsunami victims, whereas men are more likely to support national victims or an "in cause." An "in cause" is one that would positively reflect on a person's generosity or was favored by someone whom the person held in high esteem. This ties in with earlier conclusions that women are not so affected by the person asking as they are by the cause.

The spread of global giving, particularly to women in emerging countries, may well have started with microloans to women from the Grameen Foundation—women like Lucy Billingsley of Dallas, who invested through the Grameen Foundation in projects like Chiapas Women.[33]

Billingsley, the only daughter of legendary developer Trammell Crow, was on vacation in San Cristóbal de Las Casas, Chiapas, Mexico, when, while admiring the native women's talent, she also deplored the extreme poverty they endured. She was so moved by what she saw that she took thirty of her Dallas friends to Chiapas to get involved raising money to provide microfinancing (lending money to women who live and raise their family on less than $1 a day) to these women. Ultimately, Billingsley has raised $4 million through the Grameen Foundation. Billingsley reflects the view of many women when she says, "Why did I get opportunity and responsibility? I got it so I could give it again."

Also from Dallas, Trisha Wilson, interior designer for the Atlantis in the Bahamas and the Venetian in Las Vegas, says she will always remember the time when, while on safari, she went into one of the African shacks. There she found a two-year-old who looked like a newborn. "I'll never forget that sight as long as I live. He already had club fingers—his fingers were square. It was heart-wrenching."[34] That was five years ago and since then she formed the Wilson Foundation, providing education and medical help to AIDS-ravaged villages near Wilson's second home in South Africa.

There are many such stories about women who have traveled far and wide, seen the Louvre and the North Pole, ridden camels and visited Dubai. These women want more than just sight-seeing and the ability to talk about their last trip. They have looked around during their travels and seen firsthand and up close the problems of the world through women's eyes. They recognize women all over the globe as their sisters, and they feel that it's their responsibility and a major opportunity to help them break out of poverty. They know that to help a woman is to help a family, a community, and ultimately a world in which they and those they help live, no matter on what part of the globe.

A Transfer to Action. Be aware that women are interested in global causes and see a connection between what is taking place in their neighborhood and what is taking place on another continent. Are there ways that the mission of your institution or organization can embrace a global involvement, especially in Third World countries and particularly to help women and girls? There may be social networks that can be set up between your organization and a similar one in another country. Ask your women donors to help think this through. Not all will be interested in connecting globally, but the trend is definitely there.

TAKEAWAYS

Science shows that there are biological, neurological, and behavioral variations in women's and men's brains—we do think, behave, and communicate differently. Different doesn't mean right or wrong, but if there weren't these differences, we would have had no reason to write *Women and Philanthropy*. However, the fact that the Center on Philanthropy at Indiana University's preliminary research shows that younger men are thinking more like women means that noting gender differences is extremely important to those seeking money from both genders.[35]

Women are a huge and complex group. It takes an investment in time to understand women in totality and individually. But gender plays the biggest part in understanding women's giving motivations, followed by generation.

Consider these gender differences when engaging women donors:

- Women want to see the big picture.
- Women relate to causes through stories.
- Women want their gift to bring about change and make a difference.
- Women use conversation to get to know one another better.
- The cause is more important to women than who is asking.
- Women multitask and want details.
- It may take women a while to make a decision. Some call this "gestation time."
- Being properly credited for the gift is extremely important to women.
- Women are increasingly interested in having their gift publicly recognized, particularly if it serves as a role model for other women.
- Women want opportunities to be engaged with the organization—to volunteer.
- Keep a woman informed, and you can count on her loyalty.
- Women are interested in the potential impact of their bequests.
- Women are more inclined than men are to support global causes.

The Power of the Purse

Arguably, women are now the most powerful engine of global growth ... Forget China, India and the Internet: economic growth is driven by women.

—Economist, April 12, 2006

A woman's nation changes everything about how we live and work today. Now for the first time in our nation's history, women are half of all U.S. workers and mothers are the primary breadwinners or co-breadwinners in nearly two-thirds of American families.

—The Shriver Report: A Study by Maria Shriver and the Center for American Progress, 2009

WOMEN ARE NO LONGER SLEEPING BEAUTIES waiting for Prince Charmings to come. They have awakened and discovered that they must take the business of money—which includes philanthropy—into their own hands. Other significant financial changes relate to women's earnings, the outcomes of marriage and divorce, and the control of inheritance and family foundations.

THE WEALTH THAT WOMEN WILL PASS ON

Paul Schervish and John Havens's 1999 research about the transfer of wealth astonished all of us in the field of philanthropy.[1] At least

$41 trillion would be passed on from members of the World War II generation and aging Baby Boomers over the next forty-five years. Even more astounding, women would eventually control much of the nation's assets simply because they live longer than men and inherit 70 percent of all estates. A golden era of philanthropy was dawning, and women were going to be the decision makers. This staggering information certainly got a lot of attention. But that was just the tip of the iceberg. It was also reported that $6 trillion would be given that year in charitable bequests. The truth is, women have always preferred giving bequests as planned gifts—now they would have even more to give away.

Perhaps even more encouraging were the attitudes of women themselves. They began to realize their potential, their power, and especially their responsibility. And they had questions:

- How can I give my money in strategic ways?
- How can I work with others to leverage my money?
- What are society's needs where I can make a difference?
- How can I inspire others to give?
- What can I do to become a philanthropic leader?
- How can I leave a legacy?

Women Are Giving More Than Men

An ongoing study of donors released by the Center on Philanthropy at Indiana University in 2007 showed that women are more likely to give than men (85.6 percent compared with 80.7 percent), and at the highest income range (above $100,000), women give more, plain and simple. The figures at that level show men giving $3,904 and women giving $4,223 annually.[2]

A Barclays Wealth 2009 study called *Tomorrow's Philanthropist* took income to the next level (over $1 million) and showed that high-net-worth women in the United States give 3.5 percent of their total net worth to charity each year, almost double the 1.8 percent given by men.[3] Generational research from the Center on Philanthropy at Indiana University demonstrated that the Boomer generation began women's lead on giving, and it doesn't stop there: 89 percent of Boomer women give versus 85 percent men; in Gen X the ratio is 89 percent versus 83 percent; and in Gen Y, 80 percent versus 77 percent.[4]

Will this pattern continue? Most likely. At least that's the belief of thoughtful administrators like April Harris, associate vice president for advancement at the University of Alabama in Huntsville. She says, "It's contingent upon us to make sure that our alumni leadership reflects the demographics of our alumni body. Don't underestimate this. We're on the verge of the greatest unleashing of resources since the Middle Ages."[5] A pretty strong statement about women, and again, it shows that Harris realizes women now constitute 58 percent of graduates at colleges today and will be the alumni and the donors of the future.

Women's Gains in Wealth

The Boston Consulting Group, in a 2009 *Newsweek* article, projected an increase in the worldwide income of women by 2013 to $15.6 trillion, up from $5.1 in 2009.[6] That's a difference in women's earnings of $10.5 trillion in just six years. By comparison, the Chinese economy is expected to grow by only $3 trillion. These numbers cause most everyone who hears them to say, "Wow!" But it's time to pay attention not only to the numbers but also to the individual women themselves. There are real women behind the numbers, and their earning capacity and longevity favor them. Women are in line to control their husbands' and families' monies, which means they are going to control philanthropy as well.

You can use the "Women's Philanthropic Potential" questionnaire on the following page to make the point, for both yourself and others. We have found it works very well for creating "Aha!" moments at presentations to groups of women donors as well as male and female development officers, and financial advisors. The questionnaire takes three to five minutes to fill out, and anyone who does so and learns the correct answers will see that women's philanthropic potential is enormous—much more so than he or she may have realized. Not one person out of the hundreds who have taken this quiz has ever correctly answered all the questions—though as a group, the deans at University of Florida had the highest percentage of right answers. We haven't figured out what this group's performance means, other than they are certainly aware of the potential of their alumnae.

WORKSHEET 2.1

Women's Philanthropic Potential

1. One in <u>three</u>/five/eight American women considers herself more involved in financial decisions than five years ago. (Prudential, 2006)

2. Women now own almost one-third/<u>one-half</u>/three-quarters of all publicly traded stock. (The Chicago Network Census)

3. Thirty-two/<u>Forty-three</u>/Sixty-five percent of the nation's top wealth holders (individuals with assets of $1.5 million or more) are women. Assets for these 1,173,000 women were valued at $3.2/4.0/<u>4.6 trillion.</u> (Internal Revenue Service figures for 2004)

4. $5/$25/<u>$41</u> trillion will be transferred to Baby Boomers over the next forty-five years. (*Chronicle of Higher Education,* July 6, 2007)

5. Women outlive men and will inherit 50/60/<u>70</u> percent of all estates. (*Chronicle of Higher Education,* July 6, 2007)

6. Women's philanthropy has increased by more than $8/$10/<u>$15</u> billion annually since 1996. (WOW Facts 2003)

7. Women own 10.4 million firms—nearly one-fourth /one-third/<u>one-half</u>/two-thirds of the privately held businesses in the country—and generate $500 billion/$750 billion/<u>$1.9 trillion</u> in sales. (Center for Women's Business Research, May 22, 2007)

8. In the year 2000, women in the United States earned more than a billion/a billion and a half/<u>a trillion</u> dollars. (Oppenshaw, *CASE Currents,* March, 2002)

9. Women are expected to own half of the wealth in the United States by <u>2010</u>/2020/2025. (*Chronicle of Higher Education,* July 6, 2007)

10. Women of color account for 10/20/<u>27</u> percent of the $3.7 trillion buying power of all women in the U.S. (*The 85% Niche: The Power of Women of All Colors,* Miriam Muley)

11. The largest bulk of inheritance assets eventually will end up in the hands of women in the next five/<u>ten</u>/fifteen years. (*Case Currents,* March 2002)

12. Single females are 2%/5%/<u>10%</u> more likely than males to be donors. (Center on Philanthropy, 2007)

13. At incomes of <u>$100,000</u>/$250,000/$500,000, women give more than men. (Center on Philanthropy, 2007)

14. Men still control family philanthropic decision making. True/<u>False</u>. (Fidelity Charitable Gift Fund Study, 2009)

Note: For your information, the correct answers are underlined. For use as a questionnaire, download Worksheet 2.1 from www.josseybass.com/go/shaw-hardy.

The Growing Power of a Woman's Pen

Given the opportunity, women can be and are being incredibly generous—and they often wield the pen when couples or family foundations give. "Women have always had a hand in their household's charitable outreach," says Fidelity president Sarah C. Libbey, "but that role is evolving as women increasingly create their own wealth and become beneficiaries of wealth transfers because they live longer. We, and other nonprofit organizations, should pay more attention to this very influential group of donors."[7]

Libbey's remarks came after a 2009 Fidelity study indicated that most male respondents named their spouse as the primary influencer in charitable-giving decisions.[8] This is a major change from only a few decades ago, when couples almost always gave where the men wanted to and women had very little say as to philanthropic contributions. As one focus group member commented, "My daughter and son-in-law were graduates of the same school, but she's the only one interested in philanthropy. I know they will give as a couple, but it will be because of her interests in giving, not his."

Because of her background in education, Tashia Morgridge was a strong influence in the $175 million gift she and her husband, John, former CEO of Cisco System, made to the fund for Wisconsin Scholars. A retired school teacher, Tashia was a graduate of the University of Wisconsin–Madison School of Education while John graduated from the Wisconsin School of Business. The gift is designated to help public school graduates attend the state's public universities or technical schools.[9]

And according to research done by the Center on Philanthropy at Indiana University, a great deal of the "power of the pen" lies with single women. In its 2007 research on gender giving, the Center found that single women are 9 to 10 percent more likely to be donors than are single men, giving an average of $630 more per year. Among people with incomes of more than $100,000, women's average total giving was $4,223 compared with men's $3,904.[10] The Fidelity study also noted that women donate an average of 6 percent of their income, and some even up to 10 percent.

Money and Divorce

Lorna Wendt made headlines in 1998 when she sought a fair division in the settlement from her husband of thirty-two years, then a top General Electric executive.[11] Wendt's divorce request argued for half of her husband's assets, estimated at more than $100 million. Wendt explains, "When we started out with nothing, I was an equal partner. And at the end I was, too. In addition to 99 percent of the domestic workload, I was my husband's biggest supporter, married to the company but with no benefits."

Although Wendt ended up with less than half of her husband's estimated assets, the national headlines and the publicity generated about women's role in a marriage had enormous consequences for the ways in which women regard themselves as marital partners. Wendt calls this ". . . the value [women bring] to a marriage," and she established an Institute on Equality in Marriage from what she received in the divorce settlement.

Wendt also viewed the division of the assets as part of her rights as a philanthropist. And she believed she had just as much claim to the money for such purposes as did her former spouse. Fortunately, not every marriage ends as Wendt's did, although her story shows that women are taking control of the money not only outside the home, but inside it, too.

Inheriting Money

It wasn't long ago that most women were often put off by the family's money and the use and abuse of power that came with it. Only recently have women had the confidence to openly accept their inherited money and, by learning and working with others, to invest, spend, and give it away. Jennifer Ladd recalls being twenty-one in 1972 and inheriting nearly a million dollars. Ladd says, "I felt overwhelmed by that gift [from Standard Oil stocks], not liberated. I was keenly aware of the unequal distribution of wealth . . . so I struggled to keep a secret that I was sure would make me a pariah amongst my social justice friends."[12]

Fortunately, Ladd worked through her issues by aligning herself with other young people of wealth with similar values, and she learned not just to give away money, but to do so ". . . strategically and thoughtfully in collaboration with others."

Times change, and younger women are less squeamish about money. According to research published by Shaw-Hardy and Carmen Stevens in 2008, 58 percent of Gen X women (born between 1961 and 1980) expect to inherit and are preparing themselves for it.[13]

Women and Family Foundations

In addition to increasing wealth and financial control, women are also beginning to play major leadership roles in their family foundations. A recent membership survey by the Association of Small Foundations (60 percent of which are family foundations) shows that 51 percent of member CEOs and 78 percent of program staff are female. Jane Leighty Justis is trustee and executive director of The Leighty Foundation, a family foundation created by her father in 1985. She believes that the roles women often play in family communications help them develop skills critical for effective leadership of their family foundations. Justis thinks that women are sensitive to family dynamics, which makes them adept at balancing solid business decisions and grant investments for the greatest impact. "Women also care deeply about the importance of instilling a charitable ethic in the younger generations and creating ways to involve them in foundation activities as well as their own individual giving," Justis says. "It is their perspective that will keep foundation work relevant in these times of great change and into the future."[14]

THE WEALTH THAT WOMEN EARN

More women are earning the wealth versus merely inheriting it. When you earn it, you want to go that extra mile making sure it's going to be spent wisely.[15]

—*Heiress and philanthropist Abigail Disney*

Working Women

Women are earning more in the workplace than they ever have before. Figures from a 2004 Employment Policy Foundation study show that women are the fastest-growing sector of wealthy individuals, and the number of women who earn $100,000 or more has tripled over the last decade.[16] Moreover, as Witter and Chen write in *The She Spot*, women's income has risen more than 60 percent over the past thirty years, whereas men's median income has remained at around 6 percent.[17] Many of these women are graduates of business and management courses. They are savvy about investing and just as involved as men, according to Ann Kaplan, a philanthropist and chair of Circle Financial Group.[18]

Earning one's own money makes all the difference in the way people regard their own and their family financial resources, and a 2009 *Time* magazine article reports that more women than ever before (almost 40 percent) are the primary breadwinners in their households or are providing essential income for the family's bottom line.[19] The good news for development officers is that as women's incomes rise, so do their donations.

Diversity and Women's Giving

Women of color represent an economic force to be reckoned with. According to Miriam Muley, founder and CEO of 85% Niche, a marketing research firm focusing on women, 35.2 percent of the U.S. female population is of non-Anglo descent—a population as large as that of Spain or Italy.[20] Muley, a graduate of Columbia University's Graduate School of Business, expects that number will grow from the current fifty-four million to sixty-three million by 2020 and over a hundred million—or half of the U.S. female population—by 2050. Currently the spending of women of color in the United States alone equals $1 trillion, or more than the entire gross domestic product of countries such as Spain, Mexico, and Canada. Thomas J. Stanley points out in his book *Millionaire Women Next Door* that of all ethnic groups, affluent African American women give the most—about 10 percent of their income, to what he refers to as "noble causes."[21] Says Muley, "U.S. women of color have been described as a global juggernaut—an unstoppable force catalyzing sweeping change across every sector in America."

Despite this affluence, research shows that few nonprofits reach out to these women. Much, much more needs to be done to recruit women of color into the development field.

Women of color are . . . producing more wealth in this country and doing so at a rate that exceeds their population growth . . . Between 1997 and 2006 the number of privately held firms owned by women of color grew five times faster than all privately held firms (120% vs. 24%). Entrepreneurship represents the modern underground railroad used by women of color to make significant, below the radar, stealth advances into major wealth and corporate enterprise.

—Miriam Muley, *The 85% Niche*

Educated Women Will Earn More and Give More

At the tenth annual luncheon and symposium of the Chicago Foundation for Women, writer Anna Quindlen reminded the audience about careers available to women "then and now." Sometimes it takes a wake-up call like Quindlen's presentation to understand the career choices women have that didn't exist even some twenty years ago. Today we have women astronauts, partners in large law firms, surgeons, rabbis, women on fire and police forces, women Supreme Court justices, and women running for the top jobs in the nation. Most of these options are relatively new to women, and along with the choices come the means—women's earnings from their own jobs.

Education is key to women's career choices and more women today are getting a college education—the stepping stone to better jobs and better earnings. There are now more women enrolled in higher education than men, and they are more likely than men to graduate as well (63 percent compared with 55 percent.) What's more, recent studies show that women work harder in school than men and are walking off with a greater number of high honors.

True, women still earn less than men, but with more women going to college and their motivation to succeed demonstrated by graduation rates and high honors, these earning figures will change. Women's earning potential and career choices are definitely tied to higher education, and the Center on Philanthropy at Indiana University's research shows that the higher the level of education a person receives, the more the person gives. With women receiving more education, they will also be giving even more tomorrow than they are today.

Consistencies in Women's Giving

There are some consistencies among women in their giving. Studies show that women do favor giving to education, health needs, and women and girls. Often, however, the final results have depended on the wording of various studies, the women being polled, and the sources of the research. But basic needs usually also ranks high on women's lists.

Much has been written about women (and men as well) finding their passion, which ultimately defines where they give. We have found, in working with women donors in various kinds of institutions and organizations, that it is possible to find that passion within almost any group. It might be difficult for most women to discover passion in an organization established for hunting and fishing (not impossible, though), but medical centers, community organizations, art museums, and environmental groups have been able to, within their programming, attract women donors using the right approach—compassion as well as passion.

Women have moved beyond being only passionate about a cause. They know that compassion is the most important reason to give. They understand, in an unselfish, selfless way, the needs of society, and they are committing to those needs. Surely when women initiated the relief societies for refugees on the coasts at the end of the eighteenth century, and settlement houses for women and children in cities at the end of the nineteenth century, it wasn't just because of their passion for helping women and children. It was compassion for their needs—their dire circumstances.

Relevancy to their lives is a word used often by women donors, especially younger women. Debra Engle, with the Oklahoma State University (OSU) Foundation, says that OSU has found relevancy, such as environmental concerns and women's health, to be a major factor in what younger women wanted from future seminars held at the university.[22]

Women as Inspiration and Example

During the beginning of the modern women's philanthropy movement in the 1970s, it became apparent to some visionary women that their gender had the means and desire to do more, but didn't know how to give or have the right vehicle to use. Colleen Willoughby, who founded the Washington Women's Foundation in 1996, says, "After forty years of active volunteerism, I became aware of a disconnect for women donors between their capacity to give and their confidence to make major gifts. The model we created was a new form of giving. I started and focused on women because they were the unseen and unrecognized potential opportunity for new philanthropic dollars."[23]

The Washington Women's Foundation has been a model for hundreds of women's giving circles throughout the United States, with nearly five hundred members and awarding nearly $9 million as of this writing. These are five hundred women who had the potential to give but in most cases weren't giving until one of their own recognized their possibility and provided the vehicle that would encourage and excite them to become involved.

Other women have also been eager to teach women about philanthropy. Susan Ketchum, first vice president-investments at Merrill Lynch on Hilton Head Island, is one of the founders of "Women in Philanthropy," the giving circle sponsored by the Low Country Community Foundation. She says, "I like the chance to teach women about philanthropy. Philanthropy is very important to my life, and I looked at my peer group and knew that everyone didn't feel that way. I wanted to help them have the same experience I knew. That is, as I increase my giving, my life is enriched and feels much fuller."[24]

Ketchum believes that the giving circle has provided women with opportunities to become leaders:

> *I have women come up to me now who serve on boards and say they are empowered and never thought they could be a community leader before being part of the giving circle. My joy from all of this is watching how this idea became a wonderful, important, meaningful organization that has touched women's lives in a way that they didn't know was out there. The fact is we brought this to their attention and now we're seeing all these women learning and inspired to be more philanthropic. Through this leadership experience, they have become more involved in other charitable organizations as well.*

Don't ask for the needs of the organization. Be sure to find the donor's passion and stress what they will get from giving their money. This is what development officers have been taught in the past. But today passion and personal gain are no longer valid as standalone ways to reach donors. They are just two of the ways donors will respond. In these turbulent times, women are not being self-indulgent and giving just where it makes them feel good and virtuous. They are giving because of their compassion and where there is a need that can be addressed. And they are serving as examples for others as well.

Investing in Women and Changing the Culture of Giving

When Debra Engle went to Iowa State University (ISU) as senior vice president of development for the Iowa State University

Foundation in 2001, she knew that investing in women was the right course. Women represented the greatest number of students and were fast becoming the largest group of alumna, but they were not giving in commensurate numbers. Women had an unrealized potential. To Engle it seemed obvious that the culture of women's philanthropy was ready to reach a new level.

In fact, when Engle queried the spouses of the university's governing board, she found them eager to be more involved in the university. She began having breakfast meetings to find out what they were thinking and to discuss ways of encouraging women to give to the university. Out of those breakfasts came the Iowa State University Women & Philanthropy Committee, plus regional programming focused on helping alumnae acquire better financial expertise.

"We knew that women could not be as philanthropic as their potential would allow if they didn't have a sense of their own financial status," Engle says.[25] After two years of offering seminars in financial planning—including estate planning, asset management, and family-business succession planning—the Committee shifted its focus to philanthropy, with an emphasis on developing a giving plan.

Today, seminars are held once or twice a year on the campus and in conjunction with regional events. These have attracted an increasing attendance of around three hundred women at the campus event, while the regional events are aimed at smaller, more intimate groups of women and couples.

When Engle moved to a leadership position in the Oklahoma State University Foundation in 2008, her impact at Iowa State was clear in terms of increasing the number of gifts from women. From 2002 to 2007, the number of women donors had increased 37 percent, to 22,438, and the total amount of money given to the university from women had increased 138 percent, to $25.8 million.

Not only were more women giving, but women were giving more as well. From 2003 to 2007, the number of women giving $100,000-plus gifts had increased by 50 percent, while men's gifts of the same size increased only 42 percent. Iowa State University Foundation's investment had paid off, and the culture had changed. The results showed it.

Considering the incredible impact, Engle says the financial investment was small. The foundation budgets approximately $50,000 for the committee meetings and annual seminar, most of which is recouped through sponsorships and underwriting the seminar.

Staffing for the effort is not in the hands of any one office or person but is a joint venture between donor relations and events, communications, information technology and gift processing, gift planning, and the senior vice president of development's office. "While our office provided the leadership for the efforts, it was truly a jointly supported initiative, with each area working together to meet the goals of the program, ensure success, and track benchmarks for measuring impact," Engle says.

Engle says she knew the university's investment in the culture of women's philanthropy had been met when University president Greg Geoffroy spoke to women donors. "He had written the presentation himself and delivered it with great excitement and passion for what women were doing at Iowa State. He shared his own stories of women donors he had worked with and the impact their gifts were having. Immediately I knew women's giving at Iowa State was an integral part of the framework or culture of philanthropy. Women as donors had arrived and were being recognized."

Debra Engle's advice to development officers who want to change the culture of giving at their institution:

Every organization has an organizational culture, and as a leader you will often be called on to shape it. Your organizational culture can impact women's giving. Ask yourself these questions:

- Do your gifting conversations begin by exploring the donor's values?
- Do you encourage family philanthropy?
- Do you have a collaborative culture that explores donors' multiple interests rather than institutional needs?
- Do you have a culture of philanthropy, with many women's leadership and gifting role models?

TAKEAWAYS

Women's philanthropy is of utmost importance because:

- Women's potential to give is greater than ever before, and financial institutions have begun to recognize this.
- Women are already giving, and in some cases giving more than men.
- Women are often the decision-makers for family foundations.
- Women's earnings, education, and inheritance are growing. And as this happens, women's giving increases.
- Women often control the giving within couples and family foundations.
- Women are accepting control of their finances and consequently their lives.
- Women will support most causes, given the right approach.
- Women are leading the way in philanthropy.
- Minority women represent a significant and challenging new market for nonprofits.
- Women's giving is changing the culture of giving.
- Investing in women's philanthropy pays off.

These facts are very important because they challenge and correct the old stereotypes and prejudices of the past. They change the paradigm of how we think about women's philanthropic potential.

PART
TWO

The Hows and Whys of
Women's Philanthropy

CHAPTER 3

From Bag Ladies to Bold Divas: The Media and Changing Stereotypes

SOME BELIEVE THE MODERN WOMEN'S PHILANTHROPY movement reached its tipping point in the early 2000s with women's giving circles, university philanthropic initiatives, and women's funds. Not only had women's potential to give vastly increased, but the media discovered the importance of this new philanthropy and began writing about it.

In this chapter we look at the role the media played in creating the modern women's philanthropy movement, plus the old stereotypes and how they have been overcome.

THE PRESS AND THE MOVEMENT

"An extraordinary landscape." These were the words used by Joanna L. Krotz to describe what she saw when she was assigned to write a piece about family foundations: "I opened the window, stuck my head out and saw an extraordinary landscape not noticed before. I saw that women and nonprofits had not been very well covered."[1] This was in 2003, and Krotz has continued writing and speaking about women's philanthropy ever since.

Although women's philanthropy has become a full-blown movement, it would not have happened without media attention—which female writers brought about. One can hardly blame all the old stereotypes about women's giving on men in the press, but there is no doubt that until female writers discovered women's philanthropy and began writing about it, very little was printed about this new phenomenon.

For example, Anne Matthews was a stringer for the *New York Times* in 1991 when she heard about the new women's philanthropy initiative at her alma mater, University of Wisconsin–Madison. She did some investigating, liked what she saw, and wrote a feature article for the *New York Times Magazine* in April of that year titled "Alma Maters Court Their Daughters."[2] That article triggered university women development officers' enormous interest in the subject and ultimately led to the creation of the Women's Philanthropy Institute (then named the Women's Philanthropy Network).

Another catalytic writer, Holly Hall of the *Chronicle of Philanthropy*, has been reporting on women's philanthropy since 1997, when her first article, titled "Cultivating Philanthropy by Women," appeared in the newspaper.[3] Hall says she became interested in the subject when she saw the number of developments in different places where fundraisers and others were beginning to focus on women. Since 1997 she has written many more articles on the subject.

The *Chronicle of Higher Education* picked up on the subject and, in July of 2007, printed Erin Strout's article about courting and reaching female donors.[4] This was an important step for higher education women's leadership initiatives, as Strout reported on the successes of various programs at educational institutions as well as women's potential. This time the call to action couldn't be ignored, and several major institutions lined up to participate.

An article in *People* magazine, written in 1998 by Samantha Miller and Tina Kelley, propelled the movement from one giving circle to over six hundred during the next few years.[5] Seeing a photo of Colleen Willoughby of Seattle in her kitchen, throwing up her hands over the success of the Washington Women's Foundation, people all over the United States surely thought, "I could do that in my community. I could start a giving circle."

But it was Krotz, writing for *Town&Country* magazine, who helped move women's giving into seven, eight, and nine figures.

Krotz believes philanthropy is a learned behavior, and since 2003 *Town&Country* has had an annual issue on philanthropy, introducing and discussing the year's outstanding philanthropists and presenting their stories as well as outlines for how to give money more strategically.

Town&Country is the only national magazine covering women's philanthropy fully and well, and a great deal of credit goes to editor Pamela Fiori. She describes the effect of their first issue dedicated to philanthropy: "The response was truly heartwarming and gratifying. So this year we're doing it again and devoting even more of our pages to the individuals and groups that are making such a difference in the world, against all odds."[6]

Brenda Biederman of Traverse City, Michigan, was so moved by what she read in the 2008 *Town&Country* about women philanthropists addressing social causes, that she started mAIDens of Michigan, with the emphasis on AID. mAIDens is a group of Biederman's friends who gather two to three times a year at her Lake Michigan home. Guests bring a gourmet dish to share, as well as their checkbooks. Biederman plans to expand mAIDens throughout Michigan. And all because of a magazine article she read.

Even as we were writing *Women and Philanthropy*, the media was continuing to move women's philanthropy forward. The *New York Times Magazine* of August 22, 2009, focused on "Why Women's Rights Are the Cause of Our Time," with articles "X-Factor Philanthropy" and "The Power of the Purse," inspired by columnist Nicholas Kristof. Soon after, his book *Half the Sky: Turning Oppression into Opportunity for Women Worldwide*, written with his wife Sheryl WuDunn was published. These were followed by Maria Shriver's study *A Woman's Nation*, Claire Gaudiani's *Social Entrepreneurship in America: Women Building a More Perfect Union*, and *Women, Wealth, and Giving: The Virtuous Legacy of the Boom Generation* by Margaret May Damen and Niki Nicastro McCuistion.

Although Kristof has been writing about women's issues for over eight years, the irony is that once world governments, corporations, and the financial sector discovered the importance of women to the world economy, the focus turned to women and girls globally. The editor of the *New York Times Magazine*, Gerald Marzorati, says that issues confronting the world's women and what women are doing about them "was a manifesto for our times."[7] The challenge in this decade is to create policies that address the issues of women and girls.

The same type of manifesto has been issued for women's philanthropy as well. Although women's philanthropy has been around for decades, it wasn't until nonprofits saw women's potential to give that it became the focus of so much attention. In a similar vein, the discovery by corporations of women's market power has changed forever how women are approached as consumers. And financial institutions are doing this as well: modeling their approach to all their clients on what women want.

Behind this movement, the media is talking about women's potential and women's gifts such as the Women Moving Millions campaign. They are featuring the multimillion-dollar gifts that wealthy women are giving to universities, churches, and nonprofits and portraying the women behind these efforts. Rather than having reached the tipping point, the current awareness of women and philanthropy is only the beginning, and the media has played a major role in uncovering and advancing Krotz's "extraordinary landscape" by finding out more about it and helping others find out as well.

ONE BOLD WOMAN

According to Joanna Krotz, stories will grow the movement and bring it to scale. She throws out a challenge to her peers in the media to think beyond fashion and food. "Right now women's philanthropy is the condiments, not the meat and potatoes," she says. "Women and philanthropy is much too broad a topic [to be viewed so narrowly]." Krotz believes that to get the message out, there should be stories about individuals: the Hunt sisters, daughters of right-wing parents who bequeathed millions; Oseola McCarty, the African American laundress who gave away her entire savings for scholarships; or Jennifer Buffet and her husband, with their NoVo Foundation.

Darla Moore is one of those stories that merits Krotz's meat-and-potatoes scale. What could be meatier than Darla Moore's gift of $25 million to the University of South Carolina for its business school? Unlike more typical women's giving as discussed earlier, Moore neither took a long time to make her decision nor was reluctant to have her name on a building.

Moore, then a fifty-year-old investment guru running a $2 billion investment company with her husband, made the decision to give the $25 million over a single lunch with development officers from the university. She also accepted their offer to name the building for her. Moore said, "They didn't have to name it after me. There were other alternatives. But I think they wanted to make a quantum leap in the image they want to portray. The very idea that a bastion of capitalism would be named for a woman appealed to me. And the fact that this is Strom Thurmond country, well, it was just a home run."[8]

Moore used her gift to leverage change as well. With South Carolina among the poorest states in the Union, she believed that one of the most important assets of the state was the university and that an investment in the business school would help the state's economy. She hired a team of consultants to evaluate the school, got involved, pushed for a revised curriculum, instigated the search for a new dean, and advocated for the recruitment of new faculty. As a result, the school is reputed to have one of the world's best programs in international business, and for Moore it is the launching pad to grow and propel innovative business enterprise throughout the state.[9] Her combined gifts of $70 million make the Darla Moore School the beneficiary of one of the largest private donations to a U.S. business school.

Kimberly Davis, senior vice president of global philanthropy and president, JP Morgan Chase Foundation, could have been describing Darla Moore's gift when she said, "It is vital that women understand and leverage our power. We can't wait for others to give us power. We have to create the conditions and tap into our own resources and influence."[10] And to do that, women must recognize and overcome stereotypes.

STEREOTYPES AND BARRIERS

For too long women avoided being called bold or powerful. Many women had seen the use and abuse of power, often in their own families and usually around money. Other women felt that boldness wasn't feminine enough and power was something that, as a woman in one of our focus groups said, ". . . wasn't even in my vocabulary."

Fear seems to be the major factor in this reticence. Even Oprah Winfrey confessed that she was once so wary of investing her own money in the stock market that she hoarded $50 million cash, calling it her personal "bag-lady" fund.[11] Other "womanly" excuses you may have heard include:

- "I'm waiting for Prince Charming."
- "I always give where my family or financial advisors tell me to."
- "My husband made the money, so he decides where it is going."
- "I'm not comfortable talking about money," from the woman who thinks such talk is unladylike.
- "I'll have to ask my husband."
- "Well, I do give to the art museum, but not as much as my husband gives to his university."

On the receiving side are these development officer laments about women's gifts:

- "I'll be retired before we get the gift" (based on the view that women take too long to make up their minds).
- "Women don't give enough."
- "Women don't run large corporations and don't have money, know to ask for money, or leverage money," from a director who hasn't learned that women *do* have money to give and can chair a capital campaign.

Such perceptions and stereotypes are common, in both women themselves and the professionals who raise funds. Rita Hauser, chair of the Women's Leadership Challenge in the Harvard Campaign in the 1990s, set out to challenge the old stereotypes and change the face of "one of the last male bastions of supremacy," as she put it—philanthropy. The Harvard campaign raised $40 million in eighteen months, with Hauser and a few of her friends matching gifts of $25,000 to $250,000.[12] The face of philanthropy at Harvard was changed forever—and no longer would women take last place on Harvard's prospect lists.

OVERCOMING STEREOTYPES

Fortunately, the stereotypes, barriers, and misperceptions about women as givers are being eliminated as women have taken greater control of their finances and are earning their own money. But in the back of many women's minds still remain financial uncertainties. These can be addressed by development officers in the following ways.

- *Focus groups.* In the many focus groups we have conducted, we have been delighted to hear some of the women, usually the younger ones, talk about their giving and the way they make decisions—on their own or with a spouse. The older women don't generally say anything, but it is obvious from their expressions that they are taking it all in. They will leave and, after mulling it all around in their minds for a while, ask for or demand more say in the family philanthropy—at the least, an equal say and parity for the issues they believe are important. See Resource A for information about conducting focus groups.

- *Financial education sessions.* It can be very helpful to have women sit in on sessions initiated by nonprofits and conducted by financial and wealth management firms. At these sessions women can learn financial and philanthropic planning and share their feelings about money without fear of being laughed at or corrected. (Learn more in Chapter Nine.)

- *Provide ways for women to connect on the Internet.* Lisa Witter, chief strategy officer of Fenton Communications and coauthor with Lisa Chen of the book *The She Spot: Why Women Are the Market for Changing the World and How to Reach Them*,[13] talks about giving women an easy way to connect and share with one another on an organization's Web site or blog or on Facebook. These forums should be initiated by the nonprofit.

- *Use the media.* Women and philanthropy is a hot topic, and increasing media awareness has helped make this possible. Nonprofits can successfully use the media to advance their causes by using stories to get women's attention. Media attention about women donors can point future donors in the direction of self-awareness, financial independence, and bold giving.

TAKEAWAYS

- The media has helped create the modern women's philanthropy movement and is a powerful source of assistance to move it forward. Women writers are particularly interested in the subject, and they have done a great deal to create the movement. Giving circles were created in large part because of media attention, as were many other organizations focusing on women and philanthropy.

- The media is paying more attention to women as they become a powerful global economic and philanthropic force. Nonprofits are being challenged to address this potential through expanded programs for women and girls.

- Stories gain the media's attention, particularly stories that evoke readers' emotions. Women and the organizations and institutions they are associated with should work closely with the media, through stories, to take the movement even further.

- The face of philanthropy is being changed by bold women. Despite the positive press and some bold donors, however, a few stereotypes and barriers still exist. These are being overcome by generational change, positive media attention and donor education sponsored by nonprofits.

Women's Giving:
The Six Cs Plus Three

WHAT BROUGHT ABOUT THE MODERN WOMEN'S philanthropy movement? It was more than women finally having the financial means to give. What it took was a change in the philanthropic culture: an acknowledgment that women have different motivations for giving than men.

A PEACEFUL REVOLUTION

In generational research conducted by Carmen Stevens and Shaw-Hardy, published in 2008,[1] women philanthropists were asked what national or international incidents had occurred as they were growing up that most affected them. Overwhelmingly the women said it was war. No matter what generation, war was the primary influencing factor they recalled: World War II, Vietnam, or the Gulf War.

Not surprisingly, the area in which women most wanted to have influence was to create peace in the world, and 99 percent of the women we spoke with in the study thought they could make positive world change and peace occur. They said this could happen through education, philanthropy, and more compassion. Over and over women mentioned *compassion*—a word connoting empathy, concern, kindness, consideration, and care for and about others. The women felt compassionate themselves and wanted others to feel it as well.

Women do want a better world, starting with a peaceful one. After all, women have always been responsible for keeping the peace in families, so why not in the world as well? As one woman from the Baby Boomer generation (born between 1946 and 1964) told us in our 2007 research: "There can only be peace when there is economic opportunity for everyone. Real economic opportunity can only occur in an environment that works within the natural systems and fosters freedom, innovation, and individual achievement."

A Gen X woman (born between 1965 and 1976) had similar ideas: "The change we need is world peace. Understanding and appreciation of and willingness to accept the existence of different viewpoints, religions, traditions, and sexual orientations. Not homogenizing people but allowing them to coexist peacefully."

WOMEN AS A DRIVING FORCE

The United States has experienced boom times over the last two decades creating massive amounts of wealth, much of it linked to technology. From this new wealth women have emerged as a driving force. Inherited wealth has been replaced with earned wealth and with increased levels of education, opportunities, and even expectations. Women are opening the doors and assuming places in the boardrooms of business, education, and philanthropy. In many cases they are breaking down the doors to get in—or building new ones.

Not too long ago, men were expected to be the breadwinners in the family. They were the ones who went to law school, became physicians, or took over the family business. Nowadays, women are the majority of law students, they are attending medical school in droves, and they are *starting* the family business. Heavy machinery has been replaced with technology, and women are using computers as handily as men. Women are present in all forms of commerce, using their intelligence and education on an increasingly equal playing field for both genders. Our nation is unlikely to ever be an industrial strength again, and brawn is being replaced with brains.

The future of our economy rests on new solutions to old problems, new money to replace that lost in the market crash of 2008, new types of business and industry. The entrepreneurial skills and creative abilities of women are being applied to every area of work and life, including philanthropy. No longer are women relegated to volunteer work to find outlets for their abilities and talents. They are using these, plus their own money, to create new and better ways of giving.

SIX CS OF WOMEN'S GIVING

In focus groups during the early 1990s, we found that women's giving motivations can be defined by Six Cs: *change, create, commit, connect, collaborate,* and *celebrate*.

- *Change* things for the better; make a difference.
- *Create* new solutions to problems; be entrepreneurial through philanthropy.
- *Commit* through volunteerism to the organizations and institutions whose vision women share; give often to organizations to which women have volunteered.
- *Connect* with the human faces that women's gifts affect; build a partnership with people connected with the projects women fund.
- *Collaborate* with others—often other women—as part of a larger effort; seek to avoid duplication, competition, and waste.
- *Celebrate*—have fun together, celebrate women's accomplishments, enjoy the deeper meaning and satisfaction of women's philanthropy.

To our delight and amazement, these Six Cs have become part of the panoply of women's giving across the United States. Rebecca Power describes the value she and her colleagues found in the Six Cs at Impact Austin, in Austin, Texas:

> *We formed Impact Austin around the* Six Cs of women's giving. *I learned that women love to* create *something that can* change *the world for the better. It's through* collaboration *during our grant review process that women* connect *and feel really* committed *to the role they play. We also like to* celebrate *our accomplishments and our*

annual meeting gives us that opportunity. Impact Austin has given women the confidence *to increase their capacity to give because they have* control *over the decision making.*

We knew that if this was how women give, this was how women would stay in our group. We believed that if we accepted those Six Cs and kept them in front of us when we were building Impact Austin, we would continue to grow. And we still talk about them. That's why we've been so successful.[2]

Lee Roper-Batker of the Women's Foundation of Minnesota says that each day the Six Cs of women's philanthropy are a part of her leadership style at the Women's Foundation of Minnesota. "One example," she goes on, "[is] the last C, *celebrate*. I love the quote by Emma Goldman that says, 'If I can't sing and dance, I don't want to be a part of your revolution!' At the Women's Foundation, we are steeped in a culture of *celebration*."[3]

Change

Rosie Molinary, author of *Hijas Americanas: Beauty, Body Image, and Growing Up Latina*, put it this way: "We change the world despite—or perhaps because of—our understanding that the world has sometimes ostracized us."[4]

Women's funds were created in the 1970s to address and put an end to the practice of excluding women and girls from receiving corporate, foundation, government, and individual grants and monies. The funds provided opportunities for women to achieve economic independence and bring about social change and also altered funding patterns so women and girls could receive their fair share. Women were provided with opportunities to give money as well as to create women-led solutions for women's and girls' issues.

Building on the concept of delivering social change, women's funds in the United States grew from one organization in 1977 to 145 worldwide in 2009, investing $60 million annually in women and girls. The growth of women's funds has brought about the acceptance that philanthropic investments in women and girls can accelerate positive change not only in communities but also in nations and the world. Former UN Secretary General Kofi Annan put it this way: "When women are fully involved, the benefits can be seen immediately: Families are healthier, they are better fed, their income, savings, and reinvestment go up. And what is true of families is true of communities and eventually of whole countries."[5]

Carolyn Cassin: Changing Course.[6] Change is just what Carolyn Cassin knew was her job when she took the position of president and CEO of the Michigan Women's Foundation (MWF). The organization had been struggling for the previous four to five years. Although Cassin's professional practice had always been to go into an organization, figure out its essence, and turn it around, this was not an easy thing to achieve during the Great Recession years of 2008–2009, in which Michigan was hit particularly hard.

Cassin says she listened for the first five months and realized that although there was a great deal of support for the MWF, it didn't have the resources or the power that people thought it did. In fact, the MWF was having difficulty making ends meet. They had always been able to rely on the auto companies for support, but this was no longer possible, and their old-fashioned business model wasn't paying off in hard financial times.

She also found that people wanted the MWF to address problems directly, not just give money to other organizations supporting women and girls. "They told me that in the past, when giving to an organization supporting women's causes, they weren't always sure what their gifts had accomplished. I was told we needed to tap into our creative power and come up with new solutions."

One idea was to sponsor a women's enterprise fund. "I asked people what the MWF could do to recapture community support and have more impact. They kept saying to give women a start in beginning their own business to regain a financial foot. Even though women start 40 percent of new businesses they only receive 4 percent of venture capital funding and were having to work out of their kitchens because they couldn't get the financial backing from traditional sources."

A grant from the Kellogg Foundation was paramount to creating the change necessary to obtain more contributions for the MWF. The Kellogg grant enabled MWF to do a feasibility study to find out exactly what niche would work to increase funding. Cassin says the study also helped them find out what they needed to do to make the niche projects work.

As we noted earlier, change was the rationale behind the women's funds growth almost forty years ago. Their success has led to a whole new way of increasing women's giving, beginning with listening to what women want.

Create

Women are creationists by their very nature, substance, tradition, and being. They create future generations through birth. They create clothing for families, grow food in gardens and prepare it in kitchens. Traditionally, women have been responsible for creating methods of healing and, as Dr. Kathleen McCarthy discusses in her book *Lady Bountiful Revisited*,[7] creating much of the culture and many of the cultural institutions in our country.

Through women's creative efforts, relief societies were formed in the late 1700s to help immigrants arriving on the east and west coasts. In the late 1800s Jane Addams and other women founded settlement houses in cities to help women and children, and in the late 1900s women's funds were formed to help women and girls. Women have always wanted to help other women and have often gathered together to create new ways of solving problems. Giving circles (described more fully in Chapter Eight) are a modern form of women's gatherings, generally formed to help others in their community.

In these times of historic challenge and change, there are a myriad of new chances for women, men, and couples to create—to take hold of these new opportunities and create new organizations, programs, and institutions to produce a more sustainable and stable society.

Tashia and John Morgridge are examples of a couple giving creatively. Rather than exchanging traditional gifts, they celebrated their forty-first wedding anniversary by endowing two chairs at the University of Wisconsin–Madison. Tashia, a former special education teacher, gave John, the former CEO of Cisco System, a $1.6 million chair in computer science, and John gave Tashia a $1.6 million chair in reading in the School of Education. Whereas everyone may not be able to do this much, we all can think about creative and celebratory gifts to our family members' and friends' areas of interest.

Tracy Gary: Creating and Inspiring.[8] Tracy Gary has always believed in women's philanthropy as an outlet for women's entrepreneurial qualities. Gary herself has created or helped create eighteen nonprofits since inheriting a fortune in her twenties from Pillsbury stock—including the money her mother made as a stockbroker plus her great-great-grandfather's patent for the dial telephone. Her family had houses in New York, Florida, Minnesota, Wisconsin, and

Paris, France, and at one time they had thirty-six people working for them. Gary could have continued this life of luxury and spending, but instead chose to give it all away and help others through the organizations she created.

After attending Miss Porter's School and "coming out" to society in New York City, Gary graduated from Sarah Lawrence College in 1973 and volunteered at a number of organizations. Because she felt organizations weren't listening to women, she founded Resourceful Women to help wealthy women become social-change donors. From her own personal experience, she found that women needed "women-only" organizations to help them speak up and voice their ideas. Never one to accept the status quo, Gary used not only her financial capital but her creative capital as well to begin new organizations to help women, protect the environment, make peace, overcome social injustice, and enhance the opportunities for numerous disenfranchised groups across America. She has also supported gay rights causes and played a key role in supporting what is now called Funders for Gay and Lesbian Issues.

Most recently, Gary created Inspired Legacies in Houston, Texas. Gary feels that as a young woman she pursued her own "inspired legacy." The organization helps match donors with causes they feel strongly about and helps them establish long-term plans for giving. These plans for giving are described in her books, *Inspired Philanthropy: Creating a Giving Plan*[9] and *Inspired Philanthropy: Your Step-by-Step Guide to Creating a Giving Plan and Leaving a Legacy* (2nd edition),[10] as well as in donor education programs she and others have developed.

Young people are a special interest of Gary's; she believes that by educating youth to bring about social change through philanthropy, they will help make a better society. To this end, she has worked tirelessly to create a youth giving circle curriculum, "Inspiring Youth to Bring About Change: Tools for the Generosity Generation,"[11] made available through Inspired Legacies. Shaw-Hardy was honored to be a part of writing this set of philanthropic tools along with Karen Payne. But it was Gary who was unflagging in her efforts to raise the necessary money to get the curriculum written and published. She always believed it would happen. Gary's personal motivation and creativity have inspired her to tackle the really tough societal issues in a bold but reasoned and compassionate way.

Commit

A woman's commitment to a nonprofit, whether one she created or a public organization, is almost always a *total* commitment. A
woman will make a commitment to give her time and her money only
where she knows she can make a difference. Her commitment will be
to both the mission and the vision of the organization. Sometimes it
will include a commitment to saving one organization while creating
another one.

Kye Fox and Linda Paulson: Manicures and Commitments.[12] If
ever there was proof of women's potential for giving, United Way
Worldwide's successful launch of Women's Leadership Councils provides the evidence. In 125 United Way groups across the country,
separate Women's Leadership Councils raised $561 million in eight
years. In 2008, when most other philanthropic areas saw decreases
because of the challenging economy, United Way women's giving
increased by 12 percent.

In San Antonio, the Women's Leadership Council began with
a manicure. Fox, who had been active in the United Way of San
Antonio and was very committed to the United Way (UW) mission,
saw a woman at the salon whom Fox describes as "an incredible community activist." She asked Fox if she would help start a women's
group for United Way—and they were off and running.

In 1999 there were only three other UW women's philanthropic
initiatives in the United States. Fox was at a meeting in Washington,
D.C., shortly thereafter with a few other UW women. "We actually
got started over breakfast," she says. "We wanted to create something
that we thought could solve problems, and we knew women give
and think differently than men. We knew what had been happening wasn't working well for us, we were committed to United Way,
and we wanted a vehicle to truly create change by getting to the root
cause of community problems."

Each council is a separate entity and has different giving amounts
as well as ways of disbursing grants. Annual giving ranges from
$1,000 to $10,000 a year, and over 50 percent of the councils direct
their funding to special projects that are part of the overall goals of
United Way; others give directly to United Way without restricting
the money. "But I can tell you that each Women's Leadership Council
is committed to change in whatever community it is in," Fox says.

Fox, currently chair of the United Way Worldwide's National Women's Leadership Council, is proud to point out that their initiative has reached far beyond traditional UW donors to include housewives, small business owners, and major corporate leaders. A special category has been created in some councils for younger women to give annual gifts of $500 until they can grow them to $1,000. Fox likens the councils to good businesses. "We are able to raise more money because women want to know where they are investing their money, they want a say in the solution, and they want to be able to connect with other people."

Linda Paulson, director of strategic markets and investor relations for United Way Worldwide, says that advocacy, leadership, and resource development are the focuses of the councils. "It's about so much more than giving money. It's about helping women find their voice and lead change in their communities. We are enhancing leadership and harnessing the leadership skills women bring, whether it is managing a family or a multimillion-dollar corporation." Fox and Paulson both report that the women are deeply committed to the Women's Leadership Councils and have United Way as their philanthropic partner of choice.

By creating a women's philanthropic council, nonprofits can usually plan on raising more money because of increased women's giving. Paulson says that United Way Women's Leadership Councils outperform the average on every indicator of financial success; over the past three years United Way organizations with councils have enjoyed double-digit percent increases.

Even if a nonprofit is not yet ready for women's leadership councils, the fundraising methods they use can be part of any organization or institution. To appeal to women, they can

- Focus on parts of the organization that address women's caring power
- Provide ways to help women find their voice through leadership opportunities and advocacy efforts
- Use relationship-building fundraising rather than transaction-based fundraising (in which the number of contacts is valued more than the quality of the relationships)
- Put in place ways to measure impact and report results

- Ensure that fundraising goals include strategies to improve lives and address social issues

- Involve and engage donors

- Provide opportunities for advocacy for the causes women care about

Connect

Marketing expert Allison Fine, in her book *Momentum: Igniting Social Change in the Connected Age*,[13] says that the rise of the Internet is a major force of today's "connected age" for women, because they are driving this with their "innate ability to share information and collaborate."

The most successful organizations have figured out ways for their donors, both women and men, to be part of the action. They are finding out how to strengthen the bonds between their organizations and their donors: how best to connect, communicate with, and involve donors as volunteers.

The Internet provides easy ways to connect—that is, to communicate. Using social networking, many nonprofits are providing ways to connect on their Web sites. That's good, because women are using the Internet in greater numbers than men, and this trend is expected to continue. Lisa Witter and Lisa Chen, in their book *The She Spot: Why Women Are the Market for Changing the World and How to Reach Them*,[14] say, "Women use the Internet as a platform to communicate with others, whether it's with other users online or with the host organization." They suggest that Web sites today are being built both to attract women and to keep them there longer.

Linda McGurn: Connecting Beyond Football.[15] Linda McGurn—accountant, attorney, Gainesville developer, and chair of the University of Florida (UF) Foundation—understands the value of making connections. McGurn was a strong advocate for establishing the UF Women: Inspiring Leadership and Philanthropy initiative. She says, "A lot of our connection with UF has been around sports, and now we're getting women involved at another level." That new level involves regional gatherings of women to hear about the university. "We plan to bring deans, faculty, and students to meet with the women, but the gatherings will also be an opportunity for the women to meet and get to know one another," McGurn says.

Because the state is so large, seven focus groups were held in cities from Jacksonville to Miami. McGurn attended several, as did Beth McCague, cochair of the UF Women initiative and of the university's $1.5 billion capital campaign launched in 2005. McGurn knew it was important for the UF alumni as well as wives and widows of alumni to connect or reconnect with the university.

How did these two women happen to hold the positions of campaign cochair and foundation president? McGurn says it was a time of convergence of women in leadership roles. "The associate vice president of our foundation, Leslie Bram, has long been an advocate for more women in leadership positions on the campus, and it happened that not only were Beth and I in these roles, but the president of the alumni association board of directors and Gator Boosters (athletic fundraising) were also women."

McGurn attributes women's leadership at the university to enlightened staff who had been looking at increasing women's leadership for a long time: "They helped put us in those positions by giving us projects to work on and then the university found out how powerful women can be. The foundation has been adding women every year and going about it in a planned way."

McGurn recounts how surprised the wife of one of the cochairs of UF's last campaign was at being asked to join the board. "She said, 'You want me?' She was so excited to be invited and has been very pro-active and a great member: she brings to the university her own connections as well."

"There are so many more women in their fifties and sixties who have the financial wherewithal and can be asked to serve," says McGurn. "It has been a generational shift, and this generation of women have had positions in business and the means to follow through financially and with leadership capabilities. The reason we are doing the women's philanthropy leadership initiative is because we realize that if women are involved in leadership, philanthropy follows. We had to debate which comes first and felt leadership was appropriate."

UF Women are planning a monthly email to stay in touch and let the women know what is happening on campus. McGurn says, "*UF Today* recently did an article on the woman chair of Gator Boosters, and we have a new engineering dean who is a woman. We are also asking the deans if they would please send in something about what women are doing in their colleges. We're broadening our connection with women beyond football weekends."

Collaborate

To most people, "collaboration" means "working together," but it has meanings well beyond that for many women. Lovelight Foundation's cofounder, Julie Fisher Cummings, believes it is an equalizer, "one of the great levelers of society. If you're working in *collaboration*, inequities don't exist. It's the female model and nonhierarchical."[16]

Diversity has always been an important element of women's philanthropy—women working as partners and sharing stories and responsibilities. Some say collaboration is women's philanthropy's "edge," for as grants are given and funders become acquainted with those receiving the grants, they may, in many cases, actually work side by side with the grantees. Now *that* is collaboration.

Debbie Ritchie: Collaboration with Impact.[17] To Debbie Ritchie, collaboration has more than one meaning. It means giving with other women to Pensacola Bay Area IMPACT 100, a giving circle she helped organize with other women in 2003. It means using the talents women bring to the table to help the organization govern and grow. And finally, it means working with nonprofits in Pensacola to help IMPACT members learn more about the needs of their community and helping the nonprofits get the word out about what they do. Ritchie's three different types of collaboration all result in giving and working together.

Ritchie knows a great deal about collaboration as that was part of her job when she was a state representative from the Florida Keys and South Dade County. She collaborated so well with others that she was elected minority floor leader in her last two years in office.

In 1999 Ritchie moved to Pensacola. After reading an article in *People* magazine about a women's giving circle—Impact 100 in Cincinnati, begun by Wendy Steele—she decided to help organize one in her new home town. Ritchie says:

> *I found myself in a new community where I had no connections, so I reinvented myself. I wanted to make a difference in the community and get involved. I chose to make the focus on women's giving because I wanted to empower women to share ideas and to collectively make*

a difference. When we all work together and take our collection of life experiences and desires to improve a community, we can have an impact. The women of IMPACT have very clear ideas and goals of what we want, long and short term, especially about changing our community for the better.

The IMPACT Pensacola membership has grown from 233 members giving $1,000 annually to 514 women in 2009. They have awarded twenty-one $100,000 grants in the community in five areas: arts and culture, education, environment, family, and health and wellness. Overall, IMPACT Pensacola has given over $2 million in grants, with one large grant in each of the focus areas.

Collaboration is a continuing effort for IMPACT, and it has extended its work beyond funding grants by sponsoring an annual program for all nonprofits to learn not only who IMPACT is, but to also offer programming on topics such as grantmaking and how nonprofits can get their message into the media. "This past year," Ritchie says, "we talked about how nonprofits can be more successful in these tough economic times; how to identify future leaders in the organization and plan for succession. The women of IMPACT have a commitment to building stronger nonprofits in the community, not only through our grantmaking but by collaborating with the non-profits as well. We work together to meet the quality-of-life services that they strive to achieve by helping them do what they do best by doing it better."

Celebrate

The late Dame Anita Roddick, founder of the Body Shop and major philanthropist, used the word "joyful" as a way to describe her time giving away money.[18] She qualified that by saying, "To me, the joy of making this business successful is giving stuff away."[19]

Unfortunately, because Roddick died at the age of sixty-four, she did not have the "joy" of giving away and seeing the impact of all her gifts. But other entrepreneurial and corporate women are carrying on her legacy—women like those who are members of the Committee of 200.

Alison Winter: Celebrating Success.[20] Alison Winter, past chair of Committee of 200 (C200)—an exclusive leadership group of women in business—says its members are very aware of their unique and fortunate positions and want to give back. In 1986 C200 created a foundation to help women become successful entrepreneurs and corporate leaders. "We have an outreach program that encourages young college women to get an MBA," she says. According to Winter, although women represent at least half of all law and medical school students, only about a third of the MBA classes are women. "We did some research and found out that the reason more women weren't getting an MBA was because they wanted to do something worthwhile with their lives and make the world a better place. Going into business didn't seem to fit that plan."

The Outreach Seminars take C200 members into colleges and, by giving young women role models, show them that a master's degree in business can bring about success not only for themselves but through the impact they can have on others. Winter says, "First of all, we get to celebrate our own stories, and then we tell them stories of how our members overcame obstacles and achieved. We talk about what they can do for women who will ultimately work for them to help them reach their full capacity and financial independence. We also discuss philanthropy and the ways women have used their success to help others."

Celebrating their members' success is one of the missions of C200, and each year they give three or four Luminary Awards to their members. One of these, the Philanthropic Innovator Award, is given to a member who has developed an innovative funding and charitable giving program and continues her involvement with the program. They have celebrated Connie Duckworth, a former partner at a large financial firm who started Arzu, a group that helps Afghan women achieve economic independence through the sale of rugs; they have honored Judy Koch, manager of a manufacturing firm in Fremont, California, who started the Bring Me A Book Foundation by setting up a company lending library in businesses across the country, enabling employees to take new books home to their children every few days. Bring Me A Book also helps bilingual employees to become literate in reading English. "We celebrate and showcase our members as well as show other members what is possible for them to do," Winter says.

C200 members are women who have had enormous success both in the corporate world and as entrepreneurs. They understand their responsibility to give back, and they take it very seriously. Unlike many women ten to twenty years ago, C200 women don't care much about being "one of the boys." They want to be "one of the girls" and do things together as women. They also want to be good role models for younger women, perhaps because they themselves had few role models. By celebrating one another's successes, they are showing that it's fine to achieve in the corporate world because that success provides the means to do good in society. As the saying goes, "They did well and now they can do good."

THREE NEW CS: PERSONAL RESULTS OF WOMEN'S GIVING

Three more Cs have risen out of the changes we saw in women's giving from 1991 to 2000. Women now recognize they have the means to give, and their philanthropy has resulted in deeper meaning and greater satisfaction represented by:

- Taking *control* of their lives, their finances, and their philanthropy
- Gaining *confidence* in becoming philanthropic leaders
- Having the *courage* to challenge the old ways of doing things and taking risks with their giving to bring about change

Control

Control may be the most important of the three new Cs. At the very least, it's where all philanthropy begins. Without women understanding and taking control of their finances, influential philanthropy just won't happen. Women might attend a few special events and maybe even bid on an auction offering (often with their spouses), but making a true commitment to philanthropy and helping others occurs only when women comprehend their finances and the finances of their families.

Heiress and activist Tracy Gary suggests that women should spend four hours a month reading and working on financial matters, whether it be statements, options, or balance sheets. According to Gary, this time spent is as important an activity as working out in a gym. "It's getting and keeping our houses in order and empowering ourselves," she says. Gary also considers women's gaining control and financial independence to be as significant as getting the vote was to our grandmothers and driving a car to our mothers.

When a 2006 survey by Prudential showed that one in three American women consider themselves more involved in financial decisions than they were five years ago,[21] we knew those figures boded well for women's increased philanthropy—and we were right. Control of finances means women have power over their own lives and consequently enables them to help others' lives as well.

Barbara Stanny: Gaining Back a Life.[22] Barbara Stanny knows all about taking control—or at least about *having* to take control. The daughter of one of the founders of H&R Block, the income tax preparation company, Barbara grew up with wealth. But even though her father's company was all about money and finances, money was never discussed in their house. There was plenty to spend, and that was all Barbara felt was necessary to know about money.

After establishing a trust for her on her twenty-first birthday, her parents were sure that she would be fine. Her father would take care of her until she married and then her husband would take over. Take over her trust, that is. Trust meaning both her money and her faith in him.

But when her husband squandered her trust and left her with tax bills of over one million dollars, and her father refused to help, Stanny's wake-up calls wouldn't stop. She details all this in her first book, *Prince Charming Isn't Coming,*[23] published in 1997.

Reflecting on how she was forced to take control of her life, Stanny says, "I do believe this was a gift in disguise . . . Even though I have less money than I had before my husband gambled it away, I feel infinitely more secure now that I understand it."

Stanny's first move was to engage a financial planner—a person she considers her partner, not her "daddy" or her savior. Then she asked questions and interviewed women who were smart with money for a project with Tracy Gary and Resourceful Women. It was illuminating. "I found out that these women were motivated not by having money, but by what they could do with their money."

Stanny found that wealthy women who are not financially secure or knowledgeable won't give away money. "That really resonated with me. I gave away money in small dribble amounts and didn't take it seriously until I got my act together." She credits Gary with impressing on her the importance of planning her giving, something Gary writes about in her workbooks.

Stanny is a trained psychologist, so working with women had always been a part of her life; soon it became her mission. She didn't want other women to make the same mistakes she had made. Now, through her books, seminars, and Web site, Stanny helps women achieve financial independence. "It became very clear to me that I was given the family and the attention because this was what I was meant to do—to educate women. It gave me a sense of purpose as to what my life was all about. To me financial savvy means living life on your own terms and with your own values. When you take control of your money, you take control of your life."

Confidence

In the 2009 Fidelity Study about philanthropy, nearly half of the women surveyed said they were the ones who determined how much and where their households gave.[24] Even more amazing was the number of men—92 percent—who named their spouses as an influence on how much to give to charity and where to direct the funds. Bruce Flessner, founding principal of the Minneapolis philanthropy consulting firm Bentz Whaley Flessner, confirmed this study: "Our firm did some research a few years ago about who influenced giving decisions. For males it was the spouse first," he says.[25]

What has happened to produce this change from men's unilaterally choosing where the money should be directed, to women's influencing giving or actually making the decisions? Where and how did women gain this confidence? Referencing the same 2009 Fidelity study, Fidelity president Sarah C. Libbey says, "Women have always had a hand in their households' charitable outreach, but that role is evolving as women increasingly create their own wealth and become beneficiaries of wealth transfers because they live longer."[26]

Women are earning greater amounts of money and consequently believe they have the right to decide where it should go. But men should be given credit as well for having the confidence in their wives to make, or help make, these decisions.

More and more development officers are learning that, generally, there is no single donor in a couple. Savvy officers work with both spouses to finalize long-lasting commitments.

Christine Lodewick: One Woman's Journey.[27] Christine Lodewick and her husband, Philip, live in a rambling, historic farm home in Ridgefield, Connecticut, a three-hundred-year old community in the foothills of the Berkshire Mountains. Christine came from a dairy farm family in Wisconsin; Philip and his brothers were raised by their working mother in New York.

After graduating from the University of Wisconsin–Madison, Christine went on to get a degree in speech pathology at the University of Connecticut (U Conn), where she met Philip. Following his graduation from the U Conn's School of Business, Philip went to work for IBM in sales, and in 1980 founded Tradewell Corporation, a high-technology leasing company.

Philip has been enormously successful, but he makes it clear that he and Christine are a team. "Whatever I've accomplished, Christine has done it with me. We are two people working together." Philip says he is blessed in life: his wife is his best friend and now they have the opportunity to share their wealth together.

However, Christine wasn't always comfortable making decisions, nor did she always think her ideas had much worth. It is hard today to believe the same woman who chairs the Women's Philanthropy Council for the University of Wisconsin Foundation, who sits on the Foundation board and has been honored time and again for her volunteer work and philanthropy, ever felt that way about herself and her abilities. She now exudes confidence, and that confidence has helped her consider and give to the issues she really cares about, many revolving around women and girls.

Christine believes in helping other women achieve the same confidence as she has today, by taking control of their lives and their finances. She says, "Encouraging women to utilize their own financial resources for their own ideals is a very important part of equalizing society's response to women . . . to see them as equal partners, not just as adjuncts."

It helps to have a supportive husband like Philip who truly believes Christine is his partner and urges her to write the big checks, something she says still brings a lump to her throat. But she also says that being around other women and discussing money and philanthropy has been seminal in building her confidence. She says, "It was revolutionary to me when I was invited by the University of Wisconsin Foundation to attend a luncheon where women discussed their giving. And the more I talked with other women about money, the more confident I felt."

For her philanthropic and volunteer efforts, Christine received the Dr. King Ridgefield Community Service Award, named for Dr. Martin Luther King Jr. When introduced at the award ceremony, she was described as being honored for having Dr. King's spirit.[28] Spirit generally comes from confidence, and confidence is something Christine now has plenty of, as well as intellectual, financial, social, and political capital.

Courage

By the time a woman takes action to change and create, in most cases she is acting with courage. Involvement in her mission becomes so great that the last thing that crosses her mind is how brave her action is. Women who have taken control of their lives and their finances have the confidence to be courageous. This is the last of the three new Cs.

It took courage for Jane Addams to start Hull House, but her sympathy for the needs of women and children was the driving force, and she knew she would succeed. Courage has also been described as knowing that what you are doing feels intuitively right. It doesn't feel like taking a chance; rather, it's feeling focused and purposeful and undaunted.

Fortunately, because many women are entrepreneurs, and entrepreneurs have to take chances and be courageous, these qualities spill over from the business/professional arena to philanthropy.

Cheryl Womack: Seeing the World on Her Plate.[29] The third of eleven children and the daughter of a Panamanian immigrant, Cheryl Womack founded an insurance company (VCW) for independent truckers in 1983; by the time she sold it in 2002, it had become a $100-million-a-year business.

Womack's late father, who worked eighteen-hour days in a fiberglass factory, was her inspiration. She says not only did he instill in her a strong work ethic, but perhaps more important, he passed on to her an attitude that resulted in her being described as having no trouble "envisioning the world on her plate."

After teaching elementary school for a year and working at a trucking insurance company without promotion, in 1981 Womack decided to start the National Association of Independent Truckers (NAIT) in her basement. Womack says she didn't even know how to read a financial statement. When asked how she funded the company, she says, "Well, my husband certainly paid for me to live. Actually that's not true. I left that husband. I was just on a roll to change my life. What can I say? I left that husband, moved in with my sister for about three months and then got an apartment. I was making about $17,000 a year. I dated to eat . . . which was something you could do back then. And if they wanted more than dinner . . . I'd pay for the meal."

Two years later Womack founded VCW (for Very Cute Women), which sells customized insurance policies to truckers because, she says, "I listened to what the independent truckers complained about and I solved their problems. I created something and said, 'Here's what you asked for.'" One of the innovative products she developed was an alternative to workers' compensation for independent contractors.

In 2002 Womack pledged $2 million to the University of Kansas, her alma mater, to help build a women's softball stadium, the Arrocha Ballpark, named after her father, Demostenes Arrocha. Womack says, "This stadium will increase the level of confidence of the women athletes who use it because it will raise the bar for them competitively and show how much others believe in their ability."

Womack says her goal is to inspire young women around the world. To help meet that goal, she purchased and now leads the women's organization Leading Women Entrepreneurs of the World, an international group that annually honors a handful of the world's wealthiest business women.

In two male-dominated industries, insurance and trucking, Womack exemplifies the courage needed to succeed. Although her style has been described as hard-charging, she has also been lauded for her caring and nurturing management, which included day care on site and a cafeteria serving home-cooked meals for employees, mainly women. Womack's life, in both business and philanthropy, shows her boldness in trying new endeavors and her efforts to instill that courage in others as well.

TAKEAWAYS

The Six Cs Plus Three are a quick, fun, and meaningful overview of women's giving, great for use in speeches, workshops, panel discussions, or news articles. Singly they depict the essential elements of women's giving, and as a group they are a valuable tool for spreading excitement about women's philanthropy. You can tap into the Six Cs Plus Three by taking these actions:

- Develop new programs or reinvent the existing ones by using women's entrepreneurial, creative abilities. Bring women's talents to the table.
- Create projects to help women and girls.
- Provide ways, within your organization, to help solve societal issues. Be proactive with your programs.
- Ask women to become involved and be committed to the institution's mission before asking them for a major gift.
- Provide ways for women to connect with one another.
- Provide ways for corporate and entrepreneurial women to network around your cause.
- Invite corporate and business women to a focus group and ask them about ways to encourage more giving from their peers to your nonprofit.
- Ask spouses of board members to become board members.
- Develop programs that help women become role models and possible mentors for young women.
- Work with other organizations and institutions by collaborating rather than competing. Become better together.
- Involve successful women in your community, organization, or institution to honor them and celebrate their success.
- Women with money don't necessarily control the money. Women may need to meet with other women to discuss the subject of

money, philanthropy, and their lives. This format is part of donor education and can be provided by a nonprofit. (See Chapter Nine.)

- Ask a corporate or business woman to serve as executive director or development officer for a day. Cosmetic empress Bobbi Brown was asked to serve for one day as the principal of an elementary school in the Bronx. She thought that would be it, but she has been very involved since. She says, "I fell in love with the school."[30]

- Encourage women to be entrepreneurs in their philanthropy and to invest in your organization.

5

Stages, Styles, and Generations

I N THE PAST, WOMEN'S LIFE EXPERIENCES WERE NOT documented as extensively as men's. Because women historically seldom ruled countries or started wars, we know very little about their actual lives, including their philanthropic interests and actions. Fortunately, today it is understood that women bring special gifts to philanthropy, and it is important to look at their potential, their leadership qualities, and their life experiences and how these affect their giving. Women's lives are now being documented, many through their philanthropy.

Marsha Serlin, a member of C200, has been described as "a scrappy entrepreneur."[1] She owns United Scrap Metal and understands the concept of "walking a mile in someone's shoes." Any front office worker who is hired at the company has to work five weeks in the yard before claiming his or her office chair. This has kept their employee turnover rate well below the national average. Serlin also walks through the yard a couple of times a day, easily spotted in her pink hardhat, silk and cashmere Hermes scarf, and faux fur–lined wrap. She is walking in her own stilettos, but understanding on a daily basis what is going on in the lives of her employees.

The concept applies to those seeking gifts. Walking a day in a woman's shoes helps us understand her life and the factors that may make her become, or continue to be, a donor at this particular time. The reality of a woman's life today may well include divorce, becoming a second or third wife, and outliving a spouse. Other obvious factors are family background, marital status, children, occupation, and age. But along with the obvious are other, more subtle realities.

In this chapter, we try on "shoes" in three general senses: life stage, lifestyle, and generation.

Life Stages

There are five common and relevant stages in a woman's life:

Caring. Women who are raising young children are in a very different period of life from those whose children are grown and who may instead be caring for aging parents. But in both caring stages, these women are busy. Children are always on the minds of mothers, and mothers generally like to talk about their children. It's not so fun (nor socially encouraged) to talk about aging parents and/or taking care of an ill spouse. However, all caring situations need to be acknowledged in any meaningful conversation.

Receipt of life's goodness. A number of young women today come from wealthy families. They have grown up with money. They understand its importance, know that others suffer from lack of basic needs, and have had parents who instilled in them the kind of values that they are now using to shape society. These young women are hungry to find worthy causes and want to make the world a better place. They are trying new solutions and are being entrepreneurial with their inheritances. Because they're not satisfied with the status quo, these young women can be a hard sell for traditional nonprofits. They're reformers and are changing nonprofits even as they change the world.

Balancing. Every woman with a job and a family is always balancing: her time at work, her time taking care of her home, her time with her family, and, if there's any left over, time for herself. She needs information quickly and is likely to seek it from friends and family. Women trust their friends, and there's nothing more effective than one woman suggesting a particular cause that she cares about to her friend. That is much more likely to get a response than any direct mail she will ever receive. Shaw-Hardy found this to be true when she founded a giving circle in Michigan. She didn't even have to ask others to join. Her enthusiasm and her friends' trust made the job easy; most signed on without even being asked.

Climbing the ladder. If she's on any management level at a corporation, nonprofit, or her own business, being noticed is enormously important to her success. Although this woman still uses her heart when approaching philanthropy, she's also using her head. She knows the advantage of networking—of being where the action is and the people are. That means being part of the philanthropic culture in her community. She may very well be interested in chairing or being on the committee of a capital campaign or a fundraising event. Those positions not only give her visibility but also give her corporation, business, or nonprofit visibility.

The empty nest. When children leave, this is the time when many women reach out and become more direct in their approaches to issues, more active politically, and generally more outspoken. They aren't afraid of being advocates, of asking the hard questions, of taking risks in their philanthropy. Investing and getting returns are important, but more important is reaching for answers. At this stage in their lives, women know that not every investment works, but they're willing to take chances on causes so long as those causes are addressing important societal problems.

LIFESTYLES

It is also useful to take note of a woman's lifestyle. Here are some common lifestyle characteristics relevant to philanthropy:

Athletic. Unlike women born a century ago, women today are accustomed to participating in athletics—they are even expected to. Older women are urged to go to health clubs, play tennis and golf, be active. Many younger women were athletes in high school or college, and though they may not have maintained that same degree of ability, they still are supportive of athletics, particularly women's athletics. Older women may run marathons, do triathlons, or participate in walkathons, tennis tournaments, and golf leagues. These women know the benefits of being involved athletically. They want to help other women do the same by supporting athletic programs in their communities and educational institutions.

Social. Just because a woman is a member of a country club doesn't mean she's not aware of philanthropy. But it is important to keep in mind that the kind of giving that may appeal to her is something she can do with others, such as giving circles and special events. She is usually willing to offer the country club or her home as a place to hold events. If she's not employed, she no doubt is supporting her spouse socially, and what she does philanthropically reflects on him as well.

Individualist. The individualist woman has always "not quite fit in," and she is somewhat proud of this. She's not afraid to speak out and become actively involved in causes. She'll even go so far as to demonstrate for or against causes that she feels strongly about. At the very least, she'll gain signatures for petitions to change laws. She's not much for group activities, but she supports advocacy and enjoys politics. Engage the individualist by finding her a cause within the organization that doesn't necessarily involve teamwork.

Activist. Much like the individualist, the activist woman supports causes, generally those involving social action and social justice. Diversity and the environment are also important to her, and she's usually quite active in her community or has been at some point. She's a leader and a good team player and motivator. She can be counted on to perform well when asked to be part of the cause. Keeping busy is important to the activist. Key to her involvement is her understanding that what she is doing is making an impact.

Consumer. Because a consumer woman is always wearing, using, or driving the latest in brand names, appealing to her can mean tying a product to a cause. She is not unaware of the needs in the community or world, but getting closer to those needs through shopping will probably work wonders in winning her over. Take a look at the June philanthropy issues of *Town&Country*. Many of the items advertised contribute a portion of the profits to causes, from the homeless to inner city art. The items for sale include jewelry, food, wine, and clothing. Shopping can be her avocation, and knowing that some portion of it goes to charity can be both an excuse and a motivation.

Spiritualist. This can be a woman who is deeply committed to the rituals of an organized religion or a woman with strong private, individual spiritual leanings. In essence, the spiritualist wants to feel that she is deeply and personally doing good. Depending on the depth of her spiritual involvement, she also cares about making things better for others, but not necessarily in a transformational way. She is often happy at the soup kitchen or in a remote place of the world serving as a lay missionary. To involve her in your organization, you must first understand her deep-seated religious and/or spiritual beliefs.

Worthy. Once this wealthy woman focuses on something that she feels makes her life worthwhile, she's "set for life." She might stumble across something of interest when visiting another country and end up sponsoring women artisans, or she might find a unique cause right in her own neighborhood. Whatever it is, she is like the women philanthropists of the past—she wants to found the non-profit or the program and it will become her passion. Organizations seeking this woman need to find out what she is thinking and ask her opinions. They must understand, though, that this woman wants to be a pioneer in whatever she funds.

GENERATIONS

Margaret May Damen, coauthor of *Women, Wealth, and Giving* and president and founder of the Institute for Women and Wealth in Lake Worth, Florida, has done a great deal of research, particularly with Baby Boomer women. She says, "A generation is defined by a common set of lifestyle experiences that take place during a specific time in history."[2]

A woman is profoundly shaped by the generation into which she is born: her childhood experiences, her relationship with her peers, and her values are all part of that cultural history. There are extreme and very interesting differences in the generations, affecting how they give.

Analyzing the Generations

We have been developing these generational concepts for many years through hundreds of interviews, focus groups, and results of workplace gender research. In 2008 Shaw-Hardy and Carmen Stevens published the results of their research of two hundred self-selected women philanthropists.[3] This research was done primarily with Baby Boomers (born 1946–64) and Gen X (born 1965–76), with some Prime Time generation (born 1925–45) women involved.

Often it's easier to understand generational differences by looking at well-known women in each generation. For example, think how different Barbara Bush (born in 1925), Nancy Pelosi (born in 1949),

Michelle Obama (born in 1964), Tina Fey (born in 1970), Chelsea Clinton (born in 1980), and Miley Cyrus (born in 1992) are from one another. Of course, they are all women and have in common many of the unique qualities discussed in Chapter Four, but their generations also strongly define them in their spousal relationships, as parents, their choice of careers, and certainly their philanthropy.

Studies show a positive relationship between age and giving, and we have compiled as much information as possible from our own sources as well as research in the field.[4] We are pleased that the Women's Philanthropy Institute at the Center on Philanthropy at Indiana University has empirical generational research on its agenda, and we look forward to the results. Some of the Center's early results are also included in this chapter.

A word about our conclusions: not only are they generational, but they are generalizations as well. For each generation there will always be variations and exceptions.

Traditionalist Women

The women of this "Father Knows Best" generation (with a nod to the popular 1950s television show), born between 1910 and 1930, generally stayed at home raising the family while the husband went off to work. Most appeared to defer to their husbands, although many actually influenced the outcome much beyond what was seen or admitted to by their families.

Two words best describe most of the women in this generation: "preserve" and "conserve." They were profoundly affected by the Great Depression and fear losing their money; they are quite frugal. They feel a responsibility to conserve their money and pass it on to their children.

Most Traditionalist women did not bring home a paycheck, except for those who went to work during World War II. Even those women generally returned to the home when the men returned. Because of this, they can be fearful of starting over and are the most likely of all the generations to be afraid of becoming "bag ladies."

Currently a great many Traditionalists are widows or caregivers for ailing spouses. They are the least likely of all generations to regard the family money as theirs, and unless there has been a life-changing experience such as a death or divorce, they will usually continue to give, out of sense of loyalty, to the causes their spouses or families supported. Also, because Traditionalist women often don't feel the money actually belongs to them, they frequently don't want public recognition for their gifts unless it is in a family or spouse's name.

Of course, there are always exceptions; there are many women of this generation who, having no role models, boldly forged their own way to give money in their own fashion. Some well-known Traditionalist women are Sandra Day O'Connor, Margaret Thatcher, Barbara Walters, Queen Elizabeth II, Barbara Bush, Adrienne Rich, Judith Krantz, Joanne Woodward, Betty Ford, and Maya Angelou.

Traditionalist Women as Philanthropists

Fortunately, not every Traditionalist woman needs a life-changing situation to become philanthropic. Margaret Lloyd wants to live life to its fullest. She says, "To my amazement, I'm now eighty-eight years old. So many elderly people sit around having their cocktails and going to Florida, not really being alive. I want to continue to count for something no matter that I do feel my age." Lloyd donated her eight-hundred-plus acres of forest in Kershaw County, South Carolina, and about $2 million to Clemson University to implement her vision of land use. "It will become Hard Scramble Connections Center," she says, "an educational project teaching us about our vital interconnectedness, and I am very excited about it."[5] Her excitement stems, no doubt, from the fact that the land will be used as home for a world-class environmental education center and an international model for green residential development. *Not* for another golf course.

Engaging the Traditionalist Woman in Philanthropy

Try these approaches:

- *Understand her reluctance to give away her money during her lifetime and suggest bequests.* Because of her fear of running out of money during her lifetime, the woman of this generation is most interested in bequests. Help her understand what her own special interests are, then set up a program that will benefit that interest through a bequest.

- *Suggest annualizing her gift during her lifetime.* If a woman has agreed to a bequest, suggest she give an annual gift of the same amount that will eventually come out of that bequest. Explain that she will receive the joy of giving during her lifetime and be able to see where her bequest will ultimately be going. If the gift is for a scholarship, she will have the pleasure of meeting the students receiving the scholarship.

- *Be in touch and stay in touch.* Most Traditionalist women either are or will soon be widows. The smart institution, organization, or person who has worked with her when her spouse was alive will continue to stay in touch with her after he passes away. Too many gifts are lost after the spouse dies, as there has been little or no contact with the widow during his lifetime.

- *Include her family.* Because she is the conserver and preserver of the money and wants her heirs to receive the greatest benefit, involving them is key. Happily, heirs often will want her to do something in her name to realize the joy of her gift while she is alive.

- *Recognize her and how she arrived at her destination.* Although women in this generation may not mention it, they have certainly experienced some gender discrimination in their lives. If appropriate, recognize their struggles to achieve and offer ways for them to become role models while helping those who will be walking in their shoes.

Former First Lady Barbara Bush sums up the values of the Traditionalist woman: "At the end of your life, you will never regret not having passed one more test, not winning one more verdict, or not closing one more deal. You will regret time not spent with a husband, a friend, a child, or a parent." Looking ahead, she adds, "And who knows? Somewhere out there in this audience may even be someone who will one day follow my footsteps, and preside over the White House as the president's spouse. I wish him well!"[6]

Prime Time Women

Marketer and author Marti Barletta says that Prime Time women, in her book of the same name, are so called because they are in the prime of their lives.[7] These women were born between 1925 and 1945. Their children are through college, they and their spouses may have retired or be near retirement, and they are enjoying life.

This generation of women has also been called the wealthiest, most dynamic generation of women in the history of the United States.

The influence of World War II may well have provided Prime Time (PT) women with just the kind of role models they needed, even if for a relatively short time. They grew up seeing women leaving to go to work in the defense plants, offices, and elsewhere, carrying on the jobs of the males who were off to war. Of course when the males returned, the women also returned: males to the jobs and women to the homes. Nevertheless, most PT women were inspired by seeing this potential realized during the first ten years of their lives. They saw that women could work outside the home and still raise a family.

This was the first generation to commonly experience the family breakdown through divorce; many were pushed into a career whether they were ready or not. These women had to learn about money management, thus becoming the first female philanthropists in their own right.

Prime Time women were often reluctant to acknowledge there were differences, other than physical, between women and men. But as they have aged, they have mellowed and understand that it's OK to be different from men. They are proud of their accomplishments in a male-dominated world, and they especially want to help younger women succeed.

Because many a Prime Time woman was the first in her family to attend college, she is very supportive of education. She personally experienced the benefits of a college education and may have met her spouse while at college. She had a career either early on or later, after her children were raised.

Through her efforts as a volunteer or in a paid career, the PT woman helped pave the way for the enormous number of opportunities available to her daughters and granddaughters (though they don't always recognize or yet appreciate her efforts), and she wants to ensure that those opportunities continue to exist for new generations. She is often delighted to give to organizations that support young women.

Prime Time women have generally been missed by nonprofits, largely because of their earlier label: the Eisenhower or "Silent" generation. But PT women have been far from quiet. Witness just a few examples: Gloria Steinem, Diane Sawyer, Supreme Court Justice Ruth Bader Ginsburg, senators Dianne Feinstein and Barbara Boxer,

Donna Shalala, Martha Stewart, Goldie Hawn, and Jane Fonda. These women have redefined what it is to be a woman, and showcased their successes in all areas from financial to political, many while raising families as well.

Prime Time Women as Philanthropists

When a man says "I'll think about it," the sale is usually gone. When a women says "I'll think about it," she really means it.[8]

—*Anna Kate Hipp, Greenville, South Carolina*

Anna Kate Hipp, a philanthropist from Greenville, South Carolina, has thought a great deal about her personal philanthropy and her family foundation's giving. She says the recession that began in 2008 caused her to sit down and really examine what she was giving to and how much. Hipp decided to start out by writing down the issues she really cared about. As a result, she claims her giving has become planned and focused. "It is pretty exciting to see that now I am giving to exactly what I want to," she says.

Through the exercise, Hipp discovered that some of the causes she was giving to have become passions of her children. She no longer supports those causes, having turned them over to the next generation. By paring her contributions and eliminating those that were not major gifts, Hipp found what she describes as "an interesting evolution," the three areas she really cares about: education for women, the arts, and the environment.

After years of serving on boards and committees because either she thought she should, she was doing a favor for someone, or she simply wanted to serve, Hipp says she now serves only on those boards that match one of her three areas of interest. That includes her alma mater, Mary Baldwin College in Staunton, Virginia, where she has served on the board for twenty-five years and cochaired a $42 million campaign in the 1990s. Even thirty years ago, Hipp did not go to husbands for gifts. "I knew we had to connect with women, not their spouses," she says. Hipp feels so strongly about female education that she gives more to her college than her husband gives to his. At the same time, she says, "It's always been a partnership, and we've been equally generous to one another's causes."

"Although I haven't consciously thought about giving to women, much of my giving has turned out that way," she says. Brookgreen Gardens in Murrells Inlet, South Carolina, fulfills all three of Hipp's interest areas (women, the arts, and the environment), and she serves on its board. Many of the sculptures in the gardens are the work of women, and Hipp explains her interest: "Beauty appeals to women, as does creativity, and if we address the environment and the arts, we ultimately address major components of the world that are important to us all."

Engaging the Prime Time Woman in Philanthropy

Consider these ideas as you approach a Prime Time woman:

- *She is interested in breakthroughs in the traditional philanthropic ways and programs.* She has been a pathfinder and continues to be one. Prime Time women are often more like Boomer women rather than like their mothers, the Traditionalists. They have experienced extreme changes in the world, from their relatively serene childhoods to the chaotic present. They're not afraid of taking some risks in their giving and being entrepreneurial with their philanthropy.

- *She will give to already established institutions, but prefers to do so by supporting programs that are new and unique and address the problems of society.* The PT woman is particularly interested in relevancy, so consider this in any fundraising effort, particularly a capital campaign. How will her contributions to the organization or institution help solve societal issues?

- *A Prime Time woman wants to help the next generation of women.* First, identify programs that are already occurring or issues dealing with women and girls in your institution, then ask for her help. Often women don't know of the programs an institution may already have, such as child care on campus. Although it is time-consuming and requires a great deal of staff coordination, be aware that she could be interested in mentoring young women or female staff within the organization. She may also be willing to ask for money from her friends, particularly if she is deeply involved with the nonprofit.

- *Her generation is the first to have a significant influence on spousal decision making.* Because she believes her voice to be equal in the relationship, and she may make some gifts on her own, accurate gift crediting is of utmost importance to her. She wants to be acknowledged correctly, displaying her name as she wishes. (See Chapter Six for more information about the importance of crediting gifts.) Consider asking spouses to serve on committees together.

- *When calling on her husband who is already a donor, include her in the conversation unless specifically asked not to.* If the Prime Time wife has not been included in the conversations about philanthropy, she is unlikely to continue giving if she becomes a widow.

- *Propose a matching gift.* Matching gifts are favorites of this generation, who would rather give with others than be singled out as "the big donor. " Think about involving her with three or four other women to match gifts.

Suffragist Elizabeth Cady Stanton said, "The heyday of a woman's life is on the shady side of fifty, when . . . her thoughts and sentiments flow out . . . in philanthropy."[9] A century later, this still explains the Prime Time woman. She has courage, leadership, perseverance, and loyalty as well as capital; she is enjoying the results of her efforts and triumphs; and she is most willing to give.

Baby Boomer Women

This amazing group of women, born between 1946 and 1964, is the largest and best educated generation in U.S. history. They know they have the numbers, and thus the power, and they demand to be listened to.

Boomer women are not only among the leading corporate managers and executives, but according to a study by Thomas Stanley, Ph.D., author of *Millionaire Women Next Door*, there are thirty-seven to thirty-eight million women in this generation, and nine million of them are business owners with an individual net worth of more than $1 million.[10]

Television greatly affected Boomer women as they were growing up: Vietnam, war protests, the assassinations of the Kennedys and Martin Luther King Jr., the civil rights movement. As a consequence, the women of this generation became idealistic—they clamored for change. In fact, many are not done changing the world, and, thankfully for us, they are focusing on many of the important issues of today: women's economic independence, the environment, and social justice. It can be said that Boomer women always knew they were destined for great things and demand to be noticed.

According to research by Melissa Brown of the Center on Philanthropy at Indiana University, Boomer women give more than Boomer men and are the only generation for which this is true. Brown's research also showed that Boomer women were the most generous of all the generations, and Boomer and older women are more likely than Boomer men to respond to a message that urges "responsibility to help those with less."[11] Andrea Kaminski, executive director of the Wisconsin League of Women Voters, says that women in this generation question authority and do not give out of a sense of loyalty. Maintaining the status quo holds no interest for them. In fact, many would rather overthrow than preserve—after all, they were part of the 1960s social upheaval.[12]

Although their attention is on solving the big issues of today, that is not to say Boomer women aren't still supporting education and the arts—traditional areas of women's giving. But Boomer women go about giving in ways somewhat different from those of the two generations before them. For example, they would more likely support bringing to a museum an exhibit that features women of color rather than one showcasing former first ladies.

Boomer women demand accountability for the monies they give. They look on their giving as an investment and want to be sure their money is used wisely and has an impact.

This individualistic generation wants to participate in decision making; they are always asking "Why?" or "How can it be done better?" They are rewriting the rules of philanthropy and have authority within the family. They're not afraid to use their new rules and their voices of influence with female relatives. They can educate and even bring about change in the established philanthropy of their relations. Margaret May Damen—women's wealth manager, Baby Boomer expert, and author of *Women, Wealth, and Giving*—says that Boomer women "can influence the gift planning decisions of older women and nurture the philanthropic culture for younger women."[13]

While Traditionalist and Prime Time women are more likely to give with their spouses, Boomer women are the first generation to give separately as well. They are willing to give to large institutions, but less likely to do so than Traditionalist women. Public recognition is all right with them if it is for the benefit of the organization. Like almost all women, they would like hands-on involvement before giving.

Boomer women are not hard to find. They serve on city councils, county boards of commission, and hold state and national offices. These women are poised to be elected to even higher offices. Because Boomer women have graduated from law schools in record numbers, they hold judicial seats at local, state, and national levels. They are also leading the way in philanthropy. Prominent Boomer figures are Helen LaKelly Hunt, Susan Alice Buffett, Tracy Gary, Melinda Gates, and Sheila Johnson.

Baby Boomers as Philanthropists

I feel compelled to express my values through my philanthropy.[14]

—*Cheryl Rosen Weston, Madison, Wisconsin*

Cheryl Rosen Weston is a quintessential child of the '60s. Born in Chicago, she law-clerked for a Chicago firm representing Abbie Hoffman and Jerry Rubin during the Chicago 7 appeal. Granted, her experience was more "up close and personal" than that of most in her age group, but it represents what so many in her generation know: there are long-term issues that need solving, it is possible for change to rapidly occur, and we can make it happen. "The civil rights movement was happening around us and you couldn't be alive and aware and not see social injustice," she says, "especially living in a big city like Chicago. I think during the sixties we felt frustrated and powerless. We saw the assassinations of John and Bobby Kennedy and Martin Luther King Jr. We saw people dying in Vietnam on television at night. It was only natural for young people to ask themselves what could they do."

Going from being powerless to creating change happened very fast to many in the '60s, and Weston was one of them. "What the sixties taught me was that we must take responsibility for our communities, whether defined as global or just in our neighborhoods. And if we have the financial means to help, we must." Weston's philanthropy is important to her because she believes she can use it to continue making change, whether through the ACLU and its ongoing fight for people's rights, the Madison Jewish Federation with its international relief and local social services programs, or the University of Wisconsin–Madison, where she obtained her law degree.

Not only is Weston a professor at the university's law school, but she is also president and CEO of the largest woman-owned business in Wisconsin, The Douglas Stewart Company, a wholesale distributor of computer products serving the education market. The company came to her as part of a divorce settlement from her husband, who had been managing his family business during their marriage. As vice president and general counsel, Weston knew all about the organization. In 2007 The Douglas Stewart Company had sales of $300 million and 150 employees. It has also opened a subsidiary in Europe. She says she wants to encourage her employees to be philanthropic, and she matches 100 percent of any gifts they make to nonprofits. The program is run annually like a United Way campaign; Weston does have a budgetary limit, but she claims it has never been reached.

Although philanthropy is extremely important to Weston, it is not something she does without accountability. She stresses that if she gives to an organization, she holds them responsible for that gift. "I want to be sure the organization is run like a business, and I know how that goes," she says.

"My life took all these twists and turns, and I ended up with more financial resources than I ever thought I would. Certainly, in my lifetime, I've seen people become more and more focused on material things. As we are confronted with issues of sustainability—including food insecurity and climate change—people are wondering whether simply acquiring things is a rational thing to do. I really don't take much satisfaction in stockpiling money," she says. "I feel compelled to express my values through my philanthropy."

Engaging Baby Boomer Women in Philanthropy

Keep these thoughts in mind when approaching a Boomer:

- *Her family is mostly grown, so this is a reflective time of life.* She is ready to commit to her values and vision and become a loyal donor. Spend time conducting focus groups and listening to this generation of women to find out how they feel about your organization and to help them explore their own personal values and vision. (Suggestions for conducting focus groups and questions to ask are in the Resources.) Because collaboration is important to them, explain that they will be a partner with the organization—and of course provide ways for their involvement.

- *Boomer women merit respect for knowing the value of money, particularly after putting children through or currently having children in college. They generally understand finances and can read balance statements.* They are looking at the institution as an investment; they want a return on that investment and to know that the organization is well run. Treat this woman with trust and respect, and provide detailed information about the organization's budget and finances. Keep her updated on the outcome of her gift. Show how her gift has made a difference and how it has brought about change. Boomer women, particularly those who are working outside the home, understand the importance of fundraising for an organization they believe in. Present her with the challenge, then sit back and rejoice at her skills and success.

- *Boomer women are thinking legacy.* They appreciate what their mothers have done for them and want to be sure their personal values are passed on to the next generation. Women in this generation want their giving to go beyond their lifetime. Consider programs that are multigenerational, and particularly include the younger women members of Boomer families, whether daughters, granddaughters, or nieces.

- *Boomer women have multitasked in their professional and home lives and think holistically.* They want to know all the ramifications of programs and get the big picture.

- *The Boomer woman still yearns for change.* Provide opportunities for her to do more than apply a band-aid to a problem. She wants her gifts to be transformational and have a distinct positive outcome.

- *Being social has always been important to Boomer women.* They are avid users of the Internet, which has provided them with ways to reconnect with their high school and college friends. Use the Internet to help donors be in touch with one another. When they meet for the first time at focus groups, provide a Web site forum for them to continue their conversations. Offer opportunities for them to connect, network, and make friends with one another. (See Chapter Six about development and Chapter Eight about programs.)

Hillary Clinton has summed up the opportunities and obligations of this generation: "The challenges of change are always hard. It is important that we begin to unpack those challenges that confront this nation and realize that we each have a role that requires us to change and become more responsible for shaping our own future."[15]

Gen X Women

Generation X or Gen X marks the period of declining birth rate after World War II's baby boom. Born between 1965 and 1976, this is a significantly smaller generation than previous and succeeding generations. Gen X women were born and grew up during the later years of the Cold War, came of age after the Vietnam War, and watched Desert Storm on CNN. They were raised in a world of economic and domestic instability and were among the first "latchkey" children.

In an article titled "Beyond Duty and Obligation,"[16] noted philanthropy expert Sharna Goldseker identifies the following generational personality traits of Gen Xers:

- Because Gen X grew up in an era of scandals, corporate downsizing, and a tripling of the divorce rate, they learned to be skeptical of every institution, from the government to corporations—even the institution of marriage. Like the Boomers, Gen Xers are more often motivated by values of opportunity, freedom, and compassion than by duty, loyalty, and obligation.

- With the smallest numbers in their age cohort of all the generations described here, Gen Xers rarely have to compete for opportunities. They may enter leadership roles in their twenties and thirties or begin their own startup corporations and nonprofits.

- Although Gen Xers may be stereotyped as "slackers," their operational experiences demonstrate their ability to be hardworking, creative, and resourceful when they find something about which they are passionate.

Parents of Gen Xers are more likely to divorce than in previous eras, and some Gen Xers saw their parents laid off from their jobs as the security of having a lifetime career with one company began to slip away. As a result, Gen Xers tend to be independent, individualistic, resourceful, and self-sufficient. They value freedom and responsibility and a work/life balance, but enjoy playing hard as well.

Gen X Women as Philanthropists

Gen X philanthropic donors represent a new wave. They are both successful and civic-minded. Members of this generation are more ethnically diverse than earlier American generations, often have less disposable time, and want to spend that time with their growing families. Interestingly, a 2008 survey from Northern Trust[17] found that Gen X millionaires give nearly twice as much, on average, to charitable causes as their elders; they are more generous in their charitable bequests and more globally inclined or community-inclined in their giving, as opposed to giving to large institutions. Gen Xers are also more focused on honoring a loved one and creating a lasting legacy for themselves and their families than members of previous generations. The giving potential and earning power—as well as the high education levels—of Gen X women are placing them in positions of power in their communities, organizations, and institutions.

Gen Xers Versus Boomers

As is true for Prime Time and Baby Boomer women, it is important for Gen X women to know that their gifts will make a difference and change things for the better. However, Gen X women are more likely to give from personal or inherited income than to give with a spouse or partner. Shaw-Hardy and Carmen Stevens's 2008 study *Women's Giving: A Generational Perspective* revealed the following about Gen X women's giving compared with that of Boomer women's:

- Boomers on an average give between 4 and 7 percent of their income and would like to give between 11 and 25 percent.

- Gen Xers give between 1 and 3 percent of their income and would like to give between 8 and 10 percent.

- More Gen X than Boomer women expect to receive an inheritance and make more of their gifting through family wealth using family foundations.

- Boomer women are more likely to give with their spouses, whereas Gen Xers give from personal and inherited income before gifting with a spouse or partner.

- Gen Xers want to give away their money during their lifetime; Boomers want their giving to go on beyond their lifetime through their children and grandchildren.

- Boomer women felt they needed more time to become financially literate, whereas Gen Xers said they wanted more education about financial matters.

- More Gen X than Boomer women say they were influenced to give when the solicitation was made on a generational level (that is, from someone their age).

- Gen X women value their time more than their money; Boomer women were prepared to give both at least equally.

- Boomer women are more likely than Gen X women to give to large institutions.

- Boomer women are more comfortable than Gen X with public recognition of their giving. Gen Xers say they would accept recognition if it was for the pure benefit of the organization and each member who aided the organization was also recognized.

- Gen X women are not as concerned about receiving follow-up from the organization after they make a gift, whereas this is important to Boomer women.

- More Gen X than Boomer women are involved within their religious communities.

Gen X Women as Philanthropists

As a philanthropist and the COO of Associated Black Charities (ABC) of Maryland, Tanya Jones Terrell also sees a difference from previous generations in the way that Gen X women choose to spend their time and invest their charitable dollars: "I think Generation X wants to contribute talent and strengths in outcome-driven ways. For my generation, it boils down to being focused givers around very specific causes . . . [W]e want to spend our time deeply engaged in the organizations whose missions we support."[18]

Jones Terrell credits her mother as her inspiration for her own philanthropy, "not only because she is philanthropist in her own right, but because she doesn't believe what she does is anything special. All of her giving and volunteering are based on sharing and helping others." However, although Jones Terrell and her mother are both motivated to give for similar reasons, their approaches are very different. "I want my time spent on issues I care deeply about and in ways that I can have a broader impact. What I do professionally reaffirms why I give—there is so much need in the world that it's almost not an option to not help in some way." The difference? Jones Terrell considers herself a philanthropist and recognizes the power and opportunity that comes with it, whereas her mother doesn't see herself in that way.

Candace Dodson Reed, founder of the effort twentyfivefortyfive at the Columbia Foundation in Howard County, Maryland, grew up in a household that instilled in her the importance of giving time, energy, or money. Because of this, she is not only engaged in giving but also intent on being a role model for her daughter and others. However, her perspective on giving and the ways in which she is engaging in philanthropy are very different from those of her parents.

Dodson Reed explains her differences with the past generation: "My parents supported larger, national organizations like civil rights and health. For my generation, it's important that we see how our money can effect local change. I am less likely to give money to national organizations because I am not sure what my money is doing." She adds, "Our generation really wants to see how our money and time can make an impact—it's about education, engagement, awareness, networking, and building a community in a way that makes sense for our lifestyles and perspectives."[19]

As the executive director of the Reid Family Foundation in Auburn Hills, Michigan, Sheri Reid Grant has a good deal of philanthropic experience. But it's not just experience that guides her leadership; passion and caring also drive this Gen X woman's stewardship of her family's foundation. "My life has been greatly blessed with love, health, and wealth, and I want to give of myself in order to leave this world a better place while I was in it," she says. "When I give I receive so much more in return, and it's inspiring to think what would happen if more lived by this principle."[20]

The Reid Family Foundation funds educational programs encouraging kids through hands-on education. The Foundation focuses on engineering-related grants as well as scholarships. Because Reid Grant's father is the foundation's founder, she has spent time guiding their giving so as to combine both her own giving interests and passions and her father's. She believes there is a gender lens in philanthropy and that women give differently from men. She also feels strongly about the strength of women as leaders and believes they have great capacity for compassion and empathy. These strengths are a big part of her motivation to personally help others, and they serve as a guide for her stewardship of the foundation. "Many of the philanthropic leaders that I am coming into contact with are women," says Reid Grant. "Women leaders in philanthropy have their own wealth; are conscientious and ethical; are more interested in transformation, change, and impact; and as a result are becoming more visible in philanthropy."

Dictionary.com defines philanthropy as "the effort or inclination to increase the well-being of humankind, as by charitable aid or donations; love of humankind in general; someone who practices philanthropy." "These definitions fit me to a 'T,'" says Reid Grant. "I believe that I have been a philanthropist all of my life."

Engaging Gen X Women in Philanthropy

Here are some useful guidelines:

- Gen X women need to have choices that are meaningful to them and fit in with their lifestyles. They want balance in their lives. The thoughtful organization will consider how to meet Gen X women where they are in their lives. Consider reaching out to existing groups of women and inviting participation through a natural link to a book club, moms' group, or athletic group. Gen X women who can leverage their family and personal time along with community engagement and philanthropy are more likely to get and stay involved.

- This generation is the first one to grow up with computers and technology woven into their lives. Gen X women are big users of social networking and expect nonprofits to provide them with easy ways to use this to connect with one another and the organization. They use digital technology personally and professionally and are using social media tools such as Facebook and LinkedIn to stay connected. Savvy organizations will help the Gen X woman connect to causes of importance to her—on her time, in her way—while she connects to family, work, and friends through these new tools.

- Gen Xers want hands-on engagement that differs from the philanthropy and engagement of previous generations. It is not enough for Gen Xers to volunteer at the nonprofits. They want more than that. Consider providing opportunities for volunteer trips and/or learning journeys as a way to give and learn about the needs of an institution's constituents. Think about including their children as well.

- Gen Xers are a more diverse generation than preceding ones. While they expect to be treated equally, and certainly not as a minority, we have found that some women of color appreciate opportunities to network within their own ethnic group, as with the Change Fund in Baltimore.

- Leadership and networking opportunities with business associates are very important to Gen Xers as they climb the corporate ladder or develop their own businesses. Gen Xers seek ways to incorporate civic engagement with their giving. They seek opportunities to connect business and networking with giving and civic engagement, and they want to connect with other Gen X women in the workforce, providing opportunities for leadership and impact in a business setting.

Generation Y Women

Not surprisingly, Gen Y women (born between 1981 and 1999) currently give less than other generations. They are the youngest and do not yet possess the financial means of the earlier generations.

According to research,[21] Gen Y women will remain employed or working throughout their lives, even after starting a family. Yet Gen Y women crave balance in all aspects of their lives, focused on balancing their careers, families, and fulfilling personal lives. Many watched the juggling act of an earlier generation of working moms and believe they'll find a better way.[22] In any case, they are likely to rewrite the rules of the game and say they want more than just a job—they want a career they are passionate about.

Gen Y Women as Philanthropists

As Gen Y women seek meaning in their lives, they strive for meaning in their giving. They are bringing philanthropy and civic engagement to their lives in ways that previous generations never dreamed of. Sharna Goldseker says that Gen Y sees the world differently because of their experiences: "Their community takes place differently, not necessarily through Kiwanis groups, but through technology, and because of this, there is a different sense of connectedness."[23]

This different sense of connectedness is across the board— through family and friends, colleagues and peers, large and local organizations. And their community isn't just about geography. Gen Y women, particularly through philanthropy, use technology to build and join communities that are about their interests. They focus on issues of importance to them, sharing and giving in real-time using technology and social media. This new sense of connectedness is what helps to fulfill Gen Y women's desire for balance.

And although Gen Y women may be starting small, they are certainly starting early. Sara Azout, a senior at Brown University, decided she wanted to do something meaningful her final year of college and raise money for the Acumen Fund, an organization important to her that focuses on delivering affordable, critical goods and services—like health, water, and housing—through innovative, market-oriented approaches. Azout is interested in the intersection of finance and development, and when she looked for a creative way to reach members of her generation with a meaningful message and easy donation opportunity, she turned to social media technology. "It's all about social media these days," she says, adding that she doesn't like traditional philanthropy and would not respond to or send out a letter asking for money.[24]

Azout sent out a message through FirstGiving, Facebook, and her college classes that began, "So, I am trying to raise $1,000 for Acumen Fund within the next 24 hours. I want to do this by getting 100 people to donate $10. I don't really get what the deal is with the economy. Yes, we're in a recession. But hey, gas prices are low, we can still afford our tuition, we are healthy, and we are happy. This is not the case for everyone." Not only did she hit her goal, but she did so as the beginning of a quest to raise $10,000.

San Franciscan Kristin Walter calls herself a philanthropist, but to her, philanthropy means "partnership" rather than "charity."[25]

This Gen Y woman believes giving is not so much about helping people as it is about working in collaboration to create a better world. As she puts it, the term "philanthropist" has baggage, but the definition applies.

Walter is the founder of the FeelGood movement, an innovative social enterprise that engages college students in focusing on world hunger issues and becoming global citizens, socially responsible leaders, and entrepreneurs. She believes her generation has a desire to make giving part of their lifestyle. "I see it in the clothes we wear, the lunch we eat, the jobs we take, and how we express our inter-connectedness through entrepreneurial ideas . . . It's not about a tax deduction."

Walter views FeelGood donors as investors. Social networking is a component of the ways FeelGood gets the word out and, in its first year, raised almost $10,000 on Facebook. A number of "large" donations have also come from individuals who found FeelGood through word of mouth or experience with the effort. Walter believes that others will become engaged in FeelGood through efforts to make their giving personal, visionary, and an empowering part of their lifestyle. To that end, she says social networking provides a nice exchange between online and offline worlds and a way to create community on- and offline.

As a Gen Y philanthropist, Walter believes that having relationships and feeling connected is important to and engrained in women and it has been a motivator for her and her philanthropic pursuits. "I have incorporated social change through connectedness into my life, and it has empowered me—it's a very complete experience for me."

The roots of New Yorker Melissa Madzel's philanthropy are obvious to her when she thinks back to the two quarters that her grandfather always tucked into her hand for contributing at church, teaching her from a very young age that anyone can make a difference and give to others—no matter how young you are or how little money you have.

Madzel doesn't consider herself a philanthropist in the traditional sense, but she recognizes that she gives both time and money at the level that she can. Most of her donations are given online, which has been the most significant use of technology in her giving. "It's easier to learn about and give to issues beyond those in your neighborhood, thanks to technology and globalization."[26]

Madzel believes that personal experience is the best way to engage Gen Y donors. "Volunteer opportunities—as difficult as they are to coordinate for nonprofits—bring potential donors the personal experience that will stay with them as they make their giving decisions," she says. "This requires nonprofits to be extremely creative and thoughtful about ways to bring their programs to their donors."

Engaging Gen Y Women in Philanthropy

Here are some good starting ideas:

- *Gen Y women are seeking balance in all aspects of their lives.* Organizations have an opportunity to view these women with a new lens and find meaningful and engaging ways to meet them on their terms and in ways that appeal to their desire to balance their families, careers, and community engagement.

- *Some traditional messages used by nonprofits are not as effective with Gen Y.* Messages about benefiting the community, replacing or supplementing government funding, and helping meet people's basic needs aren't as interesting to this generation. But "impact" and "fun" are words that resonate. Although the words convey different concepts, they describe the benefits of giving that fit this generation's desire for balance and meaning in all aspects of their lives.

- *Gen Y donors may be an underestimated and untapped resource.* Research suggests this is the case. Many Gen Y women are both willing and able to give. But they are not being asked by nonprofits who have low expectations of their potential. Organizations should look to the future and invite these women to engage now. Gen Y women are seeking ways to give, and even if it means a smaller amount now, it can be a great start for a long-term relationship in the future.

- *Gen Y women are interested in social change and want to be engaged in giving.* They are entrepreneurial, passionate, and ready for social change across the board, including seeing a woman as U.S. president. Their dreams and aspirations can be supported by their desire for meaning in their actions, and their change will come from their philanthropic investments in social change. Engaging

Gen Y women's sense of entrepreneurial spirit and passion will bring philanthropy to a new level.

- *Gen Y women are very comfortable with technology.* Technology and social networking are part of their lifestyle, and they need to be engaged with this in mind.

A Web resource called "Nonprofit Tech 2.0: A Social Media Guide for Nonprofits" (http://nonprofitorgs.wordpress.com/) outlines some more detailed basic and distinct characteristics of Gen Y, tech-savvy donors and ways to engage them.[27] Gen Y women are not just searching for information on the Web; they also seek to share their opinions, experiences, and ideas through social media tools like blogs, Facebook, and Twitter. For the purposes of philanthropy, Web 1.0 was mostly for those who were solely reading on the Web; Web 2.0 is for those who are reading and writing and engaging in an entirely new way on the Web. Web 2.0 giving is addictive and fun, and it has been adopted by Gen Y. Nonprofits will continue to identify and nurture check writers and Web 1.0 donors, but now they must recognize that there is a new and very different generation of donors. The approach to engaging and inspiring them and the ways you thank them must be very different as well.

- Once Gen Y women start giving on social networking sites, they don't go back to Web 1.0 giving.

- Web 2.0 donors don't want to receive print materials. They are concerned about saving resources and don't want a printed thank-you letter for a $10 donation through a social networking site. They have come of age in an era in which environmental sustainability and frugality is very important; this worldview directly affects the way they give and the way they want to be approached. They do, however, want "Thank you" wall comments and compliments. When donating in public forums, they appreciate being thanked there as well.

- They often will provide only an email address and opt out of providing a mailing address. Nonprofits need to focus more on electronic communication such as an enewsletter—this may be the only way to contact and nurture Web 2.0 donors outside of social networking sites.

- They give in smaller amounts, and more often, to many nonprofits that they had not heard of until they saw them on a social networking site. If a nonprofit isn't on these sites, it may not be on the radar screen of Gen Y.

Don't be slow to address this generation. As Kristin Walter says, "Gen Y women are seeking ways to powerfully participate in philanthropy."

Takeaways

We believe the most interesting aspect of women's philanthropy is the generational differences within its ranks. Women can and do identify themselves by generation. In our presentations, focus groups, and workshops over the past twenty years, the generational theme has resonated with women more strongly than any other. When they see themselves in their particular generation, women understand more about who they are and how this knowledge relates to their philanthropy.

Even though there are many philanthropic similarities across the generations—often linked to the Six Cs Plus Three of women's motivations for giving (see Chapter Four)—the differences spark a great deal of thought and conversation among women, particularly in the areas of donor recognition and spousal giving,

We enjoy seeing women's eyes light up with recognition and awareness when they are presented with both the generational piece and the donor education as outlined in Chapter Eight. You can almost hear women thinking, "Finally, we're being paid attention to as worthwhile human beings who are different, not only from men, but from one another as well. We count because we are counted on to have capital, to be philanthropic, and to shape a better world."

PART
THREE

Building Bridges to the Other Half

6

Nonprofits' Future:
Gender-Sensitive Development

It's contingent upon us to make sure that our alumni leadership reflects the
demographics of our alumni body. Don't underestimate this: We're on the verge of
the greatest unleashing of resources—the greatest change in higher education—
since the Middle Ages. We have to be nimble to address these changes. And that's
hard when universities are so slow to respond. We're playing catch-up all the time.
Now is the time to wake up and totally rethink the way we do business.[1]

—April Harris, University of Alabama–Huntsville

CURRENTLY, WOMEN ARE AT LEAST 50 PERCENT OF the audience for most nonprofits. For some nonprofits and with higher education—because of the high number of women students—women will become the dominant audience in the future. Whether run by volunteers or professionals, development operations must be gender-sensitive to secure the support of women. All women are different, but these steps are good fundamental development principles that will apply to women and may increase success with men as well.

Here we will cover gender-sensitive principles in the development operation and then focus on how to succeed with women with different types of gifts. Women volunteers and development officers started women's philanthropy development principles, but men volunteers and development officers are now also practicing the concepts in the philanthropic field. For that reason, we interviewed both men and women for this chapter. Particularly over the past few years, as results have borne out theories, the subject of women's philanthropy has entered the mainstream of philanthropic thought.

WHERE TO START

You have read this far into *Women and Philanthropy*, so it is likely that you want to begin a program or at least take a good hard look at what is needed to gain more women donors. Clearly women have the potential and the desire to give, so where to start?

Create a Committed Group

First, you will need a committed group of women (and supportive men) who will devote themselves over a minimum period of three to five years to effect change in the organization. Many of the structures in development operations take months and years to implement. Patience, persistence, and a passion for the subject are key attributes to ensure that the changes you make will be lasting.

Once these interested and dedicated people are selected (or self-select), an institutional review is in order. No matter the size of your development operation, all fundraising includes the same basic elements that need correcting when it comes to successfully reaching women.

Run a Statistical Analysis of the Development Program

How many women and men are donors? How much money have they given and at what levels? These statistics should be run at various gift levels over the life of your data base or at least the prior five years.

Trends will begin to emerge. For example, you may discover that women give at the top and bottom of the giving levels in proportions greater than or equal to men. This has been the twenty-year trend at the University of Wisconsin (UW) Foundation. However, women do not give the same amounts or in the same numbers as men in the middle-amount ranges. This data tells us a great deal about the habits of women's giving—many are ongoing givers of under $100, then give large gifts later in life or in their estate plans. Your giving statistics may be different, but they will give you clues about where you need to place emphasis or to reinforce and expand current giving patterns. For example, the women's philanthropy program at the UW Foundation stresses women's going public with their planned gift during their lifetimes instead of encouraging competition with the men in mid-level giving. We can encourage women to give while they live, but if they are more comfortable with some major gifts during their lifetime, leaving their ultimate gift for their estate plan, then build on these giving habits and expand them to the benefit of your organization.

Develop an Initial Plan

In your planning document, point out the potential of women, their current giving patterns, and your analysis of why you believe changes would positively affect fundraising results.

Your initial planning document should spell out your hypothesis of where women find obstacles in giving to your organization. Ask yourself: What are the common obstacles women face in giving to your organization, and how can you overcome them? How can you determine where the problems are? Look at the development cycle and determine how to make your operation more welcoming to women at every stage of the cycle, as follows: identification, cultivation, the ask, acknowledgment, and stewardship. To help you discover the perhaps subtle ways in which your own organization can improve business operations, you can gather information directly from women.

You will also need to do an internal review of each step of the development process. It is up to you whether you gather information from women donors before or after the review; however, research with real live donors to your organization can more effectively and precisely make your case for change. Plus, the information-gathering process is an excellent cultivation step for the women.

GENDER-SENSITIVE PRINCIPLES IN THE DEVELOPMENT OPERATION

Gender-sensitive principles apply at each stage of the development operation: identification, cultivation, the ask, acknowledgment, and stewardship. This section is not a primer on development but rather an outline of what to do differently with women.

Identification by Staff

With the growth of prospect research departments and professional standards promoted by membership organizations such as the Association of Prospect Researchers for Advancement (APRA), processes and systems have become more gender-sensitive. Even in small organizations with no researchers, APRA has significantly influenced the field by establishing professional skill sets, ethics statements, core training curriculum, and other types of professional development programs to enhance contemporary practitioners' ways of thinking about and engaging their organization's constituents.

What are some of these standards and practices? Elizabeth Crabtree, president of APRA and director of prospect development at Brown University, says that whether you do your own prospect identification or rely on a research department, some basic procedures to include women should be followed.[2]

Specifically, when researching an individual who is married or in a partnership, be sure to conduct research on the spouse or partner. For couples, it is no longer acceptable to only focus on the business background, wealth, and philanthropic interests of the male (presumed to be) head of household. Today, in many cases, women are heads of households, or have equally lucrative careers, separate as well as joint assets, and independent philanthropic interests. Additionally, good prospect-screening or data-mining companies will return information on both the males and females in a household. More women donors are identified as a result of such research practices, as women are found to be political and philanthropic donors as well as executives, board members, leadership volunteers, and property owners in their own right.

You must also make sure that your database system is designed to capture, link, and report information on joint records or households in an appropriate and balanced way. This will help fundraisers remember the importance and interests of both members of the household as they prepare their visit. Crabtree says, "Even in households where a male executive is the primary earner and property holder, women typically play a joint role in any philanthropic decisions. In many cases, these women spearhead the family's philanthropic endeavors."

According to Robert Sharpe, planned giving consultant, the number of children is one of the highest correlations for giving.[3] When other controls are equal, the lower the number of children, the higher the ability of the family to contribute; childless people are the most likely to make gifts through their estates. However, this principle applies more to those in the middle and lower donor ranges than to very wealthy families. The wealthier the family, the more likely the parents are to be able to pick the amount they would like to leave to their children while directing any excess for charitable purposes.

Identification by Volunteers

Find informal, personal ways to get information on potential donors from volunteers. Ask them to review a list of potential supporters and give you capacity and inclination information. Often women who do not work outside the home have to be identified solely through informal volunteer networks. Having one-on-one sessions with volunteers is a friendly and confidential way to seek their input on potential supporters.

Salutations: Women's Most Frequent Complaints

One of the biggest issues with women is the way they are addressed. At the beginning of computer systems for data recording, old-fashioned rules about women were in effect. As recently as the 1980s, some older women still wanted to be addressed as Mrs. John Jones instead of Sally Jones. The address salutation may have read Dear Mr. and Mrs. Jones.

Times have changed. Not only do most women prefer Ms., but they prefer to have their own name listed as Sally Jones—such as John and Sally Jones—on the outside of the envelope and top of the letter.

Modern challenges in addressing women in automated mailings still have not been solved, so human operators must work to remove gender bias from their databases. Many women have been turned off to an organization because the salutation was not what they wanted. Women are more sensitive to this issue than you may think. Prepare your system. If you have the opportunity to do a donor survey, this salutation question is an excellent question to include.

Another issue is that when women make gifts, there is often a tendency to connect the husband to the gift. When a man makes a gift, there is a slight tendency to not link it to his female partner. If both spouses make gifts, staff may not connect the records. This skews the statistics. It is a function of convenience to attribute gifts to one person or the other, and traditional bias may choose the man. These crediting and recording problems make it difficult to properly measure women's giving or the success of women's philanthropy programs.

The need to change these biases began with those women who came of age in the mid-1960s. Does your computer system reflect the realities of these women's preferences? Ask the woman whether she wants joint credit. Women—especially those of the Baby Boom generation and younger—might want to be recognized individually and not have every gift credited jointly.

CULTIVATING WOMEN'S INTERESTS

We begin by looking closely at your communications, then cover the ask, acknowledgments, and stewardship.

Communications

One of the essential ways to interest women is through your communications—written, Web presence, email. For your publications, do a content analysis study. Look at your primary newsletter and count the number of articles about men and about women for the past three years. Count the number of pictures that show women in leadership roles. Women like human faces, personal reactions, and connections. As Wisconsin philanthropist Nancy Mead says, "I want to see the human face my gift affects."[4]

Use of language is key in cultivating a woman's interest, as well as in making an ask. Avoid sales jargon in all your communications, both printed and oral—even in-house. Make sure that all your in-house communications could be read by a donor.

Useful Content Analysis

Lutheran Social Services (LSS) of Wisconsin and Upper Michigan completely turned around their communications program. At a conference of the Association of Lutheran Development Executives in the late 1990s, Taylor led a panel on principles to secure gifts from women. She asked three organizations to undertake a content analysis of their publications over the past three years: how many photographs showed single women, how many women were featured in articles.

One of the panelists was David Larson, then director of development at LSS and now president and CEO. He was shocked at the results of the content analysis on LSS publications.[5] Most pages of the newsletter featured the male CEO in distant shots with groups or individuals. The number of women shown was small, especially considering the large percentage of women donors. Also, few articles featured women.

Larson transformed the newsletter into a four-color magazine with huge pictures of faces of the people helped as well as large photos and articles about women donors in every issue. Since this change, the organization has consistently seen increased gifts and donors.

"The exercise of content analysis I did as part of the panel at the conference not only opened our eyes about our need to better communicate with women," says Larson. "This analysis led to restructuring of our whole operation for development, media, church relations, and government relations. Previously, these areas were silos. Through content analysis, our eyes were opened that our messages were not getting across and that we weren't reaching our audiences. We also restructured our operation to put advancement functions under one executive vice president."

Take a long look at the communications for your organization. The development operation must depend on the organization for the proper image with women (as well as donors of different ages and other constituencies). Look through your annual reports. Make sure that wherever you show a woman she is identified as an individual and not just part of a couple. Your changes may not be as drastic as Larson's, but you will learn and improve your operation in reaching women and other audiences. The CARE organization is another excellent example of a campaign directed at women, with their "I Am Powerful" campaign showing close-ups of women's faces.[6]

On your Web site, photos of people, not just buildings, are important to reaching women. In your donor profile section, show minorities, women, younger and older donors. Be sensitive to not just showing women as half of a couple. Show several women as individuals. After all, single women are the most generous as a group, yet we often overlook them in communications and other aspects of the development process.

Finally, some advice from Patricia Moline, vice president of development, Oklahoma State University Foundation: "In your publications, talk less about need and more about impact. Move from talking to your donors about a menu of gifts towards creating ideas and partnership with institutions. See how your institution aligns with her values. Use language in a different way."[7]

Showing Role Models

When you are planning an event or public meeting, include women on the program. Featuring a diversity of speakers will make a real difference in how your organization is perceived. By showing women in public roles, you demonstrate that you appreciate them, their dollars, and their time, says Marion Brown, vice president, University of Wisconsin Foundation.[8]

Developing your institution's history of women philanthropists and communicating this history to your donors is another part of the cultivation process. Creative PowerPoint presentations can be organized to highlight the past and look toward the future. Show past women role models in publications, on the Web site, and in oral presentations. Their stories illustrate the proud tradition of women in your institution. Also show women who gave during times of economic challenge and what an impact these gifts made on your institution at a critical time. Identify transformative moments when a gift from a woman turned your organization in a new direction. These examples are there, waiting to be discovered, notes Claire Gaudiani, professor at New York University, former president of Connecticut College, and author of *Social Entrepreneurship in America: Women Building a More Perfect Union*. She believes that by showing the past we can inspire the future.[9]

Volunteer Involvement

Patricia Jackson, vice president of development at Smith College, says, "It is critical to have active boards and committees to involve women. As Bruce McClintock of Marts and Lundy says, 'Men like to be involved, women demand it.'"[10] Involve women in volunteer opportunities and leadership roles.

Events and Education

Women want to connect with the cause and the people they benefit, and philanthropy education seminars and activities are a foundation of women's philanthropy cultivation and involvement activities. One of the most successful cultivation events at the Divine Savior Holy Angels High School is to invite women who have made regular modest gifts ($250 to $1,000) to a scholarship event. Tracy Wayson, vice president of Institutional Advancement at the girls' school, explains, "We invite these donors to an event where scholarships are given out by other donors. The potential donors get to see how close the student is to the funder. Most women want to be close to the scholarship recipient. They don't want to talk about the scholarship, but rather want to hear about [the recipients'] experiences as a student. How do they like the teachers? What is their life like at school? The scholarship donors don't want pats on the back about their gifts—they want the relationship with recipients."[11]

Wayson admits that the event consumes a lot of staff time, and not every student is great at talking to donors. But the approach succeeds in moving women from occasional donor to invested donor. The message is to invest in an individual—through a scholarship donation.

Cultivation events should involve women as individuals and inviting women with their spouses and partners. Organizations are good at making sure couples are invited. One forgotten audience is widows or single women who may not like to drive out alone during the evening. Think of a way of providing them with rides to attend events for your organization. (See Chapter Nine for a full description of donor education programs.)

Gathering Information from Women

Finding out information about your women donors and potential donors can help you determine what ways to better reach women, and they also are a good way to cultivate donors' interest in your organization. You can conduct a survey of donors.

An easy way to seek immediate input from women and better involve them is a focus group (see Resource A.) The ideal structure is to conduct several in your areas of influence or where you have the most prospects.

Tailor your questions to your circumstances. Are you looking for basic information on how to better involve women? Include questions about how the women like to be addressed by the organization. If you desire to start women's philanthropy programming, include questions about what kind of programs the women would like to see. If you want more information about your regular development efforts, ask how fundraising efforts could better reach the women. Focus groups have been used at all sized higher education institutions, ranging from Augsburg College to the University of Connecticut. Nonprofits and hospitals have also found them to be effective.

Asking for the Commitment

Pleasant Rowland Frautschi, founder of American Girl (now owned by Mattel), is one of the leading woman philanthropists today. She has given significant gifts for children, historical preservation, and various universities and colleges. American Girl depends almost entirely on marketing to women. When consulting with her about how to ask women, she explains that you have to give women a lot of detail. She suggests that you envision a catalogue—describe the projects you are supporting or sponsoring and show them. In fact, she recommends that a "catalogue" of gift opportunities would appeal to women.[12]

Whether through the annual fund or a major gift visit, when calling or visiting a household to ask, you should ask both members of a married couple. Again, make sure you know how the woman wants to be addressed. If you are contacting the husband (or wife) on the first visit, seek to get an appointment with both on the second visit. If you are making a personal visit to ask, try to have both partners present and give adequate eye contact to both. According to Bruce Flessner, founding principal of the fundraising consulting firm of Bentz Whaley Flessner: "We know that women tend to give to change the world and are future oriented, while men—especially older men—tend to give to preserve memories and institutions. We also know that women are more focused on people than institutions, so make your story very human."[13] (Refer to Chapter One about communications with women.)

If soliciting a gift through a telefund, make sure that the individual donor's record *and* the spouse's record pop up on the caller's screen or printed information in preparation for the call. If calling for a college and both are graduates, talk to either member of the couple who answers the phone. When you are soliciting general gifts for a college, it is awkward to ask for a husband when a woman graduate answers the phone. And don't forget that single women are some of the most generous philanthropists. Ask women who have been continuing, ongoing supporters to your organization.

Acknowledging and Thanking

Earlier we discussed the solicitation salutation; the same issues apply to women when it comes time for the acknowledgment, and there can be further complications. What is your organization's crediting policy for gifts? Many women complain about organizations' crediting and acknowledging practices.

Look at the name(s) on the check! One good policy is to jointly credit all gifts on joint checks received by your organization. Some men or women may want all the credit on their records, and you must make the exception to the rule. Receipts are issued to each person as an individual. Ideally, have a box on every reply card that asks how the donor wants her salutation and her crediting.

When it comes to thanking, good stewardship practices are especially appreciated by women. Reporting on the use of a major gift is a necessity with women donors who expect accountability and transparency. Presenting photographs of people who have been helped with the donor's gift is an effective way to steward a gift. Sending letters to donors about the performance of your organization's endowment in up or down markets is another good activity. For a woman who has established an endowment fund, send an annual report on the use of the fund and the investment report.

Face-to-face stewardship is very effective for major donors—give them a report in person, bringing along the appropriate person from your organization, such as the president, chair, dean, or faculty member. An invitation to the annual student scholarship event or its equivalent is always appreciated by women—and men. Stay away from printed honor rolls of donor names. Most women donors are uncomfortable with them, and many men don't much like them either.

Send first-time donors a special welcome packet. Avoid the situation in which first-time donors just get a receipt. Send them a letter or call them and inform them how their gift has been used—this, of course, in addition to a newsletter. Email and Web sites can also be very effective in reporting the specifics of gifts to donors. The more specific you can get, the better. Even if the donor gave a general gift for operations, you can send the woman donor information about how the money was spent.

Training Staff About Women's Philanthropy

In the orientation program for your new staff or volunteers, they will appreciate a section on women as philanthropists. Include the Six Cs Plus Three of women's motivations for giving. Present information on the development cycle and how to better include women at each stage of the cycle.

Asking for colleagues' involvement in women's philanthropy presentations and staff training will help educate them and others on the subject. For example, Taylor asked colleagues to present at a staff training session on how they were involving women in their development program. One colleague was director of development for the business school. She ran statistics on women's giving to the business school and found—much to her surprise—that several of the top twenty donors were widows of business alumni. Further investigation showed that when a graduate died, she or he was automatically dropped from the mailing list and the surviving spouse—even if a donor—no longer received the school publications. After doing the self-analysis of her program, the director made sure that the policy was changed so that surviving spouses who were donors still received the school magazine and mailings.

You may find that your organization needs outside consultants on women's philanthropy to conduct the training. Despite tight budgets, consultants may save money by helping focus staff efforts and bring needed expertise.

SECURING DIFFERENT TYPES OF GIFTS

The classic three-legged stool of a strong development program consists of the annual fund, major gifts and campaigns, and planned giving.

Ultimate gifts are an additional category to be discussed—these are the largest gifts donors make, which can be a combination of major and planned gifts.

The Annual Fund: Where It All Begins

The traditional vehicles of the annual fund today are email, direct mail, and telefunding. Online giving is increasing, and the applications of Facebook and Twitter are still being explored as communication media.

Creating consistent annual fund donors is the top priority. Part of the challenge in developing these donors is their low retention rate. Erick Weber, senior director of development at the University of Wisconsin Foundation, explains:

> With only 30-percent retention, most of our first-time donors do not renew in the following year. Contrast this ominous statistic with the retention rate for five-plus-consecutive-year donors—85-percent-plus. We need to work harder on stewardship with our young and first-time donors. However, it is common for nonprofit organizations to oversolicit after a first-time gift. I have heard that some organizations will solicit first-time donors more than thirty times in a year. I would argue that less can be more. If you limit the number of solicitations by concentrating on when donors prefer to give and how they prefer to give, you may save money and address "donor fatigue" that leads to attrition. In lieu of another solicitation, consider how you are "touching" your donors with stewardship. Is it timely? Is it demonstrative of the impact of the gift you have received? Is it substantive?[14]

Yes, timing is everything. The best time to solicit a donor is around the same time she gave in the prior year. If possible, ask the donor when and how she prefers to be solicited. If you follow her lead and respect her wishes, she will most likely contribute again.

Ask for Specific Projects

Examine all of your communications and solicitations. Make sure you are using gender-sensitive messages. Don't always consider age, but consider life stage (Chapter Five). Weber recommends the application of specific, targeted requests: "On the front end, in the ask, include specific priorities and examples of how the money will be used and what it will accomplish. In stewardship mode, describe the outcomes to the donor, relating them to the communicated priorities. Consider the donor's preferred communication method and honor it."

Tracy Wayson, vice president for institutional advancement at Divine Savior Holy Angels High School in Milwaukee, Wisconsin, reaffirms the idea of asking women for a specific project in the annual fund:

> *We have found that women grads wanted to be fixers and problem solvers. In the beginning of cultivation, it is difficult for women to think at the macro level—large gifts. It is not effective to have a message about how big gifts make difference. They wanted to know if even a small gift would make an impact. They wanted to know how their gift can be the "thumb in the dam" or difference to fix a situation. You may be engaged in dialogue about generalities, but you need to provide specifics about, for example, a scholarship winner. The woman donor wants personal information about the recipient such as siblings, clubs, courses. You must build a picture in the donor's mind of the one individual she is helping.*

Survey Annual Donors

One way to learn about and increase donor motivations for annual and even major gifts is to survey donors by direct mail, phone, or email. You can find out donors' motivation for giving and learn about your organization's ongoing relationship with them. How do they want to hear from you? Involve the donor in the process of solicitation by asking them how, specifically, they'd like to be contacted—by phone, letter, email or in person. Expect 20 to 30 percent of donors to respond. In fact, there's a positive correlation between donors who answer surveys and donors who give. Lawrence Henze, managing director of Target Analysis of Blackbaud, reflects on this: "One thing we have noticed is that women are more responsive to these surveys by a factor of two to one. Why? Women in general have patterns of behavior of volunteering. They seek a higher level of involvement with the nonprofit than men. These results track with volunteerism results—women get more involved."[15] Organizations that do regular surveys will continue relationships after the initial giving commitment. If your organization follows up with a survey after initial gifts, then your giving is more likely to expand.

Major Gifts: Deeper Conversations and Commitments

Working with potential women donors on a major gift involves building a relationship over time. It is rare that a major gift is given to an organization without a prior giving record or relationship to the institution.

One of the essential parts of major gift giving for women is simply asking them. Women still perceive that they are not being asked. It is sometimes difficult to visit both members of a married couple, but treat each person as an individual prospect if you are not able to make joint visits. For example, visit the husband in his office and the wife in her office. The next visit might be an evening at their home with both of them. With so many philanthropic decisions being made jointly in married households, consider the dynamics of couple giving in which the woman plays a major role. Make sure you are involving both partners. Women want to get involved with an organization before making a major gift. Promote volunteerism and ask women to serve on boards and campaigns.

A major gift conversation includes dialogue and listening—*especially* listening. Pay attention to her emotions as well as her words. Ask what issues of society she believes are the most important to solve. Zero in on her passion and listen to her values. Avoid asking her to match someone else's gift or to put her name on something. Instead, listen to her interests and relate her values to the organization's mission. Show how she can partner with the organization to make the world a better place.

Single Women

One of the best audiences for larger gifts is single women. A study by the Center on Philanthropy showed that single women are more likely to be donors than single men. "Single females gave almost twice as much as single males," says Patrick Rooney, Executive Director of the Center on Philanthropy. And married females give significantly more than single or married males.[16] Because single women (especially those without children) are such a good audience, make sure to visit them, even if they do not have executive titles. They will appreciate the relationship to the institution.

Living Endowment

With major gifts, encourage outright or endowment giving. The most common way to create endowments is through appreciated stock. When the values of stock have dropped, however, women are less willing to make such gifts. In that case it's best to talk about the concept of the living endowment. Ask the potential donor to give the amount of money that would be the income from an endowment fund. If she pledges for three years, then give her the opportunity to have her name on the scholarship for the three-year period. Ask her to consider putting the endowment principal in her planned gift so her scholarship will continue after her lifetime.

This living endowment concept can apply to any project of a nonprofit—a specific project is the key. Women like to know about the specifics of what they fund—the details. Give them the opportunity to fund a project. They don't want to name something for the public recognition, rather for the personal satisfaction of helping an individual, providing clean water to a poor village, or giving a family the opportunity to adopt a disabled child. Give as much detail as you can about the impact of the gift. This is an excellent way to engage a woman's interests and passions with your organization, no matter whether the stock market is up or down.

Growing Major Donors

Major donors can be developed through interaction with current donors. This interaction may include survey responsiveness, volunteerism, and personal visits.

The trend over the past fifteen years is that a higher percentage of prospects identified are women, according to Henze. Nonprofits are getting better data, leading them to see that women are excellent major gift and planned giving prospects. Women are also better annuity prospects than men, as they like the security of annuities.

One of the most important issues in major gift development is maintaining staff continuity—women will have deeper conversations with people they have known over time. It is important to avoid staff turnover. According to Lynn Hubert's 2009 study of Notre Dame alumnae, part of the reason a woman made a gift was the relationship with the development officer.[17] The 2009 Center on Philanthropy study sponsored by the Bank of America showed that the nonprofit staff are some of the most important advisors in helping donors make philanthropic decisions.[18]

Robert Sharpe also points out that previously a great many major and planned gifts came from gays and lesbians with no families. They used to develop relationships with charities to replace the families that had rejected them. With the growing acceptance of gays and lesbians and their children, their giving to nonprofits has decreased. As their acceptance increases, they are likely to model the rest of the population in their giving patterns.

Capital Campaigns: The Big Push

Campaigns are structures to help nonprofits create some immediacy and momentum around giving. Use the good gender-sensitive principles outlined for annual, major, and planned gifts. Campaigns provide terrific opportunities to involve women.

Because campaigns present a special opportunity to involve volunteers, pay particular attention to recruiting women as campaign leaders. One volunteer job of great importance is campaign leadership. Women have been leaders for smaller nonprofit campaigns but are only slowly coming to the forefront for larger campaigns. Asking women and encouraging them to take these roles is critical to the future of philanthropy and women's role in society because campaign leadership is one of the last frontiers for women's leadership.

Women are now leading campaigns across the nation. Here are some examples of their superb volunteer leadership:

- Cheryl Altinkemer, associate vice president for advancement at Purdue University, used a capital campaign to help launch high-level donor meetings in selected cities across the country.[19] She held many meetings with top women donors, offering them opportunities to meet the president of the university and to connect with each other.

- Joy Picus, a former city council member and philanthropist in Los Angeles, California, is active in raising funds for Jewish causes. She says that women are prominent in leading campaigns for synagogues and Jewish social service agencies and institutions.[20]

- Beth McCague was the cochair of the recent campaign for the University of Florida. Barbara Miles, vice president for development and alumni engagement at the University of British Columbia, worked with McCague when she was at the University of Florida. Miles said: "McCague was an excellent recruiter and leader. She was a senior executive with Wachovia in Florida and thus was in an outstanding position to help us connect with others."[21]

- In 2006 the Women's Funding Network began a very successful campaign for 145 women's funds globally, called Women Moving Millions. The purpose was to inspire gifts of $1 million or more. Launched by gifts from sisters Helen LaKelly Hunt and Swanee Hunt, the campaign recruited women leaders internationally.

- The late Maddie Levitt was the only woman in America to chair two consecutive fundraising campaigns of $100 million or more in the same decade for a U.S. college or university. In addition, she contributed $10 million to the campaigns for Drake University.

- Ann Isaly Wolfe was the volunteer chair for the Columbus, Ohio Children's Hospital campaign.

Planned Gifts: The Lasting Legacy

"Understand the complexity of people's life," says Robert Sharpe. "Philanthropy is as much about making the thank-you as making the ask. Men and women alike will remember people who regularly thank them during their lifetimes. They will remember the charity that treats them like family. In turn, they will treat the charity like family in their will."

Anonymous Donors

With new charities established for pass-through giving, such as Fidelity Charitable Services and community foundations, women can be more anonymous than previously. In recent years, widely publicized anonymous gifts to higher education institutions led by women in 2009 have reinforced the concept of anonymous giving. Sharpe has noted a big drop in the number of bequest notifications to charities in 2009. He suspects that many of these are older women who are reluctant to tell the intended charitable beneficiaries about their bequest for fear that their assets may be depleted prior to their death and there may not be any remainder for charity. Continue your work, paying attention to those women who have given consistently to your organization over many years. These are often the people who have included your organization in their will.

Visits to Women

Patricia Moline has this advice about women and planned giving:

Don't be afraid to call on and visit with women. Make calls on couples. It's often helpful to staff these visits with another development officer. And finally, don't be afraid to bring up the subject of estate giving . . . Oftentimes, women won't want to tell you a dollar amount—they don't want to be on the radar. They want to be more anonymous. Take this approach about their giving: "Take care of yourself, take care of the ones you love, then take care of charities that are important to you." Include a discussion about their generosity toward other charities.

Make sure your planned giving publications show single women, not just couples. And keep asking women to be public with their giving, asking them to serve as role models. Those role models for giving planned gifts will encourage others to step forward.

Women seem to prefer bequests and annuities, says Lawrence Henze. He agrees that consecutive years of giving are the best indication of a planned gift. Many people start estate planning at younger ages, forty to sixty. You can work to reach younger women about planned giving. This applies to small nonprofits and large ones. Gender differences apply across all sizes of organizations.

Always offer to meet with the donor's children or family members. This applies equally to women and men. This action is just a fundamental in planned and ultimate gift work.

Volunteers as Good Potential Planned Givers

People who volunteer starting in their forties and fifties correlate with planned giving behavior. Individuals may say that they are volunteering because they are not in a position to give a lot of money.

Loyal donors, members, and volunteers are highly inclined to give a planned gift or annuity. They want to do something special for the institution, but writing a large check is not comfortable for them. Bequests or annuities are easier gifts for these donors, says Henze. The best prospect for a major and planned gift is a woman who has been involved or has had a long-term relationship with your organization and/or has been a consistent donor.

Ultimate Gifts: Philanthropic Planning

The philanthropy planning process has developed into a high level of work, beyond development and fundraising. When working with women, men, and families about a major planned gift—but especially an ultimate gift—a meaningful conversation about life values and self-identity must take place. Encourage development officers to get past "fundraising from a menu," says Moline. "We must encourage development officers to have relationships with a donor and listen to her core values. Then we can determine how our institution and its impact on the world can relate to her."

Planned giving officers, principal gift officers, and experienced major gift officers work with women donors to uncover the woman's most important values. They look for the best way to fulfill the donor's dream for a better world. For some who are faith-driven, the work becomes like a "ministry of money," and they are counseling donors as they might minister on any other important aspect of life. To others working at this high gift level, the work is like that of a trusted counselor and philanthropic advisor to the donor.

Many people fear talking about money. A donor appreciates a trusted advisor who truly represents her interests on all of her philanthropy. Some of the most meaningful and privileged work in the development field comes about in conversations between development officers and donors about a shared vision for a better world. Enjoy the beauty of this privileged work.

Ask Values Questions

Charles Collier, senior philanthropy advisor at Harvard University and author of *Wealth in Families*, asks donors a series of questions to help them envision their future.[22] Ellen Remmer, president of The

Philanthropic Initiative (TPI), and other philanthropic advisors use a similar series of questions to elicit reflections on the part of donors.[23] Advancement Resources, a development education firm, recommends using one question with donors to help them focus on their long-term goals: "What would you want to do with your money that is meaningful to you?"[24]

Collier helps donors understand how past family relationships influence current financial, philanthropic, and estate planning decisions. He uses Bowen Family Theory and family diagrams to help couples gain clarity about what is important to them so that they can have detailed conversations with their adult children. Bowen Theroy is used by counselors and psychiatrists to analyze family dynamics.

These conversations resonate particularly well with women. Collier explains, "Often women are more actively engaged in discussions about long-term planning for the family, and they are typically quick to zero in on the heart of the issues. In my experience, I have found that women are more attuned to the nuances of family relationships and the implications of those relationships for the well-being of the family at large."

The philanthropy planning process involves a larger discussion about the donor's life values and legacy. Represent the donor's total philanthropic interests in this discussion. In some cases, you may be asked to get information about other nonprofits, and the donor may wish to remain anonymous to them. The philanthropy planning process and diagrams showing family connections are helpful for guiding your most significant donors.

Be confident when having the big conversation with women donors. You are likely to find that they are ready and willing to talk with you.

TAKEAWAYS

Nonprofits need to secure a strong financial future by increasing women's giving. To secure more gifts from women, the first step is to analyze every step of the development process and then refine your practices and procedures to better relate to women. Also, a thorough institutional review of the development operation will uncover areas to improve gender sensitivity.

Each part of the development process should be improved to better relate to women. Consider these steps:

1. Identifying and correcting data systems—ensuring that women are being properly addressed and researched.

2. Cultivating women's interests:

   Communications—use gender-sensitive communications, and show women in leadership roles.

   Involvement—identify volunteer opportunities and cultivation activities to interest women.

   Gathering information—ask the women for their opinions through surveys and focus groups.

3. Asking—focus on the personal aspect of the impact of the gift; who is affected? Visit women and seek their support. Involve both members of a married couple in the ask, when possible.

4. Acknowledging—Make sure you are crediting women. Send personal thank-yous.

5. Stewarding—Provide meaningful reports to women and show them the results of their gifts.

Make sure you are effectively working with women when securing different types of gifts: annual fund, major gifts, capital campaigns, planned gifts, and ultimate gifts. Present women with specific projects to fund. The philanthropy planning process, helping donors identify their values and family dynamics, is especially effective with women.

CHAPTER 7

Bringing Women to the Table

Women do so much to make communities stronger. They embody the delicate balance of strength and compassion, fight for their beliefs, and are strong collaborators who know how to get things done.[1]

—Women in Philanthropy, a partnership of the United Way of the Midlands and the Central Carolina Community Foundation in Columbia, South Carolina

I think women's perspective on money and philanthropy is so very important. I have also found that the value women bring to an organization's support is often more than just their dollars.[2]

—Dune Thorne, principal, Silver Bridge Client Advisors

IN THE EARLY 1970S SHAW-HARDY WAS ELECTED TO the otherwise all-male Grand Traverse County Board of Commissioners in Traverse City, Michigan, an agricultural tourist area in Northwestern Michigan. Because of her gender, the male leaders on the board assigned her responsibilities on the social services and mental health committees—assignments they were uncomfortable with and thought "beneath" them in importance. Those early committee assignments, sexist as they may have been, fit particularly well with her interests—and a great deal more than the public safety and public works committees that the men were interested in.

She knew she brought more to the table than the men who had begrudgingly served on the "human services" committees.

When she joined forces, two years later, with a woman commissioner from a neighboring county (Connie Binsfeld, who later became Michigan's lieutenant governor), things really began happening in the health care and social services arenas because the women cared, and those issues were their issues. When Shaw-Hardy left the board, the county's prosecuting attorney told her, "Actually, it's a little difficult for me to visualize the Board of Commissioners without you present, taking the human side of the issue."

Unfortunately, during the early days there were very few female candidates who wanted to be the only woman on an otherwise all-male board. Those women who did take the leap found themselves more of a symbolic presence than a sign of the organization's willingness to move in the direction of gender equality. Other women so firmly resisted the idea that they thought or acted differently from men that they were disinclined to suggest more women to sit on what they considered "their" boards.

In the past, women weren't always intentionally and purposefully excluded from boards and committees. It was just so much easier for people to think about others like themselves when considering appointments and hiring: of the same gender, class, ethnicity, and sexual preference. The more women serve in positions of leadership, the more women candidates will be considered "like oneself" in the minds of board members. At the same time, women leaders will be able to mentor younger women and create a "virtuous circle" to bring new ideas and a fresh way of looking at age-old problems.

WHAT WOMEN BRING TO A BOARD

Granted, women bring money to the table, which is surely important, but they also bring much more: new ways of leading, thinking, and giving, as well as basic equity. These qualities are not only different, they are essential.

Their Values

David Bach, author of *Smart Women Finish Rich*, writes, "Many people manage their lives based on goals, relationships, commitments, and other stuff. Women, I have learned, are a lot more in tune with their values."[3]

Unlike goals, which are expressed by having or doing something, values are about defining a person's life—who and where we are. Over and over again we have found that the values women care most about are community, family, equality, individual worth, balanced power, and connecting with others. We have consistently found that when women define their values, they relate these values to philanthropy and as a means to help solve societal issues.

Their Spouses

Women who come to the table in any organization are very likely to bring along their spouses as well.

In an influential 2009 study, Fidelity found that nearly half the high-income women surveyed decide how much and where the household charitable contributions are given.[4] Fidelity also showed that 92 percent of the men in the study named their spouse as an influence on how much to give and where to direct the funds. That is an astounding number, and one organizations and institutions should pay attention to when recruiting leadership. As Abigail Adams famously told John, "Don't forget the women."[5] Women now acknowledge they will probably live five to seven years longer than their spouse and they might as well start making these important decisions early in their lives.

Here is a heartwarming and instructive story of the charm and influence of spouses.[6] Joyce Miles was a graduate of the Purdue University School of Consumer and Family Sciences, but after graduating she had little contact with the university until Cheryl Altinkemer, then director of development for the school, planned the annual Felker Leadership Conference (named for a previous dean of the College of Consumer and Family Sciences) to bring graduates back to campus and honor some of them. Joyce received one of the distinguished alumni awards and also spoke at the day-long event.

She had such a good time that at the next conference she brought along her husband, Bob, who had received his degree in engineering from Purdue. Bob had been to a few functions for the College of Engineering, finding them stodgy, but he began regularly attending the Felker conferences with Joyce. They were then asked to serve on the advisory council of Purdue's Center for Families. The Center had originally been funded by another graduate, Lorene McCormick Burkhart, and Joyce had learned about it when she attended the first

Felker conference to receive her award. The end result was a million-dollar Bob and Joyce Beery Miles Endowment Fund to be used by the Center and other family-focused programs.[7] Bob was enthusiastic about giving the gift because after more than thirty years in the construction business, he said he was open to supporting a field that focuses on the family. He also said that the people from the College of Consumer and Family Sciences made him feel like part of the family.

There is little doubt that Joyce brought Bob along with her to the table; subsequently they have served in several leadership positions at the university.

Intellectual Capital

In addition to financial capital, women bring along their intellectual capital as well.

Girls have long gotten better grades than boys at all levels of school and are now receiving 58 percent of all bachelor's degrees in the United States.[8] Studies done by Claudia Buchmann of Ohio State and Thomas A. DiPrete of Columbia University show that the reason for this gender gap is that women are doing better in college than men—they're not just attending college, they're shining there.[9,10] A *Women in Management Review* study predicts that by 2020, 156 women will earn bachelor's degrees for every 100 men.[11] Not only are women attending college in greater numbers, but they are also using the education and skills learned there in the workforce. In a 2005 study released in 2006, the Bureau of Labor Statistics found that half of all persons employed in management, professional, and related occupations were women—positions requiring intellect and decision-making skills.[12]

THE VALUE OF WOMEN

The proportion of women serving on nonprofit governance boards ranges from 33 to 51 percent of the total membership of a board, but most often the women serve on boards of smaller organizations with budgets of less than $500,000. This number and its leadership potential is not representative of the total population of women nor, perhaps more important, the value of what women can bring to the boardroom table financially, intellectually, and emotionally.[13]

Different Leadership

> There is growing evidence that in today's marketplace, the
> female management style is not only distinctly different
> but also essential.[14]
>
> —*Claire Shipman and Katty Kay for* Time *magazine
> in partnership with CNN*

Fortune magazine hailed Presidential Medal of Freedom award-
winner Frances Hesselbein as the best nonprofit manager in America.[15]
Hesselbein gained her reputation by using circular management during her leadership as CEO of Girl Scouts of the U.S.A. from 1976–
1990. Sally Helgesen, in her book *The Female Advantage*, describes
circular management as a web in which leaders reach out, not down.[16]
This feminine approach is very different from the top-down management favored by men. At the Girl Scouts, Hesselbein replaced the old
organizational chart with a flat or "circular" management model. The
effect of the management shift was both immediate and long term.
"It released the human spirit," she says.[17]

There are two other leadership styles that women often bring
with them: questioning and caution. Women are likely to ask more
questions than men and shy away from groupthink, in which faulty
decisions are made because of group pressure.

Groupthink decision making more often occurs when there is little diversity in a group and the group is insulated from outside opinions, writes Irving L. Janis, research psychologist at Yale University.[18]
Asking questions and not succumbing to pressure increases the
chances of alternatives being presented and better-thought-out,
defensible decisions being made. Studies from Cambridge University
and the University of Pittsburgh also conclude that women are
more likely to focus on the long term and manage more cautiously
than men.[19]

Some call these ways of leading "transformational"—meaning
very engaged, motivational, and well suited for the emerging, less
hierarchical workplace. Whatever they are called, this type of leadership is what women bring to the table—one that is more inclusive
and open to the rapid changes taking place in today's world.

Experience and a New Perspective

Women's individual experiences as mothers, daughters, wives, aunts, and grandmothers should be part of every important decision made in the nonprofit sector.

Experience is often equated with the number of years spent in a particular position or profession and what was learned from those years. But experience is also lifetime knowledge or learning. Supreme Court Justice Ruth Bader Ginsburg, in a decision involving a thirteen-year-old girl who was strip-searched, said about her male colleagues, "They have never been a thirteen-year-old girl . . . I didn't think that my colleagues, some of them, quite understood." Ginsburg strongly felt that the court needed more women and stated, "Women belong in all places where decisions are being made."[20]

Patrick Rooney, executive director of the Center on Philanthropy at Indiana University, says that in his experience, "[A]s leaders of organizations and leaders of the nonprofit sector, women bring a different perspective. I'm a big believer in 'viva la difference' and different people bring different things to the table. If we only have white men at the table, that's an important dimension of society but certainly not the only dimension. It's important to bring others into the discussion, and women are over half the population and often make the final charitable decisions in a household."[21]

Rooney also makes the case for including women by saying, "Women in general have a capacity for compassion and caring that makes them perhaps more inductively and intuitively philanthropic." These special qualities are enormously important to decisions made on boards and committees.

POTENTIAL WOMEN BOARD AND COMMITTEE MEMBERS

- Women who have started their own companies
- Women who have active roles in a family business
- Spouses of board members
- Professional women: lawyers, physicians, accountants
- Corporate women

- Women in administration/management positions
- Women's organizations such as Zonta, United Way Women's Leadership Councils, and C200
- Women in women's funds and giving circles
- Women in service organizations such as Rotary and Kiwanis
- Women board members of other organizations
- Women corporate board members

Active Listening Skills

Remember the game of Gossip, in which a brief story is whispered to the next person, who then repeats it to the next one? This takes place at least three more times before being shared to the group by the last person. Never is the story the same after the last telling. A great part of the reason is because we all listen differently—and let's face it, some of us don't listen well.

When Dr. Janie Fouke was dean of the College of Engineering at Michigan State University, she was new to development and pursuing a gift from a major prospect with the capacity to give tens of millions of dollars. Fouke says,

> On my first encounter with this donor I attended with both a male and female development officer. The senior woman development officer suggested that I really listen to what the donor was saying. I sat there listening as hard as I could to the donor's conversation, trying to understand what he meant. I'll tell you, the woman development officer just heard things completely different from what the man did. She heard verb tenses, conditions, and imperative language that he didn't hear. She heard plural and he heard singular. It was amazing to me how different the conversation was from her point of view and from the male's. It was probably the reason why we were able to be successful in our request to the donor for resources.[22]

She really listened.

The late Dr. Alma Baron, formerly professor of business at the University of Wisconsin, Madison, suggested practicing active listening by using the following exercise, Worksheet 7.1.

WORKSHEET 7.1
Active Listening Skills

by Dr. Alma Baron

1. Research indicates that you think four times faster than a person usually talks to you. Do you use this excess time to turn off your thoughts elsewhere while you are keeping general track of a conversation?

2. Do you listen primarily for facts, rather than ideas, when someone is speaking?

3. Do certain words, phrases, or ideas so prejudice you against the speaker that you cannot listen objectively to what is being said?

4. When you are puzzled or annoyed by what someone says, do you try to get the question straightened out immediately either in your own mind or by interrupting the speaker?

5. If you feel it would take too much time and effort to understand something, do you go out of your way to avoid hearing about it?

6. Do you deliberately turn your thoughts to other subjects when you believe a speaker will have nothing particularly interesting to say?

7. Can you tell by a person's appearance and delivery that she or he won't have anything worthwhile to say?

8. When someone is talking to you, do you try to make that person think you are paying attention when you're not?

9. When you are listening to someone, are you easily distracted by outside sights and sounds?

10. If you want to remember what someone is saying, do you think it's a good idea to write it down as she or he goes along?

According to Dr. Baron, if you answer "no" to all of these questions, then you are that rare individual—the perfect listener. Each "yes" means that you may have a specific bad listening habit.

Creative Approaches

As women take on bigger challenges with grander solutions and much more money, a thoughtful, creative problem-solving approach continues to appeal.

Traditionally women were excluded from access to education and boardrooms and had to find other methods to accomplish their goals. They had to be creative in their approaches to solving problems; they had to be flexible and responsive to outside changes and influences in order to get their message across or their projects funded. Out of these approaches came the special events women have so favored as well as smaller forms of fundraising whereby women could provide a personal item to sell, such as bake sales and book sales.

Philanthropy has always been a way women could use their entrepreneurial capabilities by creating organizations for the greater good of a community, a nation, or the world. They have used vision-ary approaches to start new charities and continue to bring these new strategies to solving time-worn problems.

Delivering on Change

Change happens quickly now in all areas of our economy, gov-ernment, politics, business, and philanthropy, and women are at the forefront.

Business management guru Tom Peters brought women's pur-chasing power to the forefront in 2003 when he wrote that 83 percent of all consumer decisions in the United States are made by women.[23] It makes sense then that when women change their minds about whether to buy long or short, traditional or trendy, people in many arenas must listen. And it's easier to listen to someone who's sitting at the table with you.

Think what might have happened if General Motors, Chrysler, and Ford had as many women as men on their boards and in top management. We can assure you that the long overdue change to smaller, safer, and more efficient cars would have happened much, much earlier. Although there are always exceptions, most women aren't interested in big, gas-guzzling monster cars. They want a safe car for their families and, as we've heard women say over and over, "one that always starts and won't cause me any more stress in my life than I already have." Quality and reliability are a big factor for women.

Change is fast occurring in philanthropy as well, and women are leading the way. It would be well worth it to conduct some focus groups (see Resource A) to learn where women see philanthropy headed in your organization. By including women early in these discussions, you will be providing value to men as well. America's auto industry can attest to this.

Perception of Fairness

In philanthropy, public perception can be everything.

Today, when headlines shout and the details flash by, it is hard for organizations not only to gain people's attention, but also to then persuade them that correct decision making has taken place. People's minds are often made up without all the necessary information. Opinions are made based primarily on perception, which includes the way an organization "looks."

Tough choices have to be made by universities and organizations deciding where monies will be raised, what gifts will be accepted, and who will be asked for them. Will the capital campaign include funding for scholarships or athletics or both? Will raising money for campus childcare be part of the campaign? Where does the college of education and nursing stand in fundraising efforts compared with engineering and the business college? For museums and theaters, the question may be how much income can be generated from rentals versus independent productions or whether a gift should be accepted when it was clearly given to provide the means to continue hiring a family member as staff.

Every organization and board has difficult issues. Just talk to anyone who went through the United Way or Red Cross crises about executive overspending, board laxity, and public perception. A general principal stands: you will cover numerous bases by having diversity on your boards, staff, administration, and committees. But in particular it's good for the public perception of fairness and the acceptance of new policies and change.

Diversity

Diversity has many meanings, and each segment of society brings with it important subjects, ideas that will only increase the organization's reach, scope, and success.

Women have always been concerned with ensuring there is diversity on the boards and committees on which they serve. They equate diversity with fairness and insist on it, no matter how many times they're met with "We've looked and just can't find anyone."

Anne Mosle, vice president for philanthropy and volunteerism at the W. K. Kellogg Foundation, says that when she was president of the Washington Area Women's Foundation (WAWF), the foundation "creat[ed] a new model of philanthropy with women coming together as both donors and recipients."[24] A large part of that model involved training the leaders of their partner organizations to whom the foundation gave money. Mosle recognized and accepted the responsibility of identifying and training leaders to have the background and comfort level to serve on boards.

It's not enough to make a few attempts to increase diversity; it takes a genuine effort, such as Mosle's, to seek out and train diverse communities about leadership skills. This is to help women feel more comfortable in leadership roles as well as to show them that the organization is walking their talk. Mosle says:

> It takes a community effort to create a truly inviting multicultural organization that is inclusive across class and community. For the WAWF to be meaningful and authentic in the Washington area, we needed to reach out to African American women and their wonderful history. From the beginning of our organization, we had lots of conversations about how to be multiracial and culturally competent.
>
> To be a meaningful leader and to prepare for this and tomorrow's world, you need to be able to bridge divides and bring people together across communities and constituencies. And you have to work hard to make sure everyone is at the table. [Mosle recommends a round table so everyone's voice is heard.]
>
> Leadership also involves bringing in the next generation. Those who create the vision are very different people from those who will carry the vision forward and enhance it. Good leaders know when to pass along the torch.

"You can't be what you can't see" is a general principle for Linda McGurn, chair of the University of Florida Foundation.[25] This emphasis on increasing diversity cannot consist of just one or two token women of color; it must be a genuine ongoing commitment to increasing and ensuring real diversity on boards, committees, and as donors.

> ### SOME KEYS TO HELPING GET MORE WOMEN ON BOARDS
>
> • Maintain a list of potential women candidates. Updating lists of potential members is an effort that both genders need to work hard at doing. Keep your lists handy.
> • Understand that women juggle many different roles in their lives, and you may need to change your expectations of what women board members can accomplish. Remember, when you foster an environment that adapts to families, you benefit male board members as well.
> • Be the best you can be if you want women to give their time as well as their money to your organization. Women are only going to choose nonprofits that truly speak to them and the issues and values they care about.

Consensus Building

Women have traditionally been the peacemakers and consensus builders in the family; they carry this skill to the political arena and boardroom as well.

In 2008, when the New Hampshire Senate became 54 percent female, Senate President Sylvia Larsen said that women are consensus builders and very capable of getting the job done.[26] She said getting things done through teamwork has worked very well for the New Hampshire Senate in its first year of a female majority. Larsen believes that the majority gives women an opportunity to prove their ability and their leadership style, and she feels sure the results will be positive over the next two years.

Valuing harmony has advantages for any organization. Despite the fact that in the past women may have remained silent or nonconfrontational in order to create harmony, these traits can be helpful when trying to reach consensus so long as they are not suppressive reactions or actions. Collaboration, connection, and teamwork are key and women know how to play those ways.

Volunteering

Women are more likely than men to be volunteers.[27]

Women volunteers are the lifeblood of any nonprofit organization. Ask an administrator how she or he would get along without female volunteers, and you are sure to get a horrified response, because women are crucial to the organization's success. Although volunteering was much easier for women when they weren't working outside the home, even busy working mothers are still finding the time to volunteer. Women like service and giving their time, no matter what their financial status may be. And they want to be involved and connected to an organization, especially to those where they give their money.

Volunteering has been shown to be one of the major elements leading to increased giving. Michele Minter, vice president for development at the College Board, says, "Women are . . . passionate volunteers. They volunteer at higher rates than do men in every state, and once they get involved, there are strong correlations to their financial support."[28]

The disconnect, however, is that women's high rate of volunteering doesn't translate to a high number of positions in the volunteer leadership of the organizations. A Nonprofit Governance Index found in 2007 that as an organization gets larger, with a bigger budget and increased power, the number of women in board leadership positions decreases.[29] It is in the boardroom where most major decisions are made, and women have less influence there, despite the amount of time they give.

TIPS FOR CORRECTING THE DISCONNECT
BETWEEN WOMEN'S VOLUNTEER TIME AND
BOARD LEADERSHIP

Look for the potential gift rather than an absolute requirement that a large gift be made before a person is selected for a position of leadership. Some women do not yet buy into the notion that you have to pay to play, and women often consider their time more important than their money. Some women may be overlooked in the board nomination process if it is strictly based on previous large financial contributions.

Nevertheless, stress the idea that leadership involves making a financial contribution as well as volunteering time. Talk about how a woman's credibility will be enhanced with a generous gift (which will vary according to their means) and how their influence will be made stronger by being in positions of leadership on the board, where the important issues are decided.

Invite the wife of the philanthropic couple to be on your board. No doubt she has helped make the decision about where the money should be contributed, and she may have been the primary decision maker even though the gift is in both their names. Having couples serving together on a board can help bring about more diversity and often makes the board a more sociable environment.

Create meaningful ways that women can volunteer that will put them on track for board leadership. Women respond well to mentoring, and woman board members can mentor new or existing volunteers. This plan will help the volunteer progress that includes increased opportunities and tasks leading to becoming board members.

Ensure that there is a strong commitment from the board and staff to bring more women on board—this applies also to increasing diversity and bringing in younger people. The actual number should represent more than just a token amount, and this will require a plan and a commitment reinforced on a continuing basis. Staff and board training may be necessary to reassure and convince them that greater giving potential exists through greater board diversity, and different strategies may be needed to put the plan into effect.

Financial Acumen

It is not only the traditional aspects of nurturing and caring that women bring to the nonprofit table. According to Madelyn Ringgold, senior philanthropic advisor at JP Morgan Chase Private Client Services, "When women get involved in charitable organizations . . . they're influencing the endowment and joining the board . . . Women are now business school graduates and know how to apply sound financial principle to philanthropy."[30] The workplace research group Catalyst reinforces this opinion with a study of five hundred of the largest U.S. corporations: it found that those with the most women on boards had a higher return on equities—by at least 53 percent.[31]

Nurturing and Altruism

Woman seems to differ from man in mental disposition, chiefly
in her greater tenderness and less selfishness . . . Man . . .
delights in competition, and this leads to ambition
which passes too easily into selfishness.

—*Charles Darwin in his 1871 book* The Descent of Man

Women bring both nurturing and altruism to any situation, according to Debra Mesch, director of the Women's Philanthropy Institute at the Center on Philanthropy at Indiana University. She says, "In this culture especially, they [women] are the nurturers and are charged with raising a family. Their altruism is more developed [than men's]."[32]

Nurturing and altruism are related, and both are important to society. Mesch explains that altruism is a form of prosocial behavior and a needed contrast to selfishness and egoism. Nurturing, she says, is a result of women's roles in our culture—women's socialization process leads them to be the natural nurturers and caregivers in the family social structure.

To some it is very clear that the two words go together. Joanna L. Krotz, author of *The Guide to Intelligent Giving* and writer for the annual philanthropy issue of *Town&Country* magazine, says, "Giving is what women do, of course. We nurture kids, relatives, and communities. We drop everything for friends in need. We join walkathons, sit on school boards, and donate to clothing drives. And as often as not, we also write charitable checks."[33] Nurturing and altruism: a female thing.

Taxes Versus Altruism

Our research verified what many earlier studies have shown: tax benefits are not the reason women give.

In 2009 we asked women whether their charitable giving would be affected if the federal tax provisions allowing deductions for char-itable gifts were eliminated.[34] Nearly 67 percent said their giving would remain the same. We must point out that the question did not include whether women would give less if the tax credit were less, rather whether they would continue to give if the credit were *totally eliminated*. There cannot be a truer indication that philanthropy for women is altruistic as opposed to opportunistic.

TAKEAWAYS

Every nonprofit will benefit from having women's voices, values, and leadership represented. It is up to institutions and organizations to listen to women who represent over half the U.S. population, control over half the nation's wealth, and in general have all the right values for making the world a better place. Nurturing women for positions of leadership is not only smart to do, it's the right thing as well. Women should not have to wait for permission to sit at the table; they should ask for leadership roles, and they should be asked to lead. Everyone will gain from bringing new ideas and qualities to organizational leadership—from the organization itself, to the boards, to the balance sheet, to the fellow members of the board and the constituencies they serve.

Remember the many important qualities women bring to philanthropic leadership:

- Important values
- Spouses
- Intellectual capital
- Nonhierarchical management
- Experience and a new perspective
- Listening skills
- Entrepreneurial approach
- Capacity to deliver change
- Perception of fairness
- Diversity
- Consensus building
- History of volunteerism
- Financial acumen
- Nurturing and altruism

8

Women's Philanthropy Programs and Giving Circles

T HE INFORMATION IN THIS CHAPTER IS APPLICABLE to many settings. Although the structure of the organizations and their purposes may be different, the fundamentals apply to groups such as women's funds, social service groups, religious groups, women's colleges, women's service organizations, women's health organizations, and women's athletic programs.

WOMEN'S PHILANTHROPY PROGRAMS: NEW VIGOR FOR NONPROFITS

The women's philanthropy program has given me a new and exciting way to connect to the university. I can bring my philanthropic priorities to the table where I know they will make a difference—and meet dynamic and interesting like-minded women. In just a few years, I have gone from a woman who hadn't visited the campus in thirty years to a person totally immersed in boards and philanthropy.[1]

—*Doris Weisberg, chair emerita, Women's Philanthropy Council,
University of Wisconsin Foundation; professor emerita,
The City College of New York; and a founder of the Food Channel*

Women's philanthropy programs have strengthened organizations across the nation and abroad. Programs have developed in organizations dedicated to health, social service, community improvement, religions, athletics, and higher education. A women's philanthropy program is an organized activity within a large nonprofit or institution that serves the common good.

This section of the chapter focuses on those programs that are part of nonprofits whose purpose is to serve all of society, not solely women. We will review the components for creating a successful program in a coed environment, with examples. The primary examples will be from higher education, which has been a leader in establishing women's philanthropy programs.

Programs: Popular and Purposeful

Women's philanthropy programs are becoming popular around the country. Why? When you talk to volunteers or staff involved with them, they are filled with enthusiasm and describe them with a special spirit. Volunteers find that these programs open up an institution or organization that was previously closed to them or at best a mystery. Through the program, the women learn that they are valued. The existence of the program not only positively affects those who participate in it, but gives a message that the organization validates women and their contributions. The program gives a message that women are appreciated.

Women report that the women's programs have become a real source of joy and connection in their lives, because the programs are centered on the donors and on creating a meaningful connection to institutions in a way that is comfortable for women. The programs create meaningful relationships among the women, of which philanthropy is a part, as the women meet each other and learn from the educational sessions in new and innovative ways.

The enthusiasm of staff and philanthropists is evident. Milwaukee philanthropist Judy Jorgensen said about Lori Rappe, the staff person who recruited her to the University of Wisconsin Women's Philanthropy Council: "It's amazing how one cup of coffee and one conversation can change your life and add a dimension you didn't know you needed! I am grateful!"[2]

Not all women will be interested in women's philanthropy programs, but they are another way to engage women in the life of your organization. For colleges and universities, some women have not been drawn to speeches at regular alumni events and prefer more substantive programming geared toward women.

The successful women's philanthropy programs involve the following five purposes:

- *Philanthropy*. Increase women's philanthropy of both time, talent, and money.
- *Leadership*. Raise the number of women in volunteer leadership positions.
- *Education*. Provide educational opportunities on philanthropy, finance, nonprofits, and societal issues.
- *Friendship*. Facilitate an environment for friendships and networking.
- *Joy*. Create the joy of giving.

Philanthropy

Increasing women's philanthropy of both time and money to the institution is perhaps the key internal, institutional goal. You must be clear that the program's goal is to increase philanthropy to the organization. When the word "giving" or "philanthropy" is included in the group's name, then the function is clearer. For groups that do not include the words "giving" and "philanthropy" in their title, it is important to describe philanthropy up front as part of your goal. Some names that exemplify this are Women's Leadership Initiative, Women's Giving Circle, Women Connect, and Women and Philanthropy. We also recommend providing a broader name for your program or initiative and not just focusing on the leadership group of individuals as the name. New groups should consider a title such as [name of organization] Women & Leadership, [name of organization] Women and Philanthropy, Women for [name of organization].

Women's programs fail when they are not up front that giving is a primary purpose of the organization. Do not go down the path of creating a group that merely builds better relationships with your constituency through education. Philanthropy must be a clear and present part of the equation. No one wants women's philanthropy programs to be viewed as internal competition or as marginalized auxiliaries. Women's philanthropy programs are vital add-on activities in coeducational organizations that demonstrate the organization's values. Women volunteers will sometimes want to do mentoring with students or staff. We recommend that those activities be done through alumni associations, not through the women's philanthropy program.

The inner circle of leaders is the first group of women for increased giving; the second is a larger circle of members or program participants. Your program should have a goal of increasing the total number of women giving to the organization. Another goal is increasing the number of women in leadership for boards outside of the women's program. A final goal should be increasing the total number of women on the top board. Have ways of measuring these goals and communicating them to internal and external audiences.

Those wishing to start a women's program within a coeducational institution can take lessons about marketing and development from women's colleges. Patricia Jackson, vice president for development at Smith College, reflects on women's colleges: "We think a lot of how women live their lives. We know they are concerned about the world and their legacy. We attempt to strike a balance between nostalgia for Smith and what we need today. Sixty percent of our students get need-based scholarships, and many are first-generation college students. Access to higher education is critical to us. Our goal is to make Smith College more a cause than an institution. We focus on our role of educating global women leaders—for the world."[3]

The key concept is that the institution is a cause that makes an impact in the world. This approach will attract women.

Leadership

Developing volunteer leadership is a large part of every women's philanthropy program. Members of the women's program may go on to other boards and committees within the organization. The women's program may also be a good place to engage women who have finished their service on another board or committee. The women's group should identify women outside its membership for inclusion on other boards and committees. For example, when a university is holding a women's program event in a city and a new potential school board member attends that event, the staff should bring the woman to the attention of their college colleagues. One goal of all women's programs is to increase the number of women in leadership.

Cheryl Altinkemer, associate vice president for advancement at Purdue University, reported on the development of women leaders during their capital campaign. In major cities around the country for five years, she held gatherings for top women givers at the $100,000 level. The events took place in homes and sometimes included a planned giving presentation. Each person attending talked about the impact of Purdue on her life, what kind of legacy she wanted to leave, and what kind of philanthropy she practiced. One woman came to all five events because she said she learned so much.

The internal goal of Purdue's gatherings was to invite women with the potential for million-dollar gifts. "We weren't going to change minds about women's potential until we got more million-dollar gifts," said Altinkemer. One woman increased her giving to $5 million. Follow-up visits with the 250 who attended the gatherings around the country resulted in $15 million in gifts. Many of the women went on to become campaign leaders. The group Women for Purdue—a university-wide leadership group—evolved from this campaign activity.[4]

Linda McGurn, chair of the University of Florida (UF) Foundation, was instrumental in establishing the UF Women: Inspiring Leadership and Philanthropy initiative. McGurn is proud of the education the initiative accomplished: "Our development staff had training to reach out to women, but we still needed to educate the rest of the University that women have potential and should be asked to be on advisory councils and academies. Our benchmarks revealed facts—such as many of the schools had over 50 percent women graduates, but nowhere near that number on the councils. Many of the women graduates didn't know about the councils, nor were they being asked."[5]

One of the UF Foundation goals was to get more women on volunteer boards. The Foundation board currently has eighteen women and twenty-three men as members, and McGurn points out that although board members are expected to make significant gifts to the university, the *potential* to give is as important as having already *made* a gift. This differs from many institutions that have a "pay to play" policy. By acknowledging women's desire for involvement before making significant gifts, University of Florida is in the forefront of the women's leadership movement.

Education

Women generally join a women's program to help the organization and for personal satisfaction. Part of that satisfaction comes from intellectual stimulation, and intellectual stimulation comes from education. Education from the program first must focus on philanthropy and finances—related to the purpose of the group. Education can also include programs related to issues in society, particularly related to the work of the organization. These topics might include analysis of politics, art history, social services for children, student life, women's health issues, and spiritual and religious topics. Finally, education should include components about the nonprofit or higher education institution itself. Examples can include hearing from the president of the organization about the strategic plan or learning from people within the organization—an interesting doctor doing life-saving work in a hospital, a social worker in a homeless shelter, or a faculty member who is a great artist.

Other education formats involve leadership issues and career development and mentoring as well as the steps in a woman's philanthropic journey: motivation, knowledge, action, leadership, and legacy (see Chapter Nine). These aspects should be included in every educational program.

Educational programs are a fundamental part of every women's philanthropy program and set the initiative apart from other development programs and boards. A common format is an annual conference or symposium on philanthropy, finance, leadership, and topics of interest usually related to the purpose of the nonprofit or educational institution. Suggested names for such gatherings are Women's Leadership Summit, Forum on Women and Philanthropy, and Symposium on Women and Leadership.

Friendship

Another aspect that distinguishes women's philanthropy initiatives is its purpose of networking and facilitating friendships. Developing personal friendships among the members of the women's program is a secondary result of the women working together. Over a two-, ten-, or fifteen-year period, a group of strangers become friends. We have heard women in beginning groups say, "I am too busy to make new friends," and after two years those same individuals are visiting each others' families socially. Most women like the idea of meeting new women with the potential for friendship. Linda McGurn puts it this way: "A lot of our connection with the University of Florida has been around sports, and now we're getting women involved at another level." That new level involves regional gatherings of women to hear about the university. "We plan to bring deans, faculty, and students to meet with the women, but the gatherings will also be an opportunity for the women to meet and get to know one another."

Career networking and support is another objective for some groups, even if understated. Higher education programs sometimes stress this aspect of their programming, such as California State–Fullerton, which bases its program on a leadership group of distinguished career women.[6]

Luther College in Decorah, Iowa, also hosts an annual educational seminar on philanthropy and finance for women, partnering with four local Lutheran organizations. Of the eighty to one hundred women who participate each year, many have attended the program in the past. One of the outcomes of this continued involvement is friendship and a bonding of the women participating, reports Jeanie Lovell, director of corporate and foundation relations. "Women enjoy learning together, and when they have a positive experience, they tell their friends and invite them to come along next year. This word-of-mouth marketing has been key to the growth of our program."[7] Lovell also notes that women often make new friends among the familiar faces who are active in this collaborative program. Although they may see each other only a few times each year, they share an enthusiasm for learning more about charitable giving and the financial management necessary to maximize support to their favorite organizations and causes.

Friendships and networking also take the form of mentoring. Some groups, such as the University of Notre Dame alumni office's ND Women Connect, focus on alumnae networking with each other and mentoring students. Notre Dame is also organizing a leadership group of philanthropists from the development office that will involve women who have contributed $100,000 or more, according to Lynn Hubert, director of regional development, Midwest, Notre Dame University.[8] The two aspects of the program complement each other—one is at the inclusive end, and the other at the exclusive major gift end. Mentoring students is highly staff intensive and should be undertaken only by organizations with staff time to devote to this activity.

Joy

Women volunteers and staff can work together to create meaningful giving programs for those who contribute. Each gift must be both consequential and celebrated, which addresses the core of the enjoyment and satisfaction of joining women's philanthropy programs. A meaningful giving program may take the form of each donor working with the organization to tailor her gift to the area of her interest within the organization. An example of this is Women & Philanthropy (W&P) at the University of California, Los Angeles. W&P encourages its members to give to whatever area of the university reflects the woman's values. In its publications and on its Web site, UCLA then reports on all the different ways the women have contributed. Donors find that at larger educational institutions this format works best, because personalization and relationships develop when the donor chooses and gives to a specific project.[9]

At smaller colleges, organizations may find that a more meaningful gift takes the form of an organized collective gift. Here women work with the organization to give as a group to a project they have identified. An example is Waukesha Memorial Hospital's Women Connected: women contribute an annual gift toward a collective list of projects they fund within the hospital. Kristen Freiberg, development officer at Waukesha Memorial Hospital, says that a collective gift works well for women's programs that are looking for additional donors in the community who may not have a relationship with the organization.[10]

According to "Making Philanthropy Count: How Women Are Changing the World" by the Women's Philanthropy Institute,[11] the United Way Women's Leadership Councils promote the concept that every United Way should have a women's program. Kye Fox, chair of United Way Worldwide's National Women's Leadership Council, said, "We also know that when the local United Way has a woman's program, the resource development department outperforms the system as a whole."[12] The most successful programs are those that focus on raising funds for special purposes, above and beyond the regular United Way programming but developed in conjunction with United Way. In Madison, Wisconsin, the United Way Women's Leadership Council secures funds for the Schools of Hope, a program to help children in the public schools through mentoring and developing reading skills.

Women's volunteer leadership also plays a major role in creating the joyful giver by their enthusiasm at the meetings and public events. At the larger annual public events, the volunteer chairs set the tone, inspiring confidence in giving to the organization by the joy they communicate to the audience.

Patricia Jackson believes that "women have real joy in making significant gifts to our institution. They say 'I am making this gift because I am so happy to be able to do this.' They like to set an example and model behavior—much like parenting." She also maintains that an initial good experience will enable more women to think of themselves of philanthropists: "It won't be unusual when women say 'I am a philanthropist.' They remember their first major gift and the sense of joy in giving. They experience an incredible sense of joy, an incredible sense of empowerment."

Building a Women's Philanthropy Program

The building blocks for a successful program are described shortly. But first we need to talk about the components for failure. They are simple and obvious. Lisa Johnson and Andrea Learned, in *Don't Think Pink*,[13] say it all when they point out that to engage women consumers or givers, it is not enough just to have a regular product and color it pink. Michael Silverman and Kate Sayre in "The Female Economy" in the September 2009 *Harvard Business Review* give the example of Dell's ill-fated effort to market to women.[14] The company took their regular computer and produced it in pink, putting recipes and calorie-counting tips on the Web site. Women were appalled. Attempts to start women's philanthropy programs in the same "color it pink" mind-set—by taking a regular giving program, calling it "women's philanthropy," and expecting women to give to it—simply won't work. Women's philanthropy is not a top-down activity.

You have to do the legwork and listen to the women leaders and supporters whom you are trying to attract. *They* must take the lead, not
you. Remember, one of the Six Cs Plus Three of women's philanthropy
is *create*. Women like to participate in the creation of the organization or initiative. Yes, they want to respond to a nonprofit's needs, but
they also want the joy of figuring out how to structure the response.
Give them that joy, and they will be supportive and loyal to your
organization with increased support.

Note that the nature of the women's philanthropy program will
depend on the gifting requirements. The amounts required range
from no gift, to annual gifts of $250 to $2,500, to major gifts of
$25,000.[15] Some programs require an annual gift of $1,000 to the
group's objectives and then a major gift to the area of the donor's
choosing at the institution. The Mercy Hospital System in Kansas,
Arkansas, and Oklahoma, for example, launched five women's philanthropy programs, reports Tracey Biles, Manager, Philanthropy
Services. This is the first known program across several institutions.
The programs ask for a $1,000 annual gift.[16]

Before starting or expanding a women's philanthropy program,
we recommend that you make sure you have the following components to ensure your success.

- *Staff and management commitment.* One or ideally two (or more)
  staff members envision the role of a women's program at the
  institution and decide to take it on as a project. Some organizations have formalized an internal "women's philanthropy task
  force" and involved several staff persons. Management needs
  to endorse exploring the effort and back it up later with staff
  and budget. Most women's philanthropy programs are an additional assignment for someone in the organization who has
  expressed a desire to work with women donors. Rarely have
  programs thrived just by management personnel determining
  to start a program and hiring a staff person. Instead, current
  development staff members should identify a women's program
  as a priority for themselves and believe that it is a good step for
  the organization to increase women's philanthropy. We suggest
  that the program involves at least two staff members working
  on the program part of their time. This structure is better than
  one person working full time in isolation. The more the program

can be made part of all development officers' responsibilities, the better.

- *Core group of women volunteer leadership and major donors.* Before beginning a program, you must seek the input of such a group. Brainstorm with them about how to engage women with your institution. Get their feedback and ask for their leadership behind establishing a program. All you need are four to six primary leaders to serve as a core advisory group. Some programs begin when women donors have requested a program, such as at the University of Connecticut, but most start with one or two committed staff members. At Oregon State University, thirteen women make up the steering committee. Arizona State has cochairs and a committee structure for membership, investment, and education.[17]

- *Clear vision, mission, goals, and values.* These elements help ensure a program's long-term success—indeed, these are all good standard practices in a development office. Volunteer leaders and staff should work together to formulate goals and objectives. It's critical to discover how many women are giving to your organization, how much, and at what giving level.

- *Business plan and evaluation method.* Have a business plan and analysis of how the program would fit into your development operation. This internal analysis includes benchmarking to assess your progress. Proper evaluation can be the most difficult element for a women's philanthropy program because the program is usually only one part of the relationship between the donor and the organization. However, benchmarking is effective even if joint credit with others on the staff is considered. Such benchmarking includes the number of women donors in leadership, the amount contributed, total number of gifts and amounts given by all women donors, and the number of women in leadership.

- *Organizational culture that supports women's giving.* You must complete an internal audit concerning your operations, the role of women in your organization, and the potential of women as an audience. Standard operating procedures in the organization must respect women and women's perspectives. Chapter Six describes the internal audit and how to start gender-neutral development programs. Your organization should feature women and minorities in leadership and on staff.

Listen and Talk: Focus on the Donor's Ideas

Whether starting or growing a women's philanthropy program, listening and dialogue with donors are essential. When women donors have worked with other donors to get a program started, or if a partnership of staff and donors started the program, the information from those outside the inner circle of founding visionaries is needed to understand how to shape the program. The dialogue step also engages potential members and donors to participate in the group and connect with the organization—just by the action of listening and dialogue.

Interviews with key opinion leaders and potential or current major donors will help give women volunteer leaders and staff feedback on what kind of program to undertake. Which of the purposes of women's philanthropy programs resonates with the women? The group should discuss whether to have a gift requirement group, annual gift, collective giving group, or major gift group.

Listening groups are also a good way to get feedback to start or grow your program. These groups could be small gatherings of three to six women to discuss the possibilities of a program. Surveys are also an excellent way to gather information from women donors.

The most successful way of starting a program and engaging potential participants is through focus groups. Whether you undertake the focus groups yourself or hire an outside facilitator, focus groups have proven to be an excellent way to garner information about what kind of program you should undertake, while at the same time cultivating the interest of the participants in your program. Focus groups are formal discussions with a set of questions asked of all participants. Answers between groups can be compared.

Use focus groups when you are looking to establish a new organization-wide program or to launch a separate new activity that would involve a new group of women. See Resource A for a complete description of focus groups and questions.

One unexpected result of some focus groups has been the high level of participant enthusiasm. The negative side is that you must deliver on some of the actions the women suggest in the focus groups, otherwise they will be disappointed and may not wish to continue their involvement. Meeting expectations is sometimes a challenge. Before starting the focus groups, have a few basic programming options in mind so that the organization can deliver on some of the ideas the women raise in the focus groups. Be prepared to act on their advice.

Growing the Leadership Group

One of the basic parts of a women's philanthropy program is a group of women volunteer leaders for the effort. Internal and external women leaders must work together to expand the program.

The leadership group raises awareness and visibility of women as a constituency. They serve as role models in giving. Some groups create challenge gifts. Members of the leadership group may serve as a committee for educational programming or lead women's giving circles. A leader also helps by serving as a regional coordinator who does programming and networking in her area. Examples are the United Way of American Women's Leadership Councils, the Red Cross' Tiffany Circles, and university programs such as those at Wisconsin, Princeton, Virginia, and Virginia Tech.[18]

One very important aspect of leadership development is the relationship of the women donors to the top administration, especially women, at the institution. This partnership between leaders is important for the women donors to know they are true stakeholders in the organization. The synergy between the women leaders may produce new innovative projects funded by the women's gifts. At the University of Wisconsin, one of the most important relationships for the women's philanthropy program is between donors and the women faculty and administrators. The Women's Philanthropy Council at Wisconsin has funded awards and conferences to advance women on the campus as a result of the relationship.

Regional Groups: Spreading the Word

Regional groups are a possibility for larger organizations with national or regional reach. Major donors and key volunteer leaders form the core of the activity. Bring your organization to your audience with a speaker from your institution. Provide programming with a mixture of formats.

To launch a geographic program, identify twelve women of influence in the region who are potential leaders and major gift donors. This core group is the key to success. The women connect with one another and with additional women in their areas. Engage these women with the organization, helping them to get more connected and find their interest area within the institution. Hold activities to expand connections to larger groups of donors/major gift prospects in regional areas. If your organization is a college, invite the core group leaders to the activities on campus. For large institutions with geographically dispersed staff, involve these regional staff members with the program.

A first step might be to hold a focus group with possible participants to gain their perspective on preferred programming and on their attitudes towards philanthropy. The most popular way to continuously connect the core group and others is through the women's showcase format, where the core group members get to help decide on the speaker and venue. They invite others to attend these intellectual dialogues.

At the University of Wisconsin, women faculty members and deans speak on timely topics. Recent topics have included stem cell research, democratization in the Middle East, and the campus cultural arts district. Bringing in women faculty is part of the program's mission because the women donors connect to them. Sometimes the contact continues after the event.

Another significant aspect of featuring women faculty is that the faculty gets development experience, so important to their advancement. Often women faculty are not otherwise given these opportunities. Other regional program formats are small group discussions on philanthropy. Periodic luncheons and dinners with core group members are crucial.

In priority cities, such as New York, your event can be annual. In other cities, the faculty showcase event should be periodic, with additional luncheons for the core group, as well as invitations to other events.

Constituencies: Getting the Whole Organization Involved

It is important to identify the woman donor's individual interest at the institution and connect her to that school, college, or program that may eventually lead to her involvement and to a major gift. The staff team should work with colleagues to attract women donors for their programs. Volunteer leaders are involved as leaders, emcees, and sponsors. Activities include providing mailing lists, bringing donors to events, following up with women who attend, advising on marketing to women, and speaking at special programs; for example, women in business executive leadership, children's hospital breakfasts, international studies lectures, VIP events for visiting women lecturers, human ecology, nursing, women artists events, women's history, education, letters and science, women's health, and women's athletics.

Special Fundraising Goals: To Each Her Own

Some programs seek specific fundraising goals such as scholarship support or special goals for social services. The University of Mississippi raises funds for scholarship support. The United Way Madison Women's Leadership Council seeks funds for special public school programs. Drake University raises funds for the library. Women and Philanthropy at Ohio State makes grants for scholarships and student loans.[19]

The University of Virginia Women in Leadership & Philanthropy has an online catalogue that offers a selective list of specific gift ideas from the campus. Suggested amounts may cover the entire cost of an initiative or give ideas for combined gifts. Other formats include giving circles for specific projects, which we will now discuss in detail.[20]

GIVING CIRCLES: SMART, FUN, AND TOGETHER

Throughout history, women have gathered together—in homes and churches, town squares and bodegas—to heal their communities. Perhaps it is no coincidence that when we gather as women, we gather in a circle. We sit or stand, palm to palm, shoulder to shoulder, each of us equal and able to see not just the eyes of those across from us but into the soul for which those eyes serve as doorways. It is in that circle that we collect ourselves, each other, our stories, and our purpose. It is in that circle that we nourish, encourage and empower. It is in that circle that we celebrate and grow.[21]

—*Rosie Molinary, founder of Circle de Luz, Davidson, North Carolina*

I think giving circles are important because they get women
involved who weren't involved before and they are
immediately engaged in giving.[22]

*—Eugene Tempel, president of the Indiana University
Foundation and formerly executive director of the Center
on Philanthropy at Indiana University*

Over the past decade, philanthropy has taken a new and exciting form, one that women have embraced. Increasingly, women are
coming together to give collectively—agreeing on the cause, issue, or
organization to support and deciding where the gifts will be granted.
Women's giving circles come in many varieties, from potlucks to
annual gifts of thousands of dollars.

The media first picked up on women's giving circles in 1998 when
Colleen Willoughby and her Washington Women's Foundation were
featured in *People* magazine.[23] From that point, women's giving circles
increased exponentially for several reasons: the increase in women's
philanthropy, which included and encouraged many forms of shared
giving; the rise of new donors and high-net-worth individuals who
wanted to find new ways to give back to society in which they could
be actively involved; and the increasing demand by individuals to
have a greater say in and ownership over their charitable giving.
Women like Willoughby, who initiated and embraced shared giving
and attracted press attention, were instrumental in helping establish
the trend.

Reaching the Tipping Point

When the concept of giving circles became known, it quickly
reached that magical moment when an idea or trend of social behavior
reaches a tipping point and spreads like wildfire.[24] Women's potential
to give was part of that magic moment, but mostly women flocked to
the idea of creating their own organization, giving together, pool-
ing their money, and deciding where it would be given. In 2000
the Women's Philanthropy Institute published a small handbook,
Creating a Women's Giving Circle,[25] the seminal book on the subject
that helped launch so many other circles.

From only a hundred or so giving circles in 2000 to over five
hundred some eight years later, awarding millions of dollars annually,

women have moved from quilting bees, book clubs, church circles, and investment clubs into philanthropy. It only made sense, as women like to do things together in a nonhierarchical way—and a circle represents just that. A circle is not a triangle with one person at the top and the rest of the people at the bottom; it is not a box with sharp divisive corners. A circle is a never-ending line in which everyone has the same amount of ownership and authority.

Giving circles share some commonalities. Each woman often gives the same amount of money and takes part in selecting the grant focus and awarding the grants annually. There are generally few meetings, a great deal of socializing, and little structure. The differences are not significant, although some women's giving circles do have an endowment, multiyear pledges, different giving categories and amounts, and a good deal of structure. The concept of women doing good together remains the same in all giving circles.

Women's giving circles have embraced all the Six Cs of women's giving: change, create, commit, connect, collaborate, and celebrate. There is no clearer proof of the impact of the Six Cs than women's giving circles. And, of course, the circles have contributed in large part to the three new Cs: control, confidence, and courage.

Crossing Boundaries, Spanning Generations

Multigenerational and multiethnic groups of women are coming together and making funding decisions as a group. Some meet monthly in a living room. Others meet at a dinner or other social gathering. Most hold lively conversations about their community's needs and host educational sessions to inform each other about their interest areas. Then they decide where they want their money to be invested.

Some women have used concepts from their own culture when they were forming their group, molding it into a special kind of giving circle. Hali Lee's Asian-American Women's Giving Circle and Lynn McNair's African American Women's Giving Circle (described in Chapter Ten) are two examples. Lee chose the *geh*, a social banking concept used in the South Pacific; McNair's circle members acknowledge each other's African heritage.

Rosie Molinary grew up in a Latina culture and had conflicted ideas of womanhood. Latina culture represents beautiful women as virginal in the household and sex symbols in society. Molinary started her giving circle, Circle de Luz, to award scholarships to young Latina women identified in seventh grade and who graduated from high school.

Creating Philanthropists

Most women's giving circles include women of all generations: mothers and daughters, grandmothers, and mothers of small children. Women have told us they are especially pleased to be part of their circle because there are women in it they would never have before known.[26]

—Linda Strup, Giving Circle of Hope, Reston, Virginia

A deliberate goal of many women's giving circles is to create women philanthropists—some call it "growing women as philanthropists." This goal will appear prominently in mission statements and is part of the vision held by founders. To that end, circles often pursue not only a deliberate learning agenda around issues of grant-making, but also an underlying one to help members realize the power of philanthropy and of taking their place at the table.

Giving circles engage donors to grow as philanthropists in some interesting and creative ways—an indication of their flexible and responsive nature. Creating philanthropists is part of the mission of the Women's Giving Circle (WGC) of Howard County in Maryland.[27] One way of achieving this is through their Response Network, created in response to members who wanted to directly help other women in need. A fund of the Columbia Foundation, the WGC periodically sends out emails to over one thousand donors and others, asking for contributions to address the specific need of a woman client identified by selected nonprofit agencies serving women and girls in Howard County. In 2009 Moscow Women Giving Together in Moscow, Idaho, decided to focus its giving on community organizations and projects that were responding to community needs exacerbated by the recent economic downturn, using creative solutions to address challenging problems and enhancing a sense of community.[28] This focus opened the door to many different types of projects, from art to housing to food security, but kept the circle focused on meeting pressing needs and leveraging dollars to have the greatest impact possible.

Women Giving More

We knew that people join giving circles to make a difference in their communities. Now we know that giving circles really have an impact on members' giving, knowledge, and civic participation.[29]

—Jessica Bearman, independent consultant and co-lead investigator for The Impact of Giving Together

---

A recent report released by the University of Nebraska at Omaha together with the Forum of Regional Associations of Grantmakers and the Center on Philanthropy at Indiana University finds that donors in giving circles give more, give more strategically, and are more engaged in their local communities.[30] Although the report was not specifically directed to women and women's giving circles,[31] most giving circle members are women, making these results very pertinent:

- Giving circles influence members to give more charitable donations and to give more strategically.

- Giving circle members are highly engaged in their communities. Giving circles also increase members' knowledge about philanthropy, nonprofits, and community needs.

- Giving circle members give to a greater number of organizations, compared with other donors.

- Giving circle members are more likely to give to areas less often funded by organized philanthropy, such as to organizations serving women and girls, ethnic and minority groups, and for arts, culture, and ethnic awareness.

- Giving circles can have even a greater impact in these difficult economic times, because members pool their donations and are able to make larger grants to nonprofits than they could have individually, and they are providing creative opportunities for new ways to give.

Nonprofits and Women's Giving Circles

Because women's giving circles have become an increasingly popular way for nonprofits to engage donors in exciting, creative ways, most nonprofit organizations, foundations, and associations can serve as effective hosts.

There are a number of potential benefits for nonprofits that choose to host a giving circle, including increased community visibility, new and different donors, more engagement for current donors, developing community leaders, building grant-making and endowment programs, and promoting a culture of giving.

By starting a women's giving circle, nonprofits are not only educating women about philanthropy and encouraging them to give more, but also providing leadership training and a way for women to become volunteers of the nonprofit and future board members.

It is crucial, however, that the circle be initiated by the women volunteers, with support from the nonprofit. Women want to create and not be told what to do. The most successful circles are those headed by active and dedicated volunteers who are well-respected in their community. Start the process with fewer than five women, get the organization in place, let the steering committee ask their friends to join, then watch the circle grow and the involvement (volunteers and donations) in your organization expand.

Women's Giving Circles and the Future

What do women's giving circles mean for the future? Dr. Angela Eikenberry, a professor at the University of Nebraska, author of *Giving Circles: Philanthropy, Voluntary Association, and Democracy*, and the other co-lead investigator for *The Impact of Giving Together*, says: "One of the most important findings in our study was that people in giving circles give more, the more engaged and longer they are engaged in the giving circle. This shows that we'll likely see the impact of giving circles grow in the future."[32]

Information and resources are also in the future for giving circles, as there are a number of organizations and networks now assisting circles in a variety of ways. Sandy Bettger of Washington, D.C., is an example. After reading about giving circles in the *Washington Post* in 2004, Bettger knew she had found her calling. She believed that to promote meaningful change over a long period of time, she had to start through grassroots organizations. "And what could be more grassroots than giving circles?" she asks.[33]

Because Bettger's master's thesis was on driving meaningful change and creating sustainability in organizations, she began thinking seriously about how she could apply this to giving circles. She believed that by starting a group to support and advance giving circles she would be able to create sustainability as well. Thus was born the Giving Circle Network (GCN) in 2005, a network for giving circles across the country.

Takeaways

Women's philanthropy programs are an excellent way for nonprofits to secure additional support from women. The programs are popular ways to attract new donors and reinvigorate current supporters. Programs are common in higher education, health care, and community foundations.

Giving circles are having an impact through the specific programs they fund and as catalysts for the growth of philanthropy overall. Additionally, they are proving to be successful "philanthropy incubators" for individuals who wish to leverage their dollars for greater impact while learning more about the community, grant making, and issues of importance to them. The exciting growth trend is expected to continue, with many new faces joining the philanthropic table.

9

Taught or Caught:
Donor Education

Through the years I have often thought, "I want to be a philanthropist!" Many things appear to hold me back, but the most important is just how I THINK . . . Thank you for encouraging women to think of themselves as "bigger."

—A woman who had attended a donor education session, in a note
with her annual donation to the Women's Philanthropy Institute

RESEARCH RESULTS VARY CONCERNING WHETHER philanthropy is "caught" from parents, elicited when one is personally touched by an event, or "taught" through donor education. It seems that women's philanthropic journey can be caught, taught, or a combination of both. When a woman's child is in the hospital being treated for a disease, she will mostly likely "catch" philanthropy and give to the hospital. On the other hand, women whose families were philanthropic, who attended donor education sessions, or became part of giving circles, are "taught" philanthropy and also "catch" the idea from others around them.

Philanthropy can be one of the most rewarding and meaningful parts of life. Yet some women are overwhelmed with solicitations and say they do not know how to set giving priorities or focus their giving. Others wish their philanthropy would better reflect their values and vision for a better world. Most women, as they consider the disposition of their assets, want to make sure their relatives or children are taken care of.

In this chapter we will look at all these issues as we review women's philanthropic journey. This journey is made in a very deliberate way through donor education. It is a journey that greatly benefits both the women involved and the nonprofits they support.

WHAT IS DONOR EDUCATION ALL ABOUT?

Donor education is by far the most exciting and innovative part of women's philanthropic initiatives (see Chapter Eight). Donor education programs can significantly advance women's philanthropy in nonprofits, and after women complete donor education programs, their gifts tend to become larger and less restricted.[1]

Even if nonprofits do not have formal women's philanthropy initiatives, they can sponsor programs individually or join with others in the community to support regional or citywide educational opportunities. The joint ventures have proven to build strong collaborative relationships in the community. Donor education is not only about personal learning, but also about helping unfold giving opportunities. It provides the framework for understanding philanthropic intent.

Families can be included in donor education. However, there should still be separate programs for women to provide a private and safe place for discussion about all the dynamics of giving. Women open up and discuss more in all-female groups.

Experiencing the philanthropic journey with other women gives donors the chance to learn from one another. We have seen, many times, the revealing looks in older women's eyes when they hear about couple giving in younger women's households. It was clear that some interesting conversations would be taking place in some of their homes as a result of what they heard. These moments help all women understand that they can participate in philanthropic decisions, influence their family philanthropy, and give on their own.

Through donor education programs, women experience the joy of giving by listening to other women. They become excited and open about their philanthropy as they share stories. Once the sessions begin, these stories become inspirational and motivational for everyone involved. The programs provide an unparalleled opportunity for education, learning, sharing, and networking. Women appreciate the dedicated time to talk with their peers about philanthropic values, vision, and voice in informal settings.

The sessions focus not only on philanthropy but also on related topics such as financial issues and how to achieve the joy of giving while living. Faculty, clients, administrators, and student presentations may be incorporated into the event, integrating their messages into the mission of the institution.

Donor education programs can

- *Help differentiate or distinguish your institution or nonprofit.* The organizations that engage their women donors are the ones that will succeed. If donor education is done well, women will spread the word that you care about your donors and are special in your community or way of providing service.

- *Provide value-added for the institution.* Donor education provides a double benefit where the organization is doing a favor not only for the donors but for itself as well. Donor education provides a woman with an understanding of herself, her values, and how those values translate into her giving. She also learns more about the institution, and as she is engaged with it, she is much more likely to give.

- *Create deeper relationships with donors and spouses.* A great deal that occurs during donor education leads to donors' looking at their own lives. This helps create an even closer bonding between the donor and the organization. In addition, donor education provides a means for women at the same economic level to talk comfortably among themselves and establish relationships.

- *Maximize impact and giving.* Women donors say they want involvement both before and after making gifts. Donor education provides that involvement: studies show that volunteers and those engaged with nonprofits give more. Additionally, the donors learn more about the nonprofit as they proceed on their philanthropic journey. Donors are better able to combine their values with the organization's mission.

- *Provide opportunities for individual follow-up.* Donor education gives the nonprofit an intimacy with donors and development officers as they become partners. This sharing leads naturally to working together and comfortable communication between women donors and development officers.

Before we began presenting donor education programs in conferences around the country, we talked to and learned a great deal from leaders in the field, including Tracy Gary, founder of Inspired Legacies, and Ellen Remmer, president and CEO of The Philanthropic Initiative (TPI) and a member of the Women's Philanthropy Institute's Council. We found that many development offices and financial institutions were beginning to address the financial and philanthropic techniques—the how-to's. But the modern donor education movement, developed in large part to reach audiences of women, started to become meaningful when values, inspiration, and motivation were addressed.

Women donors want to improve and change society, but also to do it wisely. And they want to learn more than just the mechanics of giving. Women want an understanding about themselves—their values and goals, the issues they care about, and their regard for money. Becoming an informed donor appeals to women. Every nonprofit could advance its own support, and that for all of philanthropy, by sponsoring women's philanthropy seminars and educational programs.

Philanthropy is the one voluntary economic decision we make in everyday life that offers a chance to put our vision and our values, our money and our morals in the right place. The result of women's donor education: finding the "right place."

VALUES, VISION, AND VOICE

Many women strive to live in tune with their values. Basing their philanthropy on those values is an important element of women's philanthropy. Women know that values-based philanthropy solves problems and makes a difference in people's lives.

Women value connection, and they feel connected with other women when they see and hear about specific examples of women philanthropists in their community—philanthropic women in history, and the growth of giving circles, women's funds, and women's initiatives, alliances, and campaigns. When Shaw-Hardy presented to 360 women after the results of the "Women Moving Millions" campaign[2] were announced, she called it an outstanding example of women's philanthropic achievements. The statement generated an enormous and spontaneous round of applause. The women in attendance were excited and proud to hear about the campaign's success and to know that they too could reach high and exceed expectations.

Voice is important. During the "Women Moving Millions" campaign, Helen LaKelly Hunt invited women to her home who were capable of giving a million dollars to help women and girls. The women were not asked to give at the session; rather, they were able to speak freely, comfortably, and confidentially with one another about philanthropy, their personal feelings about money, and the responsibilities and obligations surrounding their wealth. Of course the discussions also included the issues of women and girls, but primarily the women were being educated about philanthropy. Donor education works in the same way: a comfortable setting, confidentiality, sharing of thoughts and feelings, and interesting information presented by a caring person.

THE FIVE STAGES OF THE JOURNEY

As we learned more about donor education, we identified five different stages of the journey:

- Motivation/Inspiration
- Knowledge
- Action
- Leadership
- Legacy

We strongly recommend that each donor education program include these stages. There can be more emphasis on one than another, but to be truly successful, some aspect of each stage must be included.

Journey Stage One: Motivation/Inspiration

Stage One is reflection followed by the "Aha!" moment. It's when women look at their lives and their values and discover a passion relevant to those values.

Women at this stage frequently do not yet consider themselves philanthropists. Too often organizations jump right into the Stage Two phase of knowledge without adequately focusing on inspiration, motivation, and discovery. Without reflection and choice, follow-up education won't work very well, because the groundwork hasn't been done. This groundwork involves women finding their values, their vision, and then their voice.

Financial firms have begun adopting a "values stage" when working with their clients, in particular their female clients. These firms understand that women view their finances differently than men do; they can have emotional attachments and reactions that need exploring at the onset of the relationship. So before talking about stocks, bonds, and other options, they are having discussions about values.

Stage One sessions work best when conducted by a woman. Merrill Lynch has found that women respond best to other women when talking about personal matters; consequently, they are recruiting more female advisors to serve their increasing numbers of female clients.[3] The same holds true for programming with women donors. They are much more likely to open up to a woman than to a man conducting the session or presenting.

Participants can be asked to fill out a values questionnaire when they first arrive, with questions such as these:

- When others catch a glimpse of you, what values do they see in the first ten seconds?
- What are the differences between their values (the ways other see you) and your values (the ways you see yourself)?
- How much does your family know about your values and their own values?
- Are your collective family values the same as your personal values?
- What key values do your children or younger people who are important to you already have?
- What values would you like to pass on to them?

The Million Dollar Exercise

Taylor developed a guide through this stage that she calls The Million Dollar Exercise. (You will find it complete in Resource B.)

Women are asked to first identify their values and then the important issues of society. By bringing together their values and the "play money" they use in the exercise, and by working together, they help solve the issues and bring about social change. There is never a doubt that women will use their monies in a transformational way.

When Taylor facilitated this exercise in 1993 at the inaugural Felker Leadership Conference at Purdue University School of Consumer and Family Sciences, one of the issues the women selected was strengthening families. During the break, Lorene Burkhart, a graduate of the School, came up to Taylor and colleague Cheryl Altinkemer and said she wanted to start a Center for Families to provide decision makers with the latest research on families and children. Burkhart then astounded Taylor by saying, "And I will give the first gift—one million dollars!" Her reason: "Because you gave me permission to follow my heart."[4]

That gift resulted in a challenge to other women to give gifts to the Center, as well as additional gifts from Burkhart herself. Burkhart's values were the motivation she needed for her gift—and, she says, "When individuals make a gift, they express the values they care about."[5]

To accompany the values session and The Million Dollar Exercise, or as a standalone program, an inspirational keynote speaker about women and philanthropy is most appropriate on an annual basis at a luncheon or dinner. The values and exercise program can be done every few years with women who are new to the organization. Some of the suggested topics for a thirty-minute presentation:

- History of women's philanthropy, to help women share the pride of what has been accomplished in the past, although almost always unrecognized
- Six Cs Plus Three of women's philanthropy
- Importance of women's philanthropy in today's world
- Key women philanthropic role models and leaders
- Speaker's own philanthropic journey
- Factors in women's giving, including barriers and generations
- Ways women are giving today including giving circles, couple giving, family philanthropy, women's funds, and philanthropic initiatives in higher education

- How fortunate women are to live the lives they do and have had the life choices no other women in any time in history have enjoyed

In these presentations we often use a quotation that women very much relate to:

American women are living the best and healthiest lives that any women have ever lived . . . anywhere . . . at any time. We are the generation of women that the world has been waiting for and we should do more than soak up the good life to make up for what previous generations did to make our lives what they are.[6]

—*Dr. Claire Gaudiani, New York University professor and author of* The Greater Good and Social Entrepreneurship in America: Women Building a More Perfect Union

---

"Pursonality"

Many special events have been organized around the theme "Power of the Purse." Events, as time-consuming as they may be, seem to satisfy the desire for much that is meaningful to women: connection, collaboration, and celebration. The women in the Child Saving Institute Guild of Omaha created an event that not only raised a great deal of money but was so much fun that we wanted to be sure it was included in *Women and Philanthropy*. (See Resource E.)

Journey Stage Two: Knowledge

Women in this stage are motivated and ready to think about becoming philanthropists, or at least about giving more than they have in the past. Participants analyze personal issues and issues related to the influence of wealth on their lives and educate themselves about their financial worth. Because the subject of money can include very private issues and make some people uncomfortable, it is important to have a woman conduct the sessions. She will ensure that the women are at ease with one another and not afraid to ask questions, with confidentiality assured. The outcome of this stage is that women learn how to give away money to further their values, begin to develop a giving plan, and find out what to look for in a nonprofit. At the end of the sessions, they will identify themselves as philanthropists.

Dune Thorne, a principal of Silver Bridge Advisors, says her real passion is financial education for women.[7] She studied women's financial behavior and investing at Harvard Business School and, as a result of her research, launched the Silver Bridge "A Woman's Perspective" series, which brings women together to further educate themselves on investing, philanthropy, and a range of other wealth management topics.

Thorne found that women were clearly in need of learning how to manage money. They were going to their fathers, brothers, and friends for advice, and they said they didn't really trust advisors. Thorne says, "Women and men don't need different products and services. But women do tend to want the emphasis to be on sophisticated simplicity. They want to collaborate and not just learn from experts, but also from one another. Women learn from and share one another's experiences, such as having children, having parents in a nursing home, or being a widow." Thorne's research also adds support to the idea that women want their assets and their philanthropy aligned with their personal values.

According to Linda Descano, president and COO of Citi Women & Co., women have gone from being the family's chief purchaser to being the chief financial officer (CFO).[8] She says women are now planning for their children's education, their own retirement, and philanthropy. "Women are self-identifying themselves as CFOs and positive role models. They have taken on a much broader role and are shaping their families' financial values: one of those is giving back. They are looking at how to align their investments with their philanthropy and how to be more strategic philanthropists. How to get their kids involved. Women & Co. provides a safe place for women to talk about finances while being recognized for their economic prowess." Women & Co.'s program describes itself as a place where wisdom, wealth, and women meet—this is just the kind of atmosphere that's important to encourage during your sessions.

Following are five recommended sessions to help women feel more confident about financial matters. The first helps women look at their feelings about money; the second is structured around philanthropy; the third session features suggestions for what to look for in a nonprofit; the fourth is centered around developing a giving plan; and the last session features types of giving. The sessions build on one another and assume that the women have been a part of discussions of values and philanthropy from Stage One.

Best results will be gained from having the workshops conducted by either a woman who has been trained and is a peer of those in attendance or a carefully screened professional development officer. It is important that the attendees do not feel there is a hard sell for the nonprofit. Ideally, they will arrive at supporting your nonprofit on their own.

Session One: "What's It All About: Money and Me"

Up to forty women can effectively participate in this session. It should begin with a socializing time for a half hour followed by a fifteen- to twenty-minute presentation by a peer discussing the role of money in her life. Sharing a personal story to begin with will put the participants at ease and ready to open up in the breakout session.

Because the topic of money can be so personal, women find a questionnaire a good way of engaging their thinking in a comfortable way. Suggested questions can be found in Resource C. After the women have spent some time privately answering the questions, a facilitated one-hour discussion can be held, with four to six women per table. If it is appropriate, at the end of the hour each table can report on the conclusions that were reached during the discussion.

Follow this session with a lunch or a wine and cheese reception. This will give the women a chance not only to socialize (a very important component of women's philanthropy) but also to continue their discussions.

Session Two: "Experiences with Philanthropy"

This session can easily accommodate forty women and should be preceded by a time to socialize. Follow this with a facilitated panel of three women discussing their own personal philanthropy.

Questions for the panel should include the following:

1. Why is philanthropy important in your life?
2. Where did you learn your philanthropy?
3. What are your two favorite nonprofits and why do you give to them?

4. Describe the joy you receive from giving.

5. How are giving decisions made in your family?

The women on the panel should be recruited from donors to the nonprofit, and their stories should inspire and motivate participants to become more active givers.

Following the panel, small group discussions lasting an hour and a half, with four to eight women each, should be facilitated and include some of the topics from Resource C. One person can be appointed to report on the results of the discussion questions.

For individual women who are considering a major gift, we suggest using the questionnaire from Resource D. By asking questions of the donor, and even sending her a written report of her answers, you can assist in her planning and her communication of her plans to her family. The development officer should provide a thoughtful, calm presence to help the donor discover her true vision for a better world and how to take action.

Session Three: "My Philanthropy: Smart Giving"

It makes good sense to review a nonprofit, just as one would review a stock or business before making any kind of investment. Emotion, passion, and giving from the heart are important, of course—but so is good research. Women want to know details about the organization and are likely to be far more loyal if they have the entire story.

As with Sessions One and Two, this session can include up to forty women. Suggestions for opening the session (after the first half hour of socializing) include having a presenter discuss general information about what to look for when considering making a gift. This information should not relate specifically to the nonprofit sponsoring the presentation. Following this general session, the sponsoring nonprofit can make its presentation. Here are some of the topics for the presenter to include:

1. What is the history of the nonprofit?

2. What is the nonprofit's annual budget? What percent comes from fundraising? How much of private funding comes from the board? From the members?

3. How much is spent on administration versus programs?

4. What should I look for in an annual report?

5. Who is on the board?

6. Who are the financial supporters?

7. What should I look for in reviewing the 990?

8. What is the nonprofit's mission? Does it match mine?

9. How has the nonprofit fulfilled its mission?

10. Have the results been transformative? Have they addressed the problems rather than only providing temporary solutions?

11. Are there ways for the nonprofit to collaborate with others with the same mission?

This is an opportunity for the sponsoring organization to show itself in a good light while at the same time being fair and objective. Following the presentation, an interactive session should occur with questions and discussion.

Session Four: "My Philanthropy: Giving Thoughtfully"

This session includes both a personal look at giving and tips for developing a giving plan. For the personal part, Taylor has developed a list of ten ways for women to be more effective givers, which she calls "Being a Gifted Giver" (shown in the box). These strategies work well as handouts or bookmarks for symposiums on women's giving.

BE A GIFTED GIVER: TEN STRATEGIES FOR MORE EFFECTIVE GIVING

1. **Begin your philanthropy as early in life as possible.** Even if you can't give as much as you'd like, your gifts will add up and begin to form your legacy.

2. **Find your passion and focus your gifts** rather than scattering them. Think about two or three areas or causes you want to support with your major gifts and make this your philanthropic mission. Not only will your gifts have more impact, but you will find your giving more satisfying.

3. **Develop a giving plan.** Consider your giving as an investment needing to be carefully developed and reviewed at least annually.

4. **Work for parity in giving in your household.** You and your spouse should have equal say about which causes your contributions will support and the amount you are giving. Follow your values in your giving.

5. If you can, **give out of your assets** to the causes you are passionate about. Think of your philanthropy as you would a child—your investment in the future of our world.

6. **Give while you live,** so you can see the benefits of your action and know how to give more strategically the next time.

7. **Consider the strength of numbers.** Organize with others to provide a pooled gift that can make a project possible.

8. **Leverage your giving.** Increase your impact by challenging others to support the causes you hold dear.

9. **Teach the art of philanthropy to the next generation.** Instill in your children, and the young people you associate with, the values you treasure and your commitment to support them.

10. **Have fun with your philanthropy.** Celebrate your birthday with a philanthropic gift that you might not have thought possible. Philanthropy can be one of the most meaningful, rewarding, and joyful activities in your life. It can be your legacy.

All ten strategies are important, but the ones that will impact a woman's philanthropy the most at this particular point in her journey are numbers 3, 4, 5, and 8. We expand on each of them here.

Develop a giving plan. Former first lady Eleanor Roosevelt made a good point for a giving plan when she said, "Since you get more joy out of giving to others, you should put a good deal of thought into the happiness that you are able to give."[9]

There are excellent online resources available for developing a giving plan, including one from Tracy Gary's book, *Inspired Philanthropy,*[10] and from *The Bolder Giving Workbook*, a work by Christopher and Anne Ellinger.[11] Both help their readers decide how much they will give, to which causes, and by what process.

Having a giving plan also makes it easier to say no, says Dune Thorne: "You can say no very clearly and warmly. Not because you don't think the organization is phenomenal, but because you're personally committed to your own philanthropic mission. Otherwise you will be letting yourself down. But you can help connect them with others who have the same mission."

Giving in parity. Women usually don't give the same amounts to their alma maters as do their spouses. Frequently women don't even give to local causes they care about so much as their spouses give to their own favorite causes. Having a giving plan for the family helps equalize these disparities and sparks an honest and open discussion about them. Spouses usually will recognize the issue and encourage equality.

Giving out of assets. A big change over the last twenty years has been women moving beyond just giving out of their checkbooks. The impact of giving out of assets was best described by the late Claude Rosenberg in his book *Wealthy and Wise*.[12] Rosenberg suggested that Americans could give at least $100 billion more a year if they gave out of their assets as well as their income. Rosenberg subsequently formed the nonprofit Newtithing Group, a philanthropic research organization to educate and encourage more giving from assets. Newtithing Group points out that investment assets usually exceed income for the wealthy, with the implication that they, as well as their income, are available for philanthropy.[13]

Increasing the amount of philanthropy available per year by over $100 billion: think about it. What would that mean to the causes we most care about? To America? To the world?

Leveraging your giving. One of the stories that most resonates with women about leveraged giving is Mary Elizabeth Garrett and her "Friday Evening" group gift in the late 1880s.[14] The request came from Johns Hopkins University, asking Garrett for $354,000 to help complete its medical school. Garrett and her friends agreed to the gift under the following conditions: women would be admitted and would study the same courses as men. This offer did not set well with Johns Hopkins's president, who sided with his friend, the president of Harvard University, when he called coeducation "a thoroughly wrong idea which is rapidly disappearing."[15] Ultimately the women prevailed in what surely must have been an effort in those days, similar to today's Women Moving Millions campaign. Each was successful in spite of the naysayers.

Session Five: "Smart Planning for Smart Women"

After women have participated in the preceding four sessions, it is time to discuss the various methods of giving and which is most appropriate. The most successful way is to recruit as a presenter a woman who is a peer of the participants and familiar with various financial giving vehicles. Her presentation will resonate with the audience for two reasons: because she's a woman and because they respect her knowledge. Of course, it's important that the presenter not take advantage of the opportunity and "sell" her firm, but the fact is that some of the women will no doubt be interested in working with the presenter.

Women will look at different types of giving vehicles, depending on their stage of life and generation. (See more about this in Chapter Five.) If a woman is about to be married, is divorced, or is losing her spouse, each of these life-changing events could require a different kind of giving vehicle. For example, older women may be more interested in bequests, because many are afraid of outliving their money. Women who are climbing the corporate ladder often have family obligations and may want to do annual giving. Once a woman's children are in college, she is still likely to be most interested in annual gifts. But when college is over for her family, trusts and other planned giving instruments can be a consideration.

Women want to preserve their assets to provide enough—not too much, but enough—for their children and grandchildren. Trish Jackson, vice president for advancement at Smith College, says, "Women see themselves as guardians of that money, instead of investors of it. Women in general are more protective of their assets, not necessarily out of fear, but a sense of obligation to care for their children, in particular."[16]

At the conclusion of the session, women can fill out a questionnaire to include some of the following:

- What do I want my community to look like?
- What do I want my world to look like?
- What social change do I want to effect?
- How do I want to shape society with my giving?
- What do I want to achieve with my giving?
- What is the best way to do so?

        ° What form and type of gift?

        ° How often?

- What do I need to do to bring about these changes?
- To what type of organizations can I direct my gifts?

Journey Stage Three: Action

In the action stage, women are ready to become involved in programs at their institutions and organizations, to volunteer, and to give in an educated way. They do so first by applying their values to their giving; second, by understanding their finances; third, by having a giving plan; and finally, by knowing the different kinds of giving and what might work best for them. At this stage, women will be giving at least an annual gift.

This is the stage to provide women with opportunities for leadership to help them become philanthropic leaders. Remember, women want to be involved. Here are nine ways of involving and engaging women and helping move them to action:

- *Conduct focus groups with women donors and find out how they want to be involved in the nonprofit.* (See Chapter Six and Resource A.) In the groups, women can explore the ways they want to be involved. This is also a good time for the nonprofit to find out women's impressions of the organization.

- *Invite donors and prospects to the institution or facility for a tour.* Help them absorb the feeling and spirit of the group as well as learn about it. Show how the program is helping to solve a particular societal issue, and have contribution envelopes available on the tables. Leave plenty of time for questions, and be sure to follow up with all those in attendance. Complete the experience with a luncheon and a speaker (for example, a woman faculty member, student, physician, or director) telling interesting success stories about the programs of the nonprofit.

- *Inform women of available volunteer activities.* Almost all women want involvement, and it may be well worth the effort to create opportunities. At some nonprofits this is easy. The Child Saving Institute in Omaha had a donor contribute the money for a large garden outside their offices and daycare facility. Women and men now come to help care for the garden and teach the children about plants and other science appropriate to the children's ages.

- *Develop a list of board and committee member positions and actively recruit women for these spots.* This may mean providing leadership training discussed in Journey Stage Four: Leadership.

- *If the organization is regional, statewide, or national, hold regional meetings.* Invite women to attend, and feature topics of interest to them with time for questions and socializing.

- *Conduct panels of women givers as discussed in Session Three.* There is nothing like having a peer explain why she gives to the nonprofit to motivate others to give as well.

- *Introduce a woman to like-minded donors.* Women like giving together and inspire one another.

- *Use giving circles to include women and offer leadership experience.* (See Chapter Eight.)

- *Sponsor a book club for women.* These can even be conducted on the Internet, connecting women from outside the university or organization.

All of these methods can be personalized in different ways; for example, by bringing in students to talk about their scholarships, inviting recipients of grants to explain about how the grants helped them, or asking social workers and faculty to discuss their programs. Testimonials bring home the message better than any written piece of material. And don't forget to invite board members and executive staff. At universities, a dean is almost as important a guest as the president.

Journey Stage Four: Leadership

I like the concept of women claiming their "place at the fire," taking leadership roles in their giving and asking others to give.[17]

— *Joyce Miles, philanthropist and volunteer*

Women in the leadership stage understand they need to become role models by giving, asking, and serving on boards. They will be interested in beginning or being part of a women's philanthropic leadership initiative or a giving circle (as discussed in Chapter Eight).

Although many women still may feel they don't want their name on gifts or don't want to officially fundraise, they will recognize the importance of being role models and of asking for money. Women in the leadership stage will not only be giving an annual gift but also either be giving a major or planned gift or be prospects for the gift.

Raising Money

Philanthropist Tracy Gary (introduced in Chapter Four) has created many nonprofits and written two books on gift planning. She is an expert at fundraising and loves asking for money. Gary claims that both money management and fundraising are necessary life skills for women.[18] "To be a really good leader, women need to learn to fundraise. They may say they don't like to do it, but they should understand this is a way to leverage their own gifts." However, Gary isn't talking about the old male model whereby if a man gives $10,000 to his buddy for the buddy's cause, he can come back six months later and his buddy will give him $10,000 for his cause. Gary calls the new way not an exchange, but just plain generosity. "This is the future of philanthropy," she says, "people being generous to each other."

Gary has seen that nonprofit development officers are overwhelmed and need help raising money. She believes, "Women should do more than serve on boards. They should learn fundraising skills and make a commitment to partner with the organization."

There was a time when many organizations felt that they needed fewer volunteers for fundraising because it was too difficult to manage them. Kay Sprinkel Grace, author and consultant, disagrees: "I think this is a huge mistake [because] the very biggest thing we know about donors is that they give when they see their peers involved. So when a donor is called on by someone in the community, someone he or she knows and respects and realizes is giving up valuable time, she is more likely to give at a higher level than when approached by a staff member."[19]

As anyone who has ever raised money knows, a great deal of fundraising is organization: understanding the donor and having the right people in place. It's not a matter of "teaching" women to fundraise who are passionate about a cause. It just comes naturally when you connect the head and the heart with the voice. If women are more comfortable with a bit of role-playing, offer that. But the major points are to have the women make the introductions or the phone call if necessary and go along on visits. Before long, women understand the joy of not only giving but getting the gift as well.

Reene Bradshaw, a Gen Xer, grew up in what she described as "humble beginnings." She says, "I am Hispanic and a Catholic and was more on the receiving end of donations than the giving. I can remember standing in line for the government blocks of cheese and always getting the school-supplied yellow #2 pencils." Bradshaw now lives in Dickinson, Texas, and is the fundraising chair for the Junior League of Galveston. She says, "I enjoy fundraising, mainly for the networking. But deep down, I'm a salesperson to the core, and I get a huge thrill from raising money."[20]

Asking for the gift can also be a life stage, lifestyle, or generational issue, as women who are earning their own money know the importance of being involved in the community by serving on boards. They know that serving on a board requires members to be involved not only in policy making but in fundraising as well.

Philanthropist and former county commissioner Liz Ghrist is proud to have chaired the successful $67 million campaign in 2001 for Houston's St. Thomas University, an inner-city Catholic university with a large Hispanic population. She says, "The campaign was hard work, but a labor of love all the way, and I hope I have shown the way for other women to fundraise and chair large campaigns. Women sell themselves so short. They are so willing to be behind the scenes. We need to push ourselves forward."[21]

Influence

At this point in women's philanthropic journey, they will be truly passionate about their cause(s), have a strong sense of their financial worth, and understand why they have not only the means but also the responsibility to become more philanthropic. They will be involved in their nonprofit(s), have learned inspiring stories about other women philanthropists, and be motivated to lead others to be generous as well. Women will have found their philanthropic voice by providing leadership, becoming a role model, and influencing. They will understand that their leadership makes an enormous difference in fundraising; that because of who they are, others will be inspired to give, due to their respect for the person doing the asking.

This stage is about all that goes into leadership, including influence. Because research shows that women do have considerable influence on their spouses, consider a session where couples are invited to a donor panel made up of other married couples. The same questions listed in Journey Stage Two, Session Two: Experiences with Philanthropy can be asked of the panel. These questions are bound to elicit some interesting responses, and no doubt some will be surprised to realize that the wives have so much influence on the couple's philanthropy.

The people whom women influence to give should include friends, spouses, and other family members. Marcela Orvañanos de Rovzar, Mexican philanthropist and recipient of the 2008 Henry A. Rosso Medal for Lifetime Achievement from the Center on Philanthropy at Indiana University, shared a story about her influence with her cousin.[22] A friend of Rovzar's told her that he was unable to make an appointment with her cousin, a wealthy Mexico City resident. Rovzar was asked to intercede, so she called her cousin directly. She asked him to pay attention to what her friend had to say. Her cousin then agreed to take the call. She explains, "What happened that day when my friend spoke to my cousin about a project for children changed my cousin completely. Now he has his own foundation and has started incredible projects. He and his two daughters, his wife, and one of his sons are involved with philanthropy as well."

In addition to influencing her cousin, Rovzar also called attention to issues that he, being a male, might not have thought much about before. Linda Basch, president of the National Council for Research on Women, says, "Women have traditionally been responsible for families, community, and education. Men will respond when women bring these issues to their attention."[23]

Serving on Boards and Being Role Models

At the leadership stage, both of these actions will be important to women and completely understood. Women need to know that a "critical mass" is necessary to bring about effective change and to impact nonprofits. There must be large numbers of women giving large amounts of gifts and represented in large numbers on boards. Board positions put women in the role of deciding where monies are directed.

By this point in the journey, women will completely understand financial matters. They will not be afraid to speak up and ask questions. They will be visible and featured prominently in the nonprofit's marketing and communications to inspire other women to come forward to give and lead as well.

Journey Stage Five: Legacy

> Women use their philanthropy to enrich family life and promote connection—within the family, with the larger community, with the world. Their family philanthropy is not only a means to pay a debt to society and reinforce a family's personal values and culture, but also a way for their children to have a direct experience of giving to the larger community, an experience that helps them become more fulfilled adults.[24]
>
> *—Sara Hall, founder, New Philanthropy Advisors*

Women at Stage Five are successful philanthropists. They understand the importance of transferring their philanthropic values to the next generation and are inspired to do so. Children are women's legacy, and having charitable children is their goal. Women understand that, as the song from the Broadway musical *South Pacific* puts it, you've got to be carefully taught.

This is the final step in a woman's philanthropic journey. She will be interested in understanding how to pass her values on to her family, as well as about family philanthropy. The primary reason to discuss families is to help donors express values that will continue through the generations. The enormous growth of family foundations is part of women's philanthropy, and it is at this stage that many women will form a family foundation or consider a donor-advised fund.

Dune Thorne of Silver Bridge Advisors says that the most important part of the process of creating a strong legacy is to help the next generation have a set of sound values regarding their decision-making vehicles, and to "keep the compass true." Thorne says, "You can't predict what will happen, but family stories are very helpful to demonstrate that compass and reaffirm family values, and they resonate with everyone." She cautions that with philanthropy in particular, kids have to have independence and become responsible. "Otherwise they're not as interested and won't carry on the legacy well. It's a fine line. On the one hand you want to be clear about your values, but on the other side you need to give them independence and ownership. Be sure they are loved, well educated, and have a strong compass. Then you can feel comfortable letting them go."

Here are some legacy questions that women, either together or individually, can consider on a questionnaire that is reviewed with a development officer, a philanthropy advisor, or a peer or volunteer. Choose six to eight that will most resonate with the participants.

- What kind of a world do I want for my children?
- How can I help make that world happen with my philanthropy?
- How do I want to be remembered? What would I like my family and friends to remember about me?
- What can I do to create a legacy to help with this remembrance? What could I fund or create?
- How much is enough? Enough to earn or inherit and enough to give?
- How much is enough to leave to my heirs?
- What impact do I want to make with my philanthropy?
- What do I hope will be my philanthropic legacy?
- What values about giving and sharing do I want to pass on to the next generation?
- How can I work with my spouse or partner and children to create a family legacy?
- What institutions and people outside of my family have made a difference in my life?
- What institutions do I want to perpetuate that carry out my interests, passions, and concerns?
- What do I want to accomplish with my money that is really meaningful?

Passing on the philanthropic legacy and teaching children about money is an important aspect of this stage. Lisa Verhovek, community relations director of the Bill and Melinda Gates Foundation, enthusiastically suggests bringing children to nonprofit events: "At a recent

Women's Funding Alliance in Seattle we each brought our seventeen-year-old daughters. They could see how much we enjoyed being part of this group and what a difference the Alliance money is making in the community."[25]

To help children think about responsibility, sharing, and the relationship between values and money, we recommend that donors consider the following:

- When making decisions about philanthropy, involve children. Thanksgiving in particular is a good time to consider where to give. Find out what they care about, and be sure their choices are included. Think about giving time, toys, clothing, or a cell phone in addition to money.

- When giving an allowance, divide it into thirds and have children spend a third, save a third, and give a third. As children get older, discuss different ways of saving money: for example, to put it in a savings account and earn interest or to invest in stocks. This is also a good time to talk about ways to use or abuse credit cards.

- Put money for giving into a family fund, with each family member having a vote on how to give it. This is a great opportunity to review different kinds of solicitations and talk about their effectiveness. Encourage children to give directly to others and see the personal impact of their gifts. Involve grandparents and additional family members in the fund.

- Begin a family foundation or a donor-advised fund as the children get older. Involve the children to help decide on the family's contributions and set the goals and objectives with advisors.

- Consider a volunteer family vacation. Think about volunteering in another country or in the United States to help at a medical or educational center or help build a house. Include a side trip to a more traditionally "fun" place at the end of the volunteer vacation.

Some of the best sources of information regarding family legacy and philanthropy are Ellen Remmer's publications at The Philanthropic Initiative, Charles Collier's book *Wealth in Families*, the Center on Family Philanthropy, and the Women's Philanthropy Institute at the Center on Philanthropy at Indiana University.

TAKEAWAYS

One very gratifying aspect of working with women donors is helping them on their philanthropic journey and being aware of the steps and stepping stones—from the first step when women discover their values and passion to the last step when they use those values and passions as their legacy.

Donor education is the pathway of a woman's philanthropic journey. By providing donor education, a nonprofit has the potential to help women become more philanthropic as well as increase its own bottom line. A step-by-step women's donor education process includes the following:

- Values—what deeply held values does she have?
- Financial information—what does she need to understand about her finances to become a better philanthropist?
- Nonprofit selection—what are the tools she needs to select the nonprofit that best meet her values?
- Giving instruments—what ways of giving are best for her?
- Involvement—how can she be involved in nonprofits that fit her values?
- Leadership—how can she motivate and inspire others to be philanthropic leaders?
- Legacy—what values does she want to leave to her children and how does she want to be remembered?

PART
FOUR

The Future of Philanthropy

CHAPTER 10

Bold Women Giving Boldly: New Frontiers of Women's Philanthropy

Women are the real architects of society.[1]

—Harriet Beecher Stowe, nineteenth-century writer

Not surprisingly, it is women donors who originally took the lead in investing in women-led solutions to many of the world's greatest challenges—from climate change to food security—based on the belief that women themselves know best how to determine their needs and propose solutions for lasting change.[2]

—Betsy Brill, *Forbes*, August 18, 2009

I want to bring what I have learned from high-growth Silicon Valley companies to the philanthropic sector.[3]

—Cate Muther, creator of the Three Guineas Fund and the Women's Technology Cluster

OUT OF WOMEN-LED SOLUTIONS TO THE WORLD'S greatest challenges has arisen a new wave of women's giving:

- *With capital.* Through earnings, inheritance, and marital ties, women control the capital in the United States. Women can be philanthropic in ways never before imagined.

- *With compassion.* Women understand that in addition to giving out of passion for the cause, compassion is the predominant

reason to give: compassion for others to have better lives, result-
ing in a more peaceful world.

- *With change.* Not content with the status quo or with merely
  putting band-aids on problems, women are practicing transformational giving to get at the root causes of societal issues and
  find solutions.

- *With responsibility.* American women know they are residents
  of the United States but citizens of the world. They understand
  their responsibility and obligation to make the world better for
  future generations.

- *With emotion.* Women feel their philanthropy. It is an integral
  part of who and what they are and a way to openly display their
  values, beliefs, and ideals.

In addition to the giving circles, women's funds, and philanthropic initiatives we've discussed, women's philanthropy has created
some exciting changes in the ways women give that have impacted
all of philanthropy and the way it is conducted. This chapter features
several new iterations of women's philanthropy that can be adapted
to many nonprofits or used by women to start their own foundation,
organization, or way of giving.

Bold Women: Blending Policy with Philanthropy

The Shriver Report: A Woman's Nation, by Maria Shriver and the
Center for American Progress, deals with many of the issues that
women are concerned about and are funding.[4] Although women's
philanthropy was not a part of the *Report*, the authors do fully explain
where policies need to be changed. Yes, women are giving more philanthropically, but that does not diminish the need for new govern-
mental policies and funding to reflect a new and changed world.
As Shriver says in the report, "It's been almost fifty years since my
uncle, President John F. Kennedy, asked Eleanor Roosevelt to chair
the very first Commission on the Status of the American Woman.
We've come a long way since then. Now I'm hoping policymakers,
armed with our surveys and analysis, can develop updated policies

and practices that address and support the needs of today's American women, men, and families."

Peg Talburtt is a long-time women's funding proponent from Ann Arbor, president and CEO of the Lovelight Foundation, and executive director of the James A. and Faith Knight Foundation. She believes that a better world would include gender equity in insurance rates, more support for child care, benefits for part-time workers, and better family leave policies. She also points out the need for the government to get involved in social policies: "Many governments have taken on social programming as part of their government priorities. But most of those countries are younger democracies than the U.S. They started in different positions, and many of their governments began with departments of women and health. That kind of change is harder here because we don't have a cabinet position for women and girls, which makes rational decision making and resolution of issues far more complicated. That is why it is up to women to advocate for women and girls."[5]

Together, the public and private sectors, women and men, can transform society and make it their goal to change policies and contribute to the common good.

BOLD WOMEN: STRENGTHENING DIVERSITY IN WOMEN'S PHILANTHROPY

Women of color are often neglected and not viewed as part of the donor pool. The focus has traditionally been on older, white women. Although they are generous, women of color rarely see themselves as philanthropists and may not relate to the language of philanthropy.[6]

—*Michele Minter, formerly director of development and founding coordinator of Princeton University's Women in Leadership Initiative and currently vice president of development at The College Board*

Before anything more significant in women's philanthropy can be accomplished, it is crucial to address diversity. The contemporary women's philanthropy movement generally began as a white women's movement, and now is the time to understand and include all women, of all races, colors, ethnicities, and classes.

Although there are many common features in women's giving, there are some incredibly interesting differences depending on race and ethnicity. These differences revolve around community, family, and race and are often gender-specific. Shaw-Hardy interviewed Hali Lee, an Asian American; Rosie Molinary, a Latina; and Lynn McNair, an African American woman for the giving circle e-book *Women's Giving Circles: Reflections from the Founders*, which she wrote for the Center on Philanthropy at Indiana University.[7] Shaw-Hardy was delighted not only to get to know the women personally, but also to find that their motives for beginning a giving circle were quite different from those of other women she interviewed. (These differences and the circles are explained more fully in Chapter Eight.)

As interesting as these personal and anecdotal stories are, much more needs to be researched about women of color and their philanthropy. Very little is yet known about this important segment of American women other than the generosity of African American women to their churches.[8] This may be explained by the fact that women had an important role in the early African American churches and were permitted to be in positions of power. Their separate women's committees had great influence and spoke out against social injustices and helped promote social change. It was only natural that African American women gave to the churches that regarded them as equal members of the congregation.

A Different Vocabulary

Just as women are not small men, all women don't think in one color. Women are not a homogenous group; Michele Minter notes, "Although the strength of race and gender affiliation in philanthropy have not been studied systematically, anecdotally there is evidence that African American women are more likely to identify first as black and then as a woman. This is important because words have different meanings within different cultural traditions."[9]

Minter cites the findings from the study "Expanding the Circle," conducted by the Boston Women's Fund, the Haymarket People's Fund, and the Women's Theological Center, which suggested that the terminology used in the social justice field did not resonate strongly with African American women. She also points out that within the black church tradition, donations would more often be described as stewardship than as philanthropy. "The philanthropic language barrier is a frontier that needs to be crossed," she says.

Nonprofit communication materials is another area Minter refers to as a stumbling block for black women's giving. She says there are two issues involved. The first is that nonprofit communication materials often lack images and vocabulary that help people of color see themselves represented and included, making it difficult for them to identify with the cause. The second is that racial and ethnic communities have rich traditions of social structures and networks. "Nonprofit leaders often fail to recognize the strength of those networks and how to tap into them," Minter says. "If organizations want to engage black women, they should recognize the power of churches, sororities, and civil rights organizations as partners that have credibility with their potential donors."

A Shared History: Place-Based Giving

The African American Women's Giving Circle, part of the Washington Area Women's Fund, is a good example of ways black women choose to give. Although the grants go to women, the women in the Circle concentrate on "place" and "place-based giving." What this means is finding a place in the community where they can give and then become directly involved. Lynn McNair, one of the founders of the Circle, shares another important part of black women's giving. She says they think of their grants "as born out of our own experiences as women—as African American women." McNair says their circle particularly focuses on learning and respecting the traditions and symbols that come from African American women's shared history.[10]

But Minter cautions that there is great diversity in ethnic communities, and everyone gives differently. "You can't get everyone's targeted needs with a generic appeal. For example, it's tough to generalize, because things that matter to Latina women and Asian women often depend on how long they've been in the country." She adds: "Research shows there are over one hundred ethnicities and dialects within Asian Americans and Pacific Islanders, and caring for their extended family is a moral imperative. Hispanic/Latina women's giving is often informal, with a wariness of formal giving structures.

Native American women's giving is focused on collective wealth, and informal giving is often preferred."

According to Minter, an area of concern that affects the philanthropy of ethnic communities is the issue of remittances and the worry immigrants have about what's happening to their governments overseas. In 2008 an IBON Media Foundation study found that $7.8 billion was sent overseas from the United States, much of it no doubt from women to help relatives back in their home country.[11]

Putting Minority Women on the List

Karen Osborne, president of The Osborne Group, a management, consulting, and training firm, says, "Just as women have been ignored, so have minorities."[12] Osborne adds that she can understand this, as nine out of ten dollars given by African American, Asian American, and Latina women go to their churches. "But research shows minority women who attend religious institutions are the most generous donors." Before starting her own firm, Osborne served as vice president for College Advancement at Trinity College in Hartford, Connecticut, and director of development at Rensselaer Polytechnic Institute.

"There was a time when women were checkbook givers," she says. "But now we have become empowered and educated and give beyond our checkbooks. We have to do this same thing with minorities: educate, engage and provide relevancy." Osborne questions the efficiency of fundraisers spending so much of their time on white males who have the money and ought to give, but who are not philanthropic. "Minorities are not even on the list," she says.

More Research Is Needed

The 2007 "Expanding the Circle" study was conducted to promote philanthropy in the African American and Asian Pacific Islander communities throughout the Greater Boston area.[13] The study concluded that a lack of research or available data on the giving patterns of people of color has contributed to misperceptions. It also found that the strongest influences on giving among African American women were cultural and religious values, family and personal identity, and life experiences. The most important of the cultural influences was the idea of legacy—one's giving arising out of respect for the past and responsibility for the future. The motivations for Asian Pacific Islander women to give were family, social networks, and identity groups. Giving was often motivated by a sense of obligation rooted in their culture.

Building Critical Mass

Building a critical mass is vital to the expansion of women's philanthropy. Having a presence at the boardroom table of at least three women will usually ensure that they support one another and speak up. (See Chapter Seven.) The same rationale holds for minority representation. Large nonprofits need more than just one or two minority board or staff members expressing the values that minorities hold. Currently there is little diversity on most nonprofit staffs. Also, Minter says, "A staff that is not diverse may not value diversity, and that can translate into discomfort in trying to find a diverse group of board members."

With few exceptions, our audience is all white women when we speak to nonprofits. It is time to make sure all of us—fundraisers, donors, volunteers, presenters, and consultants—request that minorities be well-represented on our staffs, in our audiences, and on our boards. We must launch a campaign of philanthropic diversity.

Here are some things you can do:

- Create staff diversity so women of different ethnicities can relate to one another. Learn from them the best language of philanthropy.
- Search out diversity for board membership. Do so actively, not passively. (See Chapter Seven.)
- Hold focus groups with women of different ethnicities to find out their interests.
- Find women of different ethnicities as prospects and work to help engage, educate, and connect them to your cause.
- Understand that community and tradition are very important to women of different ethnicities.

Bold Women: Top Organizational Leadership

Consider the number of women who are now in positions to influence organizations as both executive directors and development officers. Paulette Maehara, president and CEO of the Association of Fundraising Professionals, says, "We've seen a significant shift in the number of women in the profession. Now 67 percent of our members are women, which is almost the reverse of when I came into the profession in the late '70s."[14] Maehara believes this has happened because "fundraising fits women's personality in nurturing and good stewardship. We have a nurturing, loving concern for our institutions and our donors. It fits with who and what we are and the connection we make with donors."

Although a 2009 study by *The Chronicle of Philanthropy* showed that only 18.8 percent of CEOs of major nonprofits were women,[15] this number is expected to greatly increase in the same way that the number of women fundraisers has swelled. The addition of more women in top leadership positions will result in women bringing not only their own type of leadership, but their special values and interests as well. In those leadership positions, women will be able to ensure that universities, community foundations, andall nonprofits recruit more women board members who will advocate for the issues women know are important.

We predict that there will be a great number of women available to head up nonprofits and chair their boards, such as women who are retiring or getting out of the corporate culture. As Linda Basch, president of the National Council for Research on Women, says, "[These women] know when they've made enough and it's time to cash out."[16] The women have the leadership skills gained in their professional days to become nonprofit and board leaders; they understand the power of money and will move into social action arenas with both their money and their skills.

Here are some suggestions for growing women's leadership:

- Understand the leadership skills and special interests women bring to the table.
- Recruit women at the peak of their careers for your boards. Not only will they be helpful now, but they well may retire early and become not only enthusiastic and committed volunteers, but leaders and philanthropists as well.

Bold Women: Addressing Needs and Finding Value

I have always dressed people, now I want to address their needs.
That's what I feel I have been given a gift to do.[17]

—*Donna Karan, fashion designer*

The value of a life should not be measured by its length.[18]

—*Lynette Huffman Johnson, photographer*

What's so gratifying is that as a foundation working in a specific
geographic region, we know exactly where our money is going, and
we see the difference we are making every day.[19]

—*Trisha Wilson, interior designer*

Because of their compassion for a particular situation or person, women from all walks of life (housewife, businesswoman, film star) are doing very bold things, such as starting their own initiatives and foundations. Here, we've included two outstanding examples. The point to take from these two women is that they needed to connect personally and emotionally to an experience in order to establish their organizations.

Lynette Huffman Johnson

For over twenty years, Seattle resident Johnson has been photographing terminally ill infants and children. In 2003 she established a nonprofit foundation, Soulumination, to "celebrate the lives of children facing life-threatening illnesses." Johnson was so moved by the experiences of women close to her who had lost babies that she quietly donated her services to two or three families a year. Now she works with two to four families a month and has a team of professional photographers providing photographs, free of charge, to parents as an enduring, positive record of their child's brief legacy. "I never knew that doing what seemed to be the simplest little act would start to change grieving in this country," she says. "It's so obvious to me that [this work] is what I'm supposed to be doing."[20]

Trisha Wilson

Trisha Wilson has been said to straddle two disparate worlds. In one, as president and CEO of the Dallas interior design firm Wilson & Associates, she caters to the rich and powerful (her work is found at the Atlantis in the Bahamas, the Venetian in Las Vegas, and palaces in the United Arab Emirates). But in the other world she serves the poor and powerless.[21]

Through her Wilson Foundation, she provides education and medical help to AIDS-ravaged villages near her second home in South Africa. "I've always believed that balance is everything in life, and I tell people at our company, 'What we do for a living here isn't saving lives. Let's not take it too seriously.' But what's amazing is that through the Foundation, we actually *are* saving lives."

A trip to South Africa fifteen years ago opened Wilson's eyes to the poverty and deprivation of the people there, and she was haunted by their extreme needs. "There are so many nonprofits in the U.S. and they are doing wonderful things. In South Africa, though, particularly in the rural areas, there are very few local nonprofits and few international organizations coming in to provide help. I was seeing these little children die from AIDS, and I knew we had to do something to help." She bought a home that was converted into an AIDS hospice house and medical clinic, and her foundation raised funds for a private school, the Waterberg Academy.

Wilson's work with the Waterberg Academy caught the attention of Oprah Winfrey, who hired Wilson Associates to complete the interior design of her school for underprivileged girls outside Johannesburg.

Although Wilson says she designs for luxury resorts and Saudi princes, "That's one side of my life. That's the work side. Then there's my foundation and South Africa. That's the side where my soul is."

BOLD WOMEN: FINDING THEIR SOULS

Churches, temples, mosques, and other religious houses are often where women learn philanthropy, for many women recall their parents, even those without means, giving to their place of worship. Surely religion opened many women's eyes to the needs of those in poverty, whether living in the United States or in Third World countries.

Jewish women have always led the way with women's philanthropy and continue to do so. Through the United Jewish Federation, the Lions of Judah was created in 1972 and awards a symbolic pin for those making personal pledges of $5,000 or more. The program has expanded and now includes other levels of giving; representative jewels indicate the amount. Jewish women are encouraged to leverage their gifts and give throughout their lives, regardless of their marital status. They are encouraged to create an identity distinct and independent from their husband, companion, or family. Former Los Angeles councilwoman and Jewish leader Joy Picus says, "Jewish women's philanthropy has been around for over forty years through the United Jewish Federation. Philanthropy is nothing new to us. The big difference is that now for family contributions, Jewish women are being asked separately from their spouses."[22]

In the Christian faith, many women believe that giving and tithing to their churches represents their total gift—they either aren't asked for more in their own names or they don't give more because they aren't directly connected or involved with a specific project. However, centers on women and spirituality have sponsored conferences on women, spirituality, and philanthropy at the national level for years.

Muslim women and their philanthropy have come to the attention of the Rockefeller Philanthropy Advisors, which has established a Muslim Women's Fund according to precepts of the Prophet Muhammad: "The rights of women are sacred. See that women are maintained in the rights assigned to them."[23]

Keep in mind these thoughts when working with spiritual or religious organizations:

- There are huge philanthropic opportunities for organizations who single women out for more than circles and Bible studies.

- Women need to feel that their giving is going to a project in which they are specifically interested, rather than just general giving.

- Religious institutions could benefit from holding focus groups with women and paying more attention to them as individuals. There are volunteer opportunities abounding in churches and ways to connect with women and obtain their commitment.

BOLD WOMEN: LEADING THE FAMILY

When Warren Buffett was asked in a January 7, 2008, interview with *Fortune* if he would have given the Gates Foundation his fortune if Melinda were not in the picture, he replied, "That's a great question. And the answer is, I'm not sure." Buffett believes that Melinda makes Bill a better decision maker. "He's smart as hell, obviously, but in terms of seeing the whole picture, she's smarter."[24]

In the same article, Gates said about his philanthropy, "I don't think it would be fun to do on my own, and I don't think I'd do as much of it."

Gates's remarks bear out what we hear across the board: in focus groups, research done by the Center on Philanthropy, as well as the 2009 Fidelity study.[25] Women have a strong influence on their spouses and on couples' philanthropy. That influence increases with women's earnings and education, and there's every reason to believe that as women gain even more education and have more resources, this influence will be even greater.

Although there is no empirical research about women's roles in creating family foundations or determining where the foundation gifts go, Ellen Remmer, president and CEO of The Philanthropic Initiative, believes women's roles will increase "as more women make substantial incomes, earn their own wealth, and become the stewards of the family's wealth. On their spouse's death, they will have significantly greater opportunities to initiate family philanthropies."[26]

Kelin Gersick, a family systems and succession specialist, noted in a report on research into why some family foundations successfully thrive through the generations, "The inclusion of women seems to have a significant impact on the grant-making process, especially if a woman is in the leadership position ... [T]hey look for support from the group. They are more accommodating and better able to tolerate multiple agendas. They are also more inclined to inclusion across branches and generations."[27]

The Council on Foundations membership surveys show a steady growth in the percentage of females as foundation board members. Remmer explains that one reason for women's governance on family foundations may be that women look at the money from the perspective of what it can do, whereas men tend to look at money as a measurement of their success.[28] The conclusion is that women regard family foundations as a way to help others and be compassionate, whereas many men are not that interested, because a family foundation isn't necessarily a way to demonstrate their success.

Women are often concerned about leaving a legacy, passing on their philanthropic values to their children, and preparing their children for an inheritance, and family foundations can provide a way to address all those issues.

When working with couples, keep in mind that, due to women's interest, influence, and special abilities, family foundations are growing in popularity and are the best way to include children in the family's philanthropy.

BOLD WOMEN: INITIATIVES AND FOUNDATIONS

Today women—especially corporate women—acknowledge that not only are they different from men, but they want their own organizations. Many corporate women have had to deal with roadblocks in their careers, and they want to help other women avoid them. They are also generally thankful for their success and want to give back. Many have been excluded from the so-called "old boy networks" and want one of their own: one that not only provides networking opportunities but also helps to advance careers. Along with these reasons, there is now a critical mass of corporate and entrepreneurial women who can speak with one voice and not be intimidated, even in a room full of men. In fact, through their philanthropic organizations, they now have "a room of their own," to adapt Virginia Woolf's phrase.

The Women of Texas Instruments Fund

The Women of Texas Instruments (TI) Fund was established in June 2001 because, as founding member Jane Schoen says, "The senior women of TI looked around at our careers and paused. We knew we had wonderful professions, but wondered why there weren't more women with us. The more we plowed into the issue, the more we found that girls were underinformed and discouraged from taking math and science. Even some of the women at TI had had very personal and unfavorable experiences with this same issue and were put off themselves from pursuing the STEM subjects of science, technology, engineering, and math."[29]

Closing the gender gap for girls in middle schools is the focus of Women in TI, and membership is open to everyone in the company. Schoen says, "Initially we recruited only women, because the case for action really resonates with women. But a couple of years ago we broadened our scope to include senior men and wondered why we hadn't done that earlier. They all have daughters, wives, and sisters." The Women of TI Fund mission is to raise and provide funds to increase the number of girls graduating from high school who are entering a university-level technical degree program.

100 Women in Hedge Funds

The "100" in 100 Women in Hedge Funds refers to the cap of the number of investors in a hedge fund. Actual membership has grown from 160 members to 10,000, with overseas groups as well. The only requirement for membership is a commitment to doing for the group one thing you are good at and another thing you enjoy.

At their first meeting in 2002, cofounder Dana Hall said, "We will have to collect those 'what I'm good at' slips and 'what I want to do' slips, and our future programs will be dictated by that."[30] Out of that meeting came the decision to focus on women's health, mentoring, and education, and to provide as many opportunities as possible for members to volunteer, network, and socialize. 100 Women has raised over $15 million in seven years through its annual galas in New York and London, plus its fundraiser and Race for the Cure.

BOLD WOMEN: TRANSFORMATIONAL LEADERSHIP

Lead organizer Diana Mendoza and her New Sanctuary Movement in California see themselves fulfilling Mahatma Gandhi's mission to "become the change we want to see" in the world.[31] Her project helps immigrant families threatened by deportation to find sanctuary in local churches. Mendoza says she is creating an atmosphere of love and acceptance, which is key to changing attitudes and turning old antagonisms into new, healthy relationships. Her work is a project of Clergy and Laity United for Economic Justice.[32]

Traditionally, foundations have been skeptical about giving to organizations that concern themselves with personal transformation. But several American foundations have taken steps to promote transformative leadership. Ana Maria Archila, executive director of Make the Road New York, explains the term as "a special kind of leadership that recognizes we are all connected and therefore have to find the places which are not functioning well and fix them by building relationships of love and trust."[33]

Mendoza says she sees the tangible benefits in their work all the time. She cites healthier relationships among nonprofit leaders, stronger coalitions, less burnout, more sustainability, and a real sense of community between organizations and those with whom they work. Paraphrasing Gandhi, she says, "Imagine how much more could be achieved if foundations also became the change they want to see."

Keep these opportunities in mind:

- Some secular and nonsecular organizations have progressed and succeeded by emphasizing personal change, connection, love, and trust.
- These organizations are on the cutting edge of transformative leadership, treating the causes of societal problems, and are more likely than before to receive foundation funding.

WHERE BOLD WOMEN WILL BE GIVING

The Women's Philanthropy Institute has always subscribed to a definition of what women give to as "all women, all causes." Women can and do give everywhere. We encourage women to give to whatever they wish: be it the arts, education, the environment, women and children, healthcare, social services, and so on. But more and more, women are giving to help one another. Paulette Maehara says she believes that with the influence of the growing number of women in philanthropy there will be more money directed to women and children. She also believes that women will be giving more to global causes as well. For example, she says, "Women are sensitive to advocacy-type causes like Amnesty International and the International Red Cross negotiating for hostage release."[34]

When women see a need, they rise to the occasion. But often they must be led by others who see not only the problem but the solution as well.

Women and Girls

Chris Grumm, president and CEO of the Women's Funding Network (WFN), is thrilled about the results of the Women Moving Millions campaign to raise money for women and girls. "For years the WFN has been thinking long and hard about women acting on big and bold ideas," she says.[35] "Women have gathered the necessary financial power, but needed to be pushed into giving larger gifts." This thinking paid off. Helen LaKelly Hunt and her sister, Swanee Hunt, came to the WFN and said they wanted to put a big gift into play that could stimulate other women to give at least $1 million each to support the work of women and girls through one of the over 150 women and girls funds around the globe.

> *Helen had done some research on philanthropy and the early U.S. suffragette movement and found that this campaign was not initially funded by women of wealth with large gifts; large gifts from women were not given until close to the end of the campaign to get women to vote. She didn't want women of wealth to miss that same opportunity to fund women and girls in the modern wave of the women's movement. Helen and Swanee knew that women had the resources but traditionally hadn't given large gifts to women and girls. The key was to get women to make high-end gifts and become leaders.*

Helen and Swanee Hunt sparked the campaign with a $10 million gift. The stunning part is that in the million-plus gift category, with a goal of $150 million, over $180 million was raised from one hundred donors in three years.

Grumm credits the campaign's success to the fact that it was connected to a very effective delivery system (women's funds) with strong leadership among both the funds and the donors. The campaign was not only about leadership, but also about building community. "We built a strategy around using women's community-building skills, women giving large gifts, and women inviting others to join them in this giving circle, showing them how, even in the midst of an economic recession, investing in women's funds would give them a good return on their investment." And she adds, "We had two incredible philanthropists at the front and in leadership positions."

The other component Grumm believed to be important was that leadership in all sectors had really failed to address the issues most affecting women and girls; there was a void, and this was an opportunity. "It was our moment in time to step up and out," Grumm says. "Donors wanted change and to be part of the solution by bringing their money, their special talents, and the women's funding organizations of the WFN together."

Actionable Knowledge

Bridget Baretta, executive director of the Martin County Community Foundation in Stuart, Florida, has conceived a new iteration of women's giving circles: a Center on Women's Philanthropy within the community foundation. The Center won't necessarily give to already established programs but create projects to address issues of importance to women and children locally, statewide, nationally, and globally. Baretta calls it "catalytic philanthropy." She says, "I want our group to create a new footprint, a high heel if you will. We don't invest in mediocrity here at the Community Foundation. We want to invent. We want to go way beyond a giving circle and grantmaking."[36]

The Center will use what Baretta calls "actionable knowledge," obtained through focused research. Once the Center's focus has been chosen, it will invest in directing its efforts towards creating new solutions to issues involving women and girls.

This iteration can be likened to the Michigan Women's Foundation's choice of making investments in women-owned businesses, described in Chapter Four. Women's organizations are listening to their constituents and reinventing not only the programs they will fund, but also their expectations for amounts raised and outcomes.

Grumm's emphasis is raising money for women and girls, Baretta's on raising money for women and children. But their strategies for successfully raising funds for women can be applied to almost any organization:

- The project or campaign must have a logical, social, and emotional component.
- Women leading the campaign must give and be highly respected by others.
- Women must understand the importance of the issues involved and that their gifts will bring about change and make a difference.
- The campaign or project should be one of special interest to women.
- Organizers need to think big and expect women to give large gifts.
- Those who give should be asked to be leaders and encourage other women to give.
- The campaign or project should be connected to an already established and responsible organization.
- Women will be more likely to give if they have the opportunity to give together.

Driving Politics—and Beyond

With the growing number of women candidates and candidates supporting causes women care about (children, peace, education, the environment, women's and girls' health), it stands to reason that more women are giving to political candidates as well as to philanthropy. Joanna L. Krotz, author of *The Guide to Intelligent Giving*, says, "I do believe when women start giving they also start advocating for social change by giving politically as well."[37]

The Women's Foundation of Minnesota's president and CEO, Lee Roper-Batker, has challenged philanthropic women to become active politically. "By aligning their philanthropy with the vision they hold for the world," Roper-Batker says, "women also need to be cognizant of local, state, and national politics. They need to do the research and align their vote with candidates who share their vision and values. This is how we will create the kind of policies and institutional changes we want to see in government."[38]

In addition to supporting the arts and in particular, contemporary art, the Barbara Lee Family Foundation is dedicated to motivating and educating women about how to run for and win political office. Her foundation researched the relationship between gender and campaigning for executive office and published their results in a four-part series called "Positioning Women to Win: New Strategies for Turning Gender Stereotypes into Competitive Advantages."

Lee believes electing a critical mass of women to public office is the most powerful way to change our society. "Research proves that Republican and Democratic women in state legislatures are more likely than their male counterparts to initiate and fight for laws to advocate for families and champion social justice," she says. "They are also more likely to fight to protect the environment and promote nonviolent conflict resolution."[39]

Not only are many women philanthropists actively participating in politics, but a number of women who have been in elective office are becoming more philanthropic as well. By using their political skills and background as well as their capital, these women are addressing issues of importance to them—issues they championed when in office. Women such as Alicia Salisbury, a member of the Kansas State Senate from 1985 to 2000, who helped start the Women's Fund in the Topeka Community Foundation, and Debbie Ritchie, a former member of the Florida State Legislature and responsible for initiating IMPACT 100 in the Pensacola Bay Area (see Chapter Four). Other similar women mentioned in *Women and Philanthropy* are Joy Picus, a former Los Angeles City Council member and university and Jewish philanthropist, and Liz Ghrist, a former Houston County Commissioner and capital campaign chair for St. Thomas University.

Women are finding themselves in positions to change social policy through both their politics and their philanthropy. And as there are an increasing number of women in both arenas, we can expect to see more focus on the issues women care about.

Supporting the Arts

Women have traditionally supported the arts, although they have not always been recognized for that support. Glorya Kaufman is one woman who not only gave a very large gift but put her name on it as well. Kaufman's gift of $20 million to the Dance Center of Los

Angeles was named "Glorya Kaufman Presents Dance at the Music Center" when announced in March 2009. "The arts are critical to the life blood of this nation," Kaufman says. "During this difficult time when art programs are barely getting by, we must do our part to protect what could be lost."[40]

Making a better world involves all areas and all issues, and the arts provide beauty in our world and help preserve a culture's heritage. John F. Kennedy said, "Art establishes the basic human truths which must serve as the touchstones of our judgment. I see little of more importance to the future of our country and our civilization than full recognition of the place of the artist."[41] That recognition includes women as artists.

Chris Grumm, president and CEO of the Women's Funding Network, says, "I think that the arts can be a very provocative and effective strategy to make social change in the world." Grumm points out that changing the structures and systems of poverty and violence in the world can come about through a multitude of strategies including art and music.[42]

Sheila Johnson, a philanthropist, founder of the Black Entertainment Network, and businesswoman, is an example of a woman combining the arts with creating social change. Her documentary *A Powerful Noise* makes a case for reaching across old ethnic divides to heal postwar tensions in order to create more jobs for women. It features a Vietnamese AIDS activist, a girls' advocate from Mali, and a woman in Bosnia-Herzegovina; a portion of the profits goes to CARE.

Johnson said she made the documentary because "people tend to ignore something unless they see that it's going on with their own eyes. I really believe documentaries are going to be the new wave of the future because I think we're in a transition phase in terms of technology. In the past, I spent a lot of time going up to Capitol Hill, trying to convince congressmen and senators to pass legislation to alleviate global poverty. I have no doubt that if we simply went up there and showed them this film on global poverty, their reaction would be, 'Okay. This is a no-brainer. Let's pass the bill.'"[43]

Global Giving

Women are finding that giving globally is not just the right thing to do but makes economic sense as well. The same holds true for nonprofit investments. Ask yourself: how much of your portfolio contains international stocks? Probably a great deal, if your U.S. stock companies are also doing business overseas. Because we have a global economy and put our money and our trust in overseas stocks, shouldn't we be doing the same with our giving? Perhaps we should give to global philanthropy the same percentage our portfolio holds in overseas stocks.

Women like Janet Shaw have discovered countless issues in the developing countries. Shaw grew up in Zimbabwe but has lived in the United States since 1989. When she returned to visit her family in Zimbabwe in 1995, she visited the Goromonzi Rural District, where she met seventeen destitute orphans who were victims of AIDS and had no money for school fees. Shaw knew she had to do something to make these children's lives better, so she created the Goromonzi Project in December 2005. Despite the political unrest in Zimbabwe, Shaw is positive about her country. "I want everyone to see Africa as a rich and vibrant continent full of possibility. Poverty in Africa is not an insurmountable problem," she says.[44]

The Project has six board members in the United States and three in Zimbabwe, as well as a project director there. Since its initiation the Project has grown; now there is a preschool program as well. Shaw is pleased that some of their funding comes from the Community Development Institute, which was cofounded by a woman, Caroline Miller.

A key reason for women's interest in giving globally is that their dollars go so much farther in the developing countries than they can in the developed countries. For example, at the Goromonzi Project $365 will pay for a child's school fees, food, school uniform, and basic medical care for a year. Another enticing feature of that program is that sponsors are encouraged to go to Zimbabwe and visit the sites of the preschools.

Shaw says that the Project has changed her life; she used to be in business to earn money for herself, now she raises it to help orphans and vulnerable children. "I don't get paid for what I do, but I am happier and more peaceful than when I was in it for myself. I laugh a lot." Besides the joy and laughter, Shaw says she gets invited to all sorts of interesting places and has exciting adventures like flying "loop the loop" in a small plane over the South Australian desert. "Sometimes it's like someone has waved a magic wand over my life."[45]

Think of the magic wand that Shaw has waved over others' lives and the happiness it has brought them. Some research shows that people who are philanthropic are also happier,[46] and she is proof of that.

Shaw offers this advice for starting your own nonprofit:

- Run the project like a business. Be organized.
- Be prepared to put up your own money if it's needed.
- Be squeaky clean when it comes to financial accountability and reporting.
- Write a strategic plan. The writing of it will help you get clear on the steps you need to take to make what you want to have happen, happen. It is also essential if you apply for grants. Find someone to cowrite it with you to get a better perspective.
- Keep up to date with legal requirements.
- Join Toastmasters—almost everyone can benefit from extra speaking skills, and you'll need public speaking skills to promote your organization.
- Choose your board members carefully—everyone should know that they're on the board to raise funds and to make financial contributions themselves.
- Keep donors informed—publishing newsletters, answering emails promptly, and so on.
- Keep educating yourself—read books, attend seminars, and listen.
- Stay true to your mission—but if necessary, have the courage to alter the means by which you make that mission happen.

MORE ADVICE ON GLOBAL INVOLVEMENT

- Review your nonprofit's current partnering efforts in developing countries and publicize them. It could be a medical effort if the nonprofit is a hospital, an agricultural program if it's a university, or an exchange if it's an art program. There are many possibilities you may not even know about.

- If you don't have an overseas effort, consider collaborating with a global organization that has a connection with your nonprofit's mission. Publicize your effort so everyone knows about it.
- Services for children, women, and girls are important program areas to gain women's philanthropic support as well as corporate and foundation support. Conduct a focus group to find out what your nonprofit is or can be doing to positively affect the lives of children, women, and girls outside your own country.
- Women today have extensive experience with world travel for business and pleasure. Now they want to travel and do good at the same time, often bringing their children along. Is there a way your nonprofit can provide this kind of experience with a program in another country?
- Contact some of the organizations women have created. We have mentioned several throughout this *Women and Philanthropy*: the Goromonzi Project, the Wilson Foundation, Chiapas Women, and Soulumination. Learn more about the founders' vision and how this could be applied to your nonprofit.

Takeaways

This is an exciting time for women's philanthropy. Women are making great strides in creating their own ways of giving, whether through traditional organizations or by forming their own nonprofits. They are acting boldly and showing the way for all of philanthropy.

- Women's philanthropy cannot take the place of government funding. The two must complement one another.
- Women of other ethnicities and color give differently than Caucasian women.
- Women see and feel the needs around them and are establishing their own foundations and initiatives to meet those needs.

- Organizations would do well to look at the Jewish model for involving more women.

- Women and girls are receiving a number of large gifts from women, which has resulted in groundbreaking and record-breaking fundraising done by the Women's Funding Network.

- As women give more philanthropically, they are giving more politically as well.

- Many women are interested in giving globally.

The Age of Women's Philanthropy

I do not believe that women are better than men. We have not wrecked railroads,
nor corrupted legislatures, nor done many unholy things that men have done;
but then we must remember that we have not had the chance.[1]

—Jane Addams, Nobel Peace Prize winner

IN *WOMEN AND PHILANTHROPY*, WE HAVE LOOKED EVERY WHICH way at women's philanthropy: the history, leaders, and programs; the potential and motivations; the impact of gender, generations, and the ways women give. This last chapter asks, "What if?" *What if* the ways women give became the ways everyone gives? What would the world look like? Let's take a look at what some women are already achieving through their giving.

PEACEFUL COEXISTENCE

Liberia's head of state, Ellen Johnson Sirleaf, had this to say when asked: if women ran the world, would wars still exist? "No," she answered. "It would be a better, safer, and more productive world. A woman would bring an extra dimension to that task—and that's a sensitivity to humankind. It comes from being a woman."[2]

Peace was the biggest concern expressed by women in the 2007 research conducted by Shaw-Hardy and Stevens.[3] Peace was usually the first thing women talked to us about in informal conversations. Los Angeles resident Liz Levitt Hirsch feels that before we can stop shooting and start talking, we need to get to know one another.

"Getting to know you" is exactly what Hirsch had in mind when, in 2002, she broadened the concept of the Levitt Pavilion Programs, a free summer concert series her father began in 1974 in Connecticut. There are now five Levitt Pavilions throughout the country providing free concerts for people of all ages, colors, and classes at amphitheatres. Hirsch says, "The concept lends itself to people socializing in a relaxed way. I can be sitting on the lawn next to someone who parks cars for a living but we're all equal here. This is a class breaker, gives people their dignity, and is a tremendous forum of enriching humanity at the same time."[4]

The requirement for funding from the Levitt Pavilion Programs is that it must be a partnership with the community and provide at least fifty free concerts annually, featuring a variety of professional performers. "It appeals to me because it combines social justice and joy," Hirsch says. "It's the kind of program that gets unanimous votes in city hall and has done a lot to address racial tension in the south. It's music in a communal space. It gives everyone dignity."

Other ways women work at "getting to know you" are taking their children to help out in soup kitchens and planning family vacations that include volunteer work in the United States and other countries. These experiences provide both adults and children with knowledge about what is happening outside of their comfortable life—firsthand knowledge that builds tolerance through understanding. It is important not only to oppose poverty but to understand it and spend time observing it directly, say Nicholas Kristof and Sheryl WuDunn in their book *Half the Sky: Turning Oppression into Opportunity for Women Worldwide*.[5] When we observe and understand, then we lose our fear, and the outcome is a more peaceful coexistence for all.

A SUSTAINABLE WORLD

Julie Weeks, former managing director and director of research for the Center for Women's Business Research, believes that when women are empowered philanthropically, when they are engaged in communities and in charge of their own lives economically and socially, there will be more collaborative decision making and less harshness in national politics. "More people will be talking around the water cooler," she says, and "women will see to it that businesses are taking the triple bottom line approach."[6]

"Triple bottom line" is a method of decision making advanced by John Elkington in his 1997 book *Cannibals with Forks: The Triple Bottom Line of 21st Century Business*.[7] The concept holds companies responsible to all their stakeholders, including everyone who is directly or indirectly involved with the company as well as the planet we live on. It asks businesses to consider these three questions: (1) Am I making money? (2) What is my corporate responsibility? (3) What is the impact of my company on the environment? Weeks believes that adopting this method can bring about enormous change. "Businesses, whether for-profit or not, will be doing something for human kind as opposed to just making money."

We look forward to a world where all companies, institutions, and nonprofits will understand the importance of addressing societal issues and mandate programs to create more stability, security, and equity in the world. For too long institutions have considered "leaving a legacy" only as something donors could do for them. It is time for those same organizations to consider the legacy *they* wish to leave: one that is not all about buildings and making money, but about creating and funding programs that will really make a difference to those who follow. This is women's challenge and opportunity: to challenge their institutions to become bold. To seize the opportunity and realize their potential to bring about the kind of change that the world needs. It is up to all of us to work together to create a sustainable world as a legacy to future generations.

A COMPASSIONATE WORLD

In 2007 Marcela Orvañanos de Rovzar, philanthropist and winner of the Center on Philanthropy at Indiana University's 2008 Hank Rosso award, moved to New York with her husband. Rovzar looked around to see what she could do to help in her new city. "I wanted to get closer to the community," she says.[8]

What Rovzar found was an incredible number of Hispanics who needed financial education. They didn't understand the concepts of budgets, bank accounts, investing, saving, and retirement. Many couldn't work because they didn't have a green card, but they did want to better their lives and that of their families. By the end of that first year, Rovzar had helped provide financial education and worked with five hundred people, 75 percent of them women.

Rovzar claims her accomplishments come from her sense of her compassion and her global perspective. "We are a global society," she says. "I no longer see my kids being just from Mexico. They have been raised to care about everyone in the world. It is really important to start visualizing ourselves as part of a world of all countries and all races. We are all struggling for the same thing. We want to survive and give our kids the best."

QUALITY EDUCATION FOR ALL

Linda Basch, president of the National Council for Research on Women, says, "Research by the World Bank shows that when people have access to quality education, they thrive."[9] The World Bank study emphasizes that education is of special benefit for girls. " [Education] profoundly affects reproductive health, and also improves child mortality and welfare through better nutrition and higher immunization rates. Education may be the single most effective preventive weapon against HIV/AIDS."[10]

"At least 70 percent of people living in poverty around the world and in the United States are women and children," says Chris Grumm, president and CEO of the Women's Funding Network.[11] Providing an education is one of the first steps, along with quality health care, to help bring about a better life for women, their families, and their communities.

QUALITY HEALTH CARE FOR ALL

Women are the majority of health care providers in this nation, as well as the ones making most of the health care decisions for their families.[12] They understand that health care is a basic right. First Lady

Michelle Obama, who stumped hard for health care reform in 2009, said, "Women play a unique and increasingly significant role in families, with eight in ten mothers reporting they are the ones responsible for choosing their children's doctors. More than 10 percent of women in this country are caring for a sick or elderly relative."[13]

Women have used their compassion and their philanthropy to bring about better health care in the past and continue to do so. The death of Anna Clise's young son from inflammatory rheumatism in 1898 made her tragically aware of the lack of specialized care for children—and inspired her to take action. Clise's husband, James, was a real-estate developer, banker, and international trader. With the help of twenty-three female friends, Clise established the first facility in the Pacific Northwest to treat children suffering from this disease, most of whom would otherwise have been left to endure a life of pain and disability. Clise's original vision—to care for children regardless of race, religion, gender, or a family's ability to pay—still guides the Seattle Children's Hospital today.[14] Until just a few years ago, all of the hospital board members were women.

Other women who were moved to action after the death of a loved one are Patricia Miller and Barbara Bradley Baekgaard, who established the Vera Bradley Foundation for breast cancer research at the Indiana University after a close friend died of breast cancer, and Nancy Brinker, who founded the Susan G. Komen for the Cure Foundation after her only sister, Susan, died from breast cancer in 1980 at the age of thirty-six.[15] Many more women have used their wealth, compassion, and energy to found cancer treatment facilities, clinics, and medical schools, fund disease research, and endow professorships and scholarships that benefit children, women, and men.

MORE PHILANTHROPY

For years we have been discussing the need for a language of philanthropy, one that doesn't make people uncomfortable talking about money. We wanted a way to talk about philanthropy in the same way that people talk about shopping and investments. Philanthropy, shopping, investments. A place to begin was suggested years ago by Tracy Gary at a Women's Philanthropy Institute board meeting: whatever the board members had spent shopping for clothes that day, they had to give that same amount to the Women's Philanthropy Institute (WPI). It worked. We didn't stop shopping, and the contributions to WPI increased. Not only that, but we talked about it as well.

But surely one day's shopping wasn't our full potential to give.

"So many of us, even those who are passionate about philanthropy, are giving just a fraction of our capacity," says philanthropist Anne Ellinger.[16] She and her husband, Christopher, started a Web organization called Bolder Giving in Extraordinary Times, helping people explore how to become more bold, effective, and fulfilled as givers.[17] "Bolder Giving's mission is to inspire us to give at our full lifetime potential by providing remarkable role models and practical support. There's nothing to counteract a feeling of scarcity like generosity," Ellinger says. She believes that women are going to give more now because the issues are critical. "There are a lot of urgent issues—global warming particularly—that are time sensitive. Sure, I might still want to be a giver in my seventies, but what kind of a world is that going to be? Might it be wiser to give more now?"

MAKING TRANSFORMATIONAL CHANGES

The Shriver Report calls the United States today "a woman's nation."[18] What does that mean for women's philanthropy? For all of philanthropy? What are the changes that will result from this transformational moment? And if we like the way women are already changing the world, how can we make this happen on a bigger scale—and faster?

Approaching Critical Mass

Some historical and current women in power haven't behaved in quite the nurturing ways we attribute to women in earlier chapters. Consider these "Iron Ladies": Queen Elizabeth I, Golda Meir, and Margaret Thatcher. They were all by themselves in a man's world. And when women are in a male-dominated environment like government and business, they often act more like men. "Only when women are a critical mass will they be able to act more like women," says Julie Weeks, president of Womenable, whose clients include the World Bank, American Express, and Booz Allen Hamilton. "If there is only one woman, she has to act like a man. But once there's a critical mass, then women are more comfortable with bringing up alternative views and different decisions."

Reaching critical mass means having enough women philanthropists with enough money to change the culture of philanthropy—change it so that women's voices are heard and listened to, women's values are expressed and acted on, and a woman's viewpoint and life experiences are as valued as a man's.

Women are already powerful as consumers. We know that women make 83 percent of all consumer decisions[19] and that women's projected increase in worldwide income is expected to increase by $10.5 trillion by 2013.[20] The challenge and opportunity is for women to use this power to help change the world as well.

Women have proven themselves more than capable of collaborative leadership, consensus building, and building relationships rather than empires. When given the chance, women's philanthropic leadership will be a winner for everyone. But there must be a critical mass for this to happen.

Institutionalizing Women's Philanthropy

Debra Mesch, director of the Women's Philanthropy Institute at the Center on Philanthropy, Indiana University, thinks that women's philanthropy will become the norm only through strong research. "Building an empirical base is critical," Mesch says. "If you look at any type of field, like management, and how people understand what being a good manager means, the whole discipline behind that is how the research gets translated so everyday practitioners can use it."[21]

Mesch believes that by understanding the nature of women's philanthropy through research and translation, more women will understand themselves as philanthropists. This understanding will affect men as well, as they learn how over 50 percent of the population is giving. "We're not talking about small change," Mesch says. "We're talking about making the world change."

Think Pink

A popular book on marketing to women suggests that corporate America shouldn't "think pink" because it is dated, full of stereotypes, and turns off men; it makes one think too much of butterflies, hearts, and flowers; it is too full of good intentions and sincerity.

Although there is much we agree with in the book (see Chapter Eight), let's reconsider. Surely pink represents all things good in the campaign to fight breast cancer. It is seen in products from Hershey chocolate to iPods to cell phones. It is a color free from representing anything unpleasant or aggressive. It is a color representing women and girls.

Many little girls have had pink bedrooms and dresses, and most women have at least one pink item in their wardrobe and their home. So let's "think pink" and see what the world might look like if a color representing women and girls also meant a world of peace, prosperity, a clean environment, social justice, equality, good health care, and quality education for all.

Does this sound too full of good intentions and sincerity? Well, maybe not too full. Just brimming over with what women care about, the legacy they want to leave.

ALL GOOD THINGS

Women are using their wealth deliberately and systematically as well as generously and boldly. Women are uniting their resources behind a resolution of societal issues. Each day another couple's gift is influenced by a woman, each week a new women's giving circle is created, and each year more millions are given by women to the causes they care about—causes that will determine the outcome of the twenty-first century.

Women understand we are all codependent; that what occurs in one block, one community, city, state, or nation affects what happens in the world. And power is a word that is now in women's vocabulary. The power to bring about change through leadership. This is the message women want nonprofits to hear, to understand, and to act on. They want nonprofits to know that diversity is as important to philanthropy as working intergenerationally.

The old nursery rhyme tells us, "The king was in his counting house, counting out his money; the queen was in the parlor, eating bread and honey." Now the queen is also in the counting house, giving away the money with the king, and she shares the parlor with him as they eat bread and honey and drink milk while making this a land of "all good things," as the Old Testament says. The land of all good things will be a place of great abundance and sharing because of women's philanthropy—because of the philanthropy of women and men today and in the future. The way of giving that means peace, justice, sustainability, and equality for all.

Resource A:
Focus Group Sample Questions

THE FOLLOWING ARE QUESTIONS TO ASK WOMEN IN FOCUS groups of eight to twelve. You can also have separate tables of eight at a larger event. A recorder should be appointed for each table, in addition to the facilitator. In some situations, as appropriate, each recorder makes a report to the larger group at the end of the focus group discussion time.

1. What was your first meaningful philanthropic gift—of time or money?

2. How does your charitable giving represent what is important to you and/or your family?

3. As you determine whether to make a contribution, how important is it to see the direct result of your contribution?

4. What kind of ongoing relationship with the nonprofit do you want?

5. How do you believe donors like to find out about giving opportunities—by mail, letters, email, events, personal visits?

6. Have any of you been visited personally by a development officer from a university or nonprofit?

7. In making a decision about a financial contribution, how much do you consult with your family members and others? Whom do you consult—spouse, children, parents, friends, financial advisors?

8. How do you like to be addressed in a letter or phone call?

9. How do you like to be acknowledged for a gift? What was the most meaningful thank-you that you have received?

10. Do you believe there is a difference in how women and men approach philanthropic giving? If so, in your opinion, what is one such difference?

11. What are three causes that you support or would be interested in supporting?

12. How high a priority does the [your organization] have in your giving? What are your areas of interest to fund at [your organization]?

13. What is your interest in supporting women's advancement at [your organization]?

14. What are ways that our organization can better connect to you as a woman?

15. Describe the characteristics you would like to see in a special women's philanthropy initiative affiliated with [your organization]. For example, would you be interested in inspiring and stimulating talks, small group meetings, leadership development, educational programs on family philanthropy and finance?

    • What times and venues would be most comfortable for you? For example, a certain day of the week; breakfast, lunch, early supper, or dinner; downtown or in the suburbs.

    • If speakers were invited, what are some of the topics you would like to see addressed?

Resource B
The Million Dollar Exercise

Supplies needed:

Up to ten sheets of poster or butcher paper

Up to ten markers to write issues on the sheets

Three small sticky notes for each attendee's votes

Paper to tabulate results

Paper and a pen on each table for someone to take notes and to record group decisions

$1 million play money bill for each attendee

People needed:

One to lead the discussion of societal issues and call on each table to report on their results

One to write the issues on the large sheets of paper

Two or three vote tabulators

The Million Dollar Exercise

This full version takes one and a half hours.

Preparation: Post up to ten large sheets of butcher paper on the walls around the room where all will be able to view them.

Five minutes	Participants get situated at their tables; three sticky notes are handed out to each.
Five minutes	The facilitator asks women to call out loudly issues of concern to society (education, environment, at-risk kids, and the like); the scribe posts one issue on each sheet.
Ten minutes	Participants "vote" by getting up from their tables and putting their sticky notes on the sheet with the issues they most care about. Women can put all three sticky notes on one sheet or spread them around three sheets; they may not cut or tear up their sticky notes to create more votes!
Ten minutes	Votes are tallied and the results shared (it's helpful to have two or three people tabulate the results so they can be shared fairly quickly). The three or four top selections are the ones women work on at their tables and direct their money toward in specific programs.
Forty minutes	Each table chooses a leader and a scribe who will report out at the end. This can be done by having the leader be the person whose first name starts closest to A in the alphabet, and the scribe, the person whose name starts closest to Z.
	Each table works on its giving plan. A table of eight will have $8 million, a table of twelve will have $12 million, and so on. Participants must decide how much of their dollars to allocate to each societal issue and what kinds of specific programs within the organization or institution to support for that issue. These can be existing programs or new ones. To make a real impact with their money, they may choose only one or two issues to deal with, and this will elicit a great deal of discussion.
Twenty minutes	Tables report back to the whole group. The scribe at each table shares the way or ways in which the participants are making a difference with their allocations of financial resources. The facilitator may also suggest that if the same issues are addressed at various tables they could combine their resources, showing collaboration. Outcome: Collaboration, Strategic philanthropy, Empowerment

SHORTER VERSION

A shorter version of the exercise can be done in twenty to thirty minutes.

- The facilitator asks the women which societal needs they think are the most important to resolve.
- The facilitator writes the answers on a flip chart.
- The facilitator then gives each woman a piece of paper that says "Today I am giving one million dollars to _____"; women fill in one to three designated purposes, one of which is the nonprofit that sponsored the seminar.
- The women are given five minutes to determine the designations and write them on their slips of paper. They then report out individually. Depending on the group size and time limit, only a sampling will likely be able to report out.
- As the women report their designations, the facilitator writes a slash mark for every million next to the societal need that the gifts address.
- After adding up the slash marks, the facilitator discusses the total designation and the problems that the group has determined have top priority.
- The participants are empowered when they see the societal problems they collectively have addressed with their gifts. The facilitator asks for all the designation slips for the causes that will be helped. These give a good snapshot of the women's philanthropic priorities.

Resource C
What's It All About? Money and Me

More and more women are becoming the chief financial officers for themselves and their families. Because women haven't traditionally discussed money, we hope you will give thoughtful consideration to the following questions about financial and thus philanthropic topics.

1. How did your parents handle money? Mother? Father?
2. What does "having money" mean to you?
3. How do you and your spouse differ in the treatment of money?
4. Does your money bring you satisfaction? How?
5. How do you talk about money with your family?
6. What are you saving for now?
7. How is an aging population impacting you financially?
8. Are you comfortable talking about money with your friends and why or why not?
9. Under what circumstances do you discuss money with your friends?
10. Do you feel you are knowledgeable about investing and finances?

11. How are you going to prepare your children for a financial inheritance and what impact will it have on their families?

12. When is it best to give children a financial inheritance?

Topics for Donor Breakout Sessions

• Where and from whom did you learn about giving and philanthropy?

• Was philanthropy a part of your family when you were growing up? If so, in what ways?

• What is your favorite gift that you have made? Describe how you felt about making the gift.

• What do you see as the relationship between a woman's values and her philanthropy?

• What was your first philanthropic gift?

• What are some of the barriers to Americans' reaching their full potential as philanthropists?

• What are some of the unique barriers to philanthropy for women?

• What are some of the barriers to philanthropy in your life?

• How are you working to overcome these barriers?

Resource D
Experiences with Philanthropy: Current Giving Patterns and Family Values

THE FOLLOWING IS A SAMPLING OF QUESTIONS THAT CAN be used when asking women philanthropists about their giving. You can use some of these with a donor panel, in a group setting, or one on one. They help women envision their philanthropic journey. For further in-depth questions on philanthropy for families, please refer to *Wealth in Families* by Charles Collier (published by Harvard University), The Philanthropic Initiative, the Center on Philanthropy at Indiana University, and *The Guide to Intelligent Giving* by Joanna Krotz (published by Hearst).

- Talk about your family—spouse, parents, grandparents, siblings. What are some of the values you learned from your parents and others in your lifetime?

- How do you view the philanthropy of your parents?

    Obligation _____ Social _____ Passionate _____
    Strategic _____ Entrepreneurial _____

- Talk about your parents' philanthropy.

- How do you identify yourself as a philanthropist now?

    Obligation _____ Social _____ Passionate _____
    Strategic _____ Entrepreneurial _____

- Explain your giving philosophy.

- What organizations are you currently supporting and why?

- What are your giving practices? For example, do you work from a budget in your giving? Give from your checkbook? Give from income only? Give from principal (stocks, other assets)? Each year do you tithe? Give 5 percent or another percentage as a goal?

- What is the most effective use of philanthropy? Giving to fewer groups or more groups? Scattered or focused giving? (Some studies have shown that women give to twice as many organizations as men do, yet they give the same total amount.)

- What is most joyful for you—giving small gifts to many organizations or larger gifts to fewer organizations? Why?

- What values about giving and sharing do you want to pass on to the next generation—your relatives and others?

- What institutions and people outside of your family have made a difference in your life?

- What institutions do you want to perpetuate that carry out your interests/passions/concerns?

- What do you want to accomplish with your financial resources?

- How do you want to be remembered?

- What impact do you want to make with your philanthropy?

- What do you hope will be your philanthropic legacy?

Resource E
The Power of the Purse

For hundreds of years, women provided the energy, labor, and passion for solving societal needs, and the men controlled the funds. Today's women don't ask permission to make philanthropic decisions. They are willing to use their own financial power to address their community's needs.

The Child Saving Institute Power of the Purse Scholarship Luncheon was developed to celebrate the philanthropic influence of Nebraska women. When women aren't busy volunteering, working, and caring for their families, they are frequently pursuing a personal passion—the perfect purse! The Power of the Purse event appeals to women on two levels: raising funds for youth to advance their education and an opportunity to purchase that perfect purse. Purses create a community buzz, a "purseOlicious" environment.

The event theme includes the invitation design, the PurseOnalities (honorary chairpeople), silent auction, Purses with Pizzazz, and dessert—cakes shaped and frosted to represent designer bags.

Event details:
- Schedule in August to correlate with local school calendars and college classes and to encourage women of all ages to attend.
- Determine scholarship criteria; appoint committee.
- Prepare forty to fifty silent auction purse packages (donated); retail values of $50 and up. Packages include:

Source: Child Saving Institute, Omaha, Nebraska, www.childsaving.org, 866-400-4CSI (866-400-4274).

- o One-of-a-kind purses
- o Items collected and donated from guild or board members' travels
- o Purses and special accessories solicited from local retailers
- Designate five to ten "Purses with Pizzazz." These purse packages are typically designer bags—Chanel, Coach, Dolce & Gabbana.
- Select "PurseOnalities": one or two local women whose philanthropic actions have made a significant positive impact in the community—particularly for children.
- Engage a guest speaker with a philanthropic background, locally or nationally recognized.

TIME LINE

Twelve months
- Recruit committee chairpeople (three).
- Begin purse solicitation.

Six to nine months
- Book event speaker.
- Select and invite PurseOnality(ies).
- Select and secure date and location.
- Design "save the date" card and invitation.
- Mail "save the date" card.
- Continue collecting and creating purse packages.
- Recruit event emcee.

Four months
- Finalize list of scholarship recipients; invite to event for special recognition.
- Determine event site details—table size, linens, menu, special equipment, and so on.
- Print invitations and envelopes.
- List event on agency and networking Web sites: Facebook, Twitter, and the like.

Three months

- Complete travel arrangements for guest speaker.
- Finalize decoration concept.
- Continue collecting purses, accessories, and raffle items.

Six weeks

- Hand address and mail invitations.
- Process reservations, checks, and credit card charges.
- Confirm logistics with location, speaker, guest(s) of honor, and emcee.

Four weeks

- Confirm menu and decorations.
- Confirm auction items and finalize bid sheets.
- Confirm speaker arrangements; assign volunteer liaison to assist speaker.
- Confirm volunteers.
- Set agenda.
- Handle logistics:

    o Produce name tags and seating arrangements for guests.
    o Finalize program and PowerPoint presentation.
    o Secure credit card machines to process bids.
    o Complete a backup plan for inclement weather.

Event day

- Set up silent auction.
- Set up reservation table.
- Have volunteers in place thirty minutes before start time.
- When all is done, savor the successes; take off shoes.

Resource F
Resource Papers

The following are papers on women as philanthropists, written by women at higher education institutions.

Beeson, Melisa Jane Ellis, Indiana University. "Women's Giving Circles: A Case Study in Higher Education Philanthropy." 2006. Melisa.beeson@yahoo.com.

Bressi, D. E., University of Tennessee. "Women and Philanthropy: Making a Difference in Higher Education." Retrieved from ProQuest Digital Dissertations (AAT 9962245). 1999.

Diehl, Betsy Duncan, Hood College. "Philanthropy as an Expression of Feminism: Aligning a Traditionally Masculine Concept with a Decidedly Feminist Ideal." 2010.

Hubert, Lynn, University of Notre Dame. "Emerging Donors: The Reliability and Validity of the Survey of Women Donors at the University of Notre Dame." 2009.

Lovell, Jeanine M., St. Mary's University of Minnesota. "Women's Philanthropy Programs at Coeducational Colleges and Universities: Exploring the Concept at Luther College." June 2004. lovellje@luther.edu.

Pumphrey, Kathryn, University of Virginia Curry School of Education. "Characteristics That Motivate Alumnae Giving at a Research 1 Public University." 2004. kathryn.pumphrey@centrahealth.com.

Rhodes, Nichole D., University of Illinois Foundation. "Women's Philanthropy in Higher Education." 2006.

Simari, Rosalie, Hofstra University. "Philanthropy and Higher Education: Women as Donors." Retrieved from ProQuest Digital Dissertations (AAT 9530157). 1995.

Swift, Holly, Washington University. "Why Women Give—An Exploration of Women's Philanthropy." 2009.

Notes

ACKNOWLEDGMENTS

1. Center on Philanthropy at Indiana University, *Women and Philanthropy: Gaining Momentum*, Aug. 2005 and *Moving Women's Philanthropy Forward: Influences, Intent, Impact*, Nov. 2008.
2. Von Schlegell, A., and Fisher, J. *Women as Donors, Women as Philanthropists*. San Francisco: Jossey-Bass, 1998; Conry, J. *Women as Fundraisers: Their Experience in and Influence on an Emerging Profession*. San Francisco: Jossey-Bass, 1998; Taylor, M., and Shaw-Hardy, S. *The Transformative Power of Women's Philanthropy*. San Francisco: Jossey-Bass, 2005; Krotz, J. *Making Philanthropy Count: How Women Are Changing the World*. Women's Philanthropy Institute at the Center on Philanthropy at Indiana University, 2009. Available online: Shaw-Hardy, S. *Women's Giving Circles: Reflections from the Founders*, Women's Philanthropy Institute at the Center on Philanthropy at Indiana University, Aug. 2009; *Women's Philanthropy on Campus: A Handbook for Working with Women Donors*, Women's Philanthropy Institute at the Center on Philanthropy at Indiana University, Dec. 2009.

CHAPTER ONE: WOMEN ARE NOT LITTLE MEN

1. Falk, Edith. Personal interview. Aug. 8, 2009.
2. Gilligan, C. *In a Different Voice: Psychological Theory and Women's Development*. Boston: Harvard University Press, 1982.
3. Brin, D. "Men's Brains Shrink as They Age, Study Says." *Detroit News*, Apr. 11, 1996.
4. Ryan, J. "Brains of Women and Men Only Part of Story in Science." *San Francisco Chronicle*, Mar. 3, 2005.

5. Gramza, J. "Girls Vs. Boys at Math." *ScienCentral Archive.* [http://www .sciencentral.com/articles/view.php3?article_id=218393226&cat=1_5]. June 2, 2009.

6. Hyde, J., and Mertz, J. "Gender, Culture, and Mathematics Performance." [http://itp.wceruw.org/Hyde%20PNAS09.pdf]. April 2, 2009.

7. Barnett, R., and Rivers, C. "Data on Scientists Hushes Media Echo Chamber." *Women's enews.* Oct. 3, 2007.

8. Warner, J. "The Inner Lives of Men." *New York Times.* [http://warner. blogs.nytimes.com/2006/01/24/the-inner-lives-of-men/?scp=6&sq= corpus%20callosum%20larger%20in%20women&st=cse]. Jan. 24, 2006.

9. Tannen, D. *You Just Don't Understand: Women and Men in Conversation.* New York: Ballantine Books, 1991.

10. Curan, D. "Wooing Women." *Worth*, Apr. 2007.

11. Basch, Linda. Personal interview. Sept. 17, 2009.

12. *Women in Fund Management.* National Council on Research on Women. 2009.

13. Kavanagh, Thomas. Personal correspondence. Jan. 9, 2010.

14. "A Philanthropy of Their Own." *Giving Matters: Vanguard Charitable Endowment Program*, Spring 2004.

15. Brown, M., and Rooney, P. "Men, Women, X and Y." The Center on. Philanthropy at Indiana University. [http://www.google.com/search?client =safari&rls=en-us&q=center+on+philanthropy+younger+men+give+more+ like+women&ie=UTF-8&oe=UTF-8]. 2008.

16. Nichols, Judith. Personal correspondence. Dec. 10, 2009.

17. Tannen, D. *You Just Don't Understand: Women and Men in Conversation.* New York: Ballantine Books, 1991.

18. Ballard, K. "Marketing to Older Women: Ideas and Opinions from the Trenches." *Journal of Gift Planning*, Volume 4, Number 1, 1st Quarter 2000.

19. Conway-Welch, C. "Does Sex Make a Difference?" [http://www.nursing. vanderbilt.edu/dean/2003/04_uwc/full.pdf]. 2003.

20. Flessner, Bruce. Personal correspondence. Dec. 8, 2009.

21. "Philanthropy Among Business Women of Achievement: A Summary of Key Findings." National Foundation for Women Business Owners (now the Center for Women's Business Research), The Committee of 200. 1999.

22. Krotz, J. "Revolution REDUX." *Contribute: The People and Ideas of Giving*, Jan./Feb. 2008.

23. Lodewick, Christine and Philip. Personal correspondence. July 17, 2009.

24. Gienow, M. "Wanted: More Men Committing More Time to Charities." *Chronicle of Philanthropy*, Oct. 1, 2009.

25. Mesch, Debra. Personal interview. Aug. 29, 2009.

26. Slania, J. "A Woman's Touch." *Crain's Chicago Business.* [http://www.chicago business.com/cgi-bin/article.pl?article_id=19765&seenIt=1]. Mar. 31, 2003.

27. Pactor, Andrea. Personal interview. Aug. 27, 2009.

28. Swank, J. D. "What Women Want." *Target Analytics.* [http://www.black-baud.com/files/resources/downloads/WhitePaper_WhatWomenWant.pdf]. Mar. 2009.

29. Wasley, P. "New Research Sheds Light on Bequest Giving." *Chronicle of Philanthropy News Updates.* [http://philanthropy.com/news/updates/7698/ new-research-sheds-light-on-bequest-giving]. Apr. 1, 2009.

30. Association of Healthcare Philanthropy. [http://www.lllsearches.com/resources-dev-professionals/Development%20News%20Importance%20of%20Fundraising%20During%20Recession-mayjune2009.pdf]. May/June 2009.

31. Preston, C. "Women are More Inclined to Support Charities Overseas, Study Finds." *Chronicle of Philanthropy, Prospecting News and Tips on Fund Raising.* June 15, 2009.

32. Shaw-Hardy, S., and Stevens, C. *Women's Giving: A Generational Perspective.* Traverse City, MI: The Falconer Group Press, 2008.

33. Hall, C. "The Search for Significance." *Dallas Morning News.* [http://www.dallasnews.com/sharedcontent/dws/dn/latestnews/stories/122406dnbusaltruists.2b1c1b5.html]. Dec. 24, 2006.

34. Ibid.

35. Brown, M., and Rooney, P. "Men, Women, X and Y." The Center on Philanthropy at Indiana University. [http://www.google.com/search?client=safari&rls=en-us&q=center+on+philanthropy+younger+men+give+more+like+women&ie=UTF-8&oe=UTF-8]. 2008.

CHAPTER TWO: THE POWER OF THE PURSE

1. Schervish, P., and Havens, J. "The Markets May Be Down, But the Largest Intergenerational Transfer of Wealth in History Is Still Coming to Town." [www.bc.edu/research/cwp/meta-elements/pdf/41trillionpressrelease.pdf]. Jan. 6, 2003.

2. Brown, M., Rooney, P., Hao, H., and Miller, S. "Men, Women, X and Y." The Center on Philanthropy at Indiana University, 2007.

3. "Tomorrow's Philanthropist." Barclays Wealth in association with Ledbury Research. [http://www.barclayswealth.com/tomorrows-philanthropist.htm]. July 13, 2009.

4. Brown, M., Rooney, P., Hao, H., and Miller, S. "Men, Women, X and Y." The Center on Philanthropy at Indiana University, 2007.

5. Scully, M. "The Pendulum Swings." *Case/Currents Magazine*, July/Aug. 2009.

6. The Boston Consulting Group. [http://www.bcg.com/media/PressRelease Details.aspx?id=tcm:12–24864]. Sept. 28, 2009.

7. Dempsey, S. "Fidelity Study Finds Women Shaping the Future of Philanthropy." [http://www.onphilanthropy.com/site/News2?page=News Article&id=7819]. May 22, 2009.

8. Ibid.

9. McConnona, A., and Delevingne, L. *Bloomberg Businessweek.* "The 50 Top American Givers." [http://images.businessweek.com/ss/08/11/1124_biggest_givers/15.htm]. Dec. 8, 2009.

10. Mesch, et al. The Center on Philanthropy at Indiana University. [http://www.philanthropy.iupui.edu/PhilanthropicServices/WPI/docs/MeschResearch Agenda.pdf and http://www.philanthropy.iupui.edu/PremiumServices/Demo/current_research_copps.html]. 2007.

11. Benjamin, M. "Lorna Wendt." *U.S. News and World Report*, Mar. 30, 2005.

12. Ladd, J. "Giving It Away: The Challenge of Inheriting a Fortune." *Women's Times.* [http://www.classism.org/pdf/resources_giving.pdf]. Feb. 2000.

13. Shaw-Hardy, S., and Stevens, C. *Women's Giving: A Generational Perspective.* Traverse City, MI: The Falconer Group Press, 2008.

14. Justis, Jane Leighty. Personal correspondence. Jan. 4, 2010.

15. Krotz, J. "Revolution REDUX." *Contribute: The People and Ideas of Giving,* Jan./Feb. 2008.

16. Toppo, G., and DeBarros, A. "Women Feed the Jump in College Enrollment." *USA Today.* [http://www.usatoday.com/news/education/2007–09–12-census-college-enrollment_N.htm]. Aug. 12, 2007.

17. Witter, L., and Chen, L. *The She Spot: Why Women Are the Market for Changing the World and How to Reach Them.* San Francisco: Berrett-Koehler, 2008.

18. "High Net Worth Women and Men Investors." Center for Business Research. [http://www.nfwbo.org/press/details.php?id=47]. Dec. 10, 2002.

19. Gibbs, N. "What Women Want Now." *Time,* Oct. 26, 2009.

20. Muley, M. "The 85% Niche: The Power of Women of All Colors." [http://85percentniche.com/newsblog/?p=8]. June 6, 2008.

21. Stanley, T. *Millionaire Women Next Door.* Kansas City, KS: Andrews McMeel, 2004.

22. Engle, Debra. Personal interview. June 6, 2009.

23. Shaw-Hardy, S. *Women's Giving Circles: Reflections from the Founders.* Women's Philanthropy Institute at the Center on Philanthropy at Indiana University. [http://www.philanthropy.iupui.edu/PhilanthropicServices/WPI/docs/IU_GivingCircle_082809.pdf]. Aug. 2009.

24. Ketchum, Susan. Personal interview. Mar. 3, 2009.

25. Engle, Debra. Personal interview. June 6, 2009.

CHAPTER THREE: FROM BAG LADIES TO BOLD DIVAS: THE MEDIA AND CHANGING STEREOTYPES

1. Krotz, Joanna L. Personal correspondence. May 25, 2009.

2. Matthews, A. "Alma Maters Court Their Daughters." *New York Times Magazine,* Apr. 7, 1991.

3. Hall, H. "Cultivating Philanthropy by Women." *Chronicle of Philanthropy,* July 10, 1997.

4. Strout, E. "Courting Female Donors." *Chronicle of Higher Education,* July 6, 2007.

5. Miller, S., and Kelley, T. "Charity Belle: Colleen Willoughby Helps Women Give Money Away." *People,* Nov. 30, 1998.

6. Fiori, P. "New Orleans Now." *Town & Country,* June 2006.

7. Marzorati, G. "Editor's Notes." *New York Times Magazine,* Aug. 17, 2009, p. 8.

8. Forest, S. "Darla Moore: The Lady Is a B-School." *BusinessWeek,* Mar. 30, 1998.

9. Parker, A. "State's Future Moore's Passion." *Charleston Post and Courier*, Nov. 11, 2008.

10. Krotz, J. "Making Philanthropy Count: How Women Are Changing the World." Women's Philanthropy Institute at the Center on Philanthropy at Indiana University, May 2009.

11. Sellers, P. "The Business of Being Oprah." *Fortune*, Apr. 1, 2002.

12. "$15M Matching Fund Encourages Women to Make Their Mark at Harvard." *The Harvard University Gazette.* [http://www.news.harvard.edu/gazette/1998/05.21/15MMatchingFund.html]. May 21, 1998.

13. Witter, L., and Chen, L. *The She Spot: Why Women Are the Market for Changing the World and How to Reach Them.* San Francisco: Berrett-Koehler, 2008.

CHAPTER FOUR: WOMEN'S GIVING: THE SIX CS PLUS THREE

1. Shaw-Hardy, S., and Stevens, C. *Women's Giving: A Generational Perspective.* Traverse City, MI: The Falconer Group Press, 2008.

2. Shaw-Hardy, S. *Women's Giving Circles: Reflections from the Founders.* Women's Philanthropy Institute at the Center on Philanthropy at Indiana University. [http://www.philanthropy.iupui.edu/PhilanthropicServices/WPI/docs/IU_GivingCircle_082809.pdf]. Aug. 2009.

3. Roper-Batker, Lee. Personal correspondence. Jan. 4, 2010.

4. Molinary, Rosie. Personal correspondence. Dec. 8, 2009.

5. Annan, K. "To Save Africa, We Must Save Africa's Women." *Independent.* [http://www.independent.co.uk/opinion/commentators/kofi-annan-to-save-africa-we-must-save-africas-women-612484.html]. Jan. 1, 2003.

6. Cassin, Carolyn. Personal interview. June 26, 2009.

7. McCarthy, K. *Lady Bountiful Revisited.* Piscataway, NJ: Rutgers University Press, 1990.

8. Gary, Tracy. Personal interview. Sept. 14, 2009.

9. Gary, T., and Kohner, M. *Inspired Philanthropy: Creating a Giving Plan.* San Francisco: Jossey-Bass, 1998.

10. Gary, T. *Inspired Philanthropy: Your Step-by-Step Guide to Creating a Giving Plan and Leaving a Legacy* (2nd ed.). San Francisco: Jossey-Bass, 2008.

11. Gary, T. "Inspiring Youth to Bring About Change: Tools for the Generosity Generation." Inspired Legacies [www.inspiredlegacies.org/youthgiving/]. 2009.

12. Fox, Kye, and Paulson, Linda. Personal interview. June 18, 2009.

13. Fine, A. *Momentum: Igniting Social Change in the Connected Age.* San Francisco: Jossey-Bass, 2006.

14. Witter, L., and Chen, L. *The She Spot: Why Women Are the Market for Changing the World and How to Reach Them.* San Francisco: Berrett-Koehler, 2008.

15. McGurn, Linda. Personal interview. July 21, 2009.

16. Shaw-Hardy, S. *Women's Giving Circles: Reflections from the Founders.* Women's Philanthropy Institute at the Center on Philanthropy at Indiana University.   [http://www.philanthropy.iupui.edu/PhilanthropicServices/WPI/docs/IU_GivingCircle_082809.pdf]. Aug. 2009.

17. Ritchie, Debbie. Personal interview. July 16, 2009.

18. Moore, M. "Anita Roddick's Will Reveals She Donated Entire 51 Million Pound Fortune to Charity." *Telegraph.co.uk.* [http://www.telegraph.co.uk/news/uknews/1895768/Anita-Roddicks-will-reveals-she-donated-entire-51m-fortune-to-charity.html]. Apr. 16, 2008.

19. Hughes, D. "An Interview with Anita Roddick." *Share Guide.* [http://www.shareguide.com/Roddick.html].

20. Winter, Alison. Personal interview. June 22, 2009.

21. "2006 Prudential Financial's Study on Financial Experience and Behaviors Among Women." Prudential Financial. [http://www.aauwtexas.org/docs/2006PrudentialWomensFinancialStudy.pdf]. 2006.

22. Stanny, Barbara. Personal interview. July 16, 2009.

23. Stanny, B. *Prince Charming Isn't Coming: How Women Get Smart About Money.* New York: Penguin Group, 1997.

24. Dempsey, S. "Fidelity Study Finds Women Shaping the Future of Philanthropy."   [http://www.onphilanthropy.com/site/News2?page=NewsArticle&id=7819]. May 22, 2009.

25. Flessner, Bruce. Personal correspondence. Dec. 8, 2009.

26. Wasley, P. "Women Take the Lead in Couples' Charitable-Giving Decisions." *Chronicle of Philanthropy.* [http://philanthropy.com/news/updates/8307/women-take-the-lead-in-couples-charitable-giving-decisions]. May 19, 2009.

27. Lodewick, Christine and Philip. Personal correspondence. Dec. 15, 2009.

28. Reid, M. "Christine Lodewick Honored for Having Dr. King's Spirit." *The RidgefieldPress.com.*   [http://www.acorn-online.com/joomla15/index.php?view=article&id=18804%3Achristine-lodewick-honored-on-martin-luther-king-day&option=com_content&Itemid=767]. Jan. 24, 2009.

29. Womack, Cheryl. Personal correspondence. Dec. 18, 2009.

30. Ernst, A. "Q&A With Bobbi Brown: How to Give Back." *ForbesWoman Q&A.*   [http://www.forbes.com/2009/06/24/bobbi-brown-philanthropy-forbes-woman-q-and-dress-for-success.html]. June 25, 2009.

CHAPTER FIVE: STAGES, STYLES, AND GENERATIONS

1. Gajilan, A. "Scrap Mettle." CNNMoney.com. [http://money.cnn.com/magazines/fsb/fsb_archive/2005/12/01/8365394/index.htm]. Jan. 20, 2006.

2. Damen, Margaret May. "Women as Philanthropists: Gender and Generational Synergy for Effective Gift Planning." *Journal of Gift Planning.* [http://ohiononprofits.org/services.asp?page=ONN-51]. Dec. 2007.

3. Shaw-Hardy, S., and Stevens, C. *Women's Giving: A Generational Perspective.* Traverse City, MI: The Falconer Group Press, 2008.

4. Brown, M., Rooney, P., Hao, H., and Miller, S. "Men, Women, X and Y." The Center on Philanthropy at Indiana University, 2007.

5. "Margaret Lloyd of Kershaw County, Bolder Giving in Extraordinary Times." [http://www.boldergiving.org/inspiring_stories/profile.php?cat=ages& value=over60&id=56].

6. Brainy Quote. [http://www.brainyquote.com/quotes/authors/b/barbara_bush.html].

7. Barletta, M. *PrimeTime Women*. Chicago: Kaplan, 2007.

8. Hipp, Anna Kate. Personal interview. Aug. 13, 2009.

9. Brainy Quote. [http://www.brainyquote.com/quotes/authors/e/elizabeth_cady_stanton.html].

10. Stanley, T. "Women Baby Boomers May Boost Your Dollars." Ohio Association of Nonprofit Organizations, Sept. 2006.

11. Krotz, J. "Advancing Women's Philanthropy through Research." *Making Philanthropy Count*. Women's Philanthropy Institute at the Center on Philanthropy at Indiana University, May 2009.

12. Damen, M., and McCuistion, N. *Women, Wealth, and Giving: The Virtuous Legacy of the Boom Generation*. San Francisco: Wiley, 2010.

13. "Women as Philanthropists: Gender and Generational Synergy for Effective Gift Planning." *Journal of Gift Planning*. [http://ohiononprofits.org/services .asp?page=ONN-51]. Dec. 2007.

14. Weston, Cheryl Rosen. Personal interview. Sept. 9, 2009.

15. Brainy Quote. [http://www.brainyquote.com/quotes/authors/h/hillary_clinton_2.html].

16. Goldseker, S. "Beyond Duty and Obligation." *Council on Foundations, Foundation News & Commentary*. Jan./Feb. 2006.

17. Marquardt, K. "New Money." *US News & World Report*, Aug. 12, 2009.

18. Terrell, Tanya Jones. Personal interview. Aug. 14, 2009.

19. Reed, Candace Dodson. Personal interview. Aug. 17, 2009.

20. Grant, Sheri Reid. Personal interview. Sept. 21, 2009.

21. Harrin, L. "10 Tips for Managing Gen Y." *The Glass Hammer*. [http://www.the glasshammer.com/news/2009/09/02/10-tips-for-managing-gen-y/]. Aug. 2, 2009.

22. Bay, W. "What a Generation Y Woman Really Wants?" *Huffington Post*. [http://www.huffingtonpost.com/willow-bay/what-a-generation-y-woman_b_44132.html]. Mar. 23, 2007.

23. Goldseker, Sharna. Personal interview. Aug. 28, 2009.

24. Azout, Sara. Personal interview. Sept. 24, 2009.

25. Walter, Kristin. Personal interview. Sept. 17, 2009.

26. Madzel, Melissa. Personal interview. Aug. 17, 2009.

27. "Five Things Your Nonprofit Needs to Know About Web 2.0 Donors." Nonprofit Tech 2.0: A Social Media Guide for Nonprofits. [http://nonprof-itorgs.wordpress.com/]. Sept. 17, 2009.

CHAPTER SIX: NONPROFITS' FUTURE: GENDER-SENSITIVE DEVELOPMENT

1. Scully, M. K. "The Pendulum Swings." *Council for Advancement and Support of Education Currents*, July/Aug. 2009.

2. Crabtree, Elizabeth. Personal interview. July 10, 2009.

3. Sharpe, Robert. Personal interview. July 13, 2009.
4. Mead, Nancy. Personal interview. Oct. 8, 2009.
5. Larson, David. Personal interview. July 13, 2009.
6. "I Am Powerful." CARE Web site. [http://mycare.org/site]. July 2009.
7. Moline, Patricia. Personal interview. July 9, 2009.
8. Brown, Marion. Personal interview. Oct. 21, 2009.
9. Gaudiani, Claire. Personal interview. July 17, 2009.
10. Jackson, Patricia. Personal interview. Aug. 26, 2009.
11. Wayson, Tracy. Personal interview. July 8, 2009.
12. Rowland Frautschi, Pleasant. Personal correspondence. Feb. 5, 2010.
13. Flessner, Bruce. Personal interview. July 10, 2009.
14. Weber, Erick. Personal interview. July 8, 2009.
15. Henze, Lawrence. Personal interview. July 8, 2009.
16. *Making Philanthropy Count: How Women Are Changing the World.* Women's Philanthropy Institute at the Center on Philanthropy at Indiana University, May 2009.
17. Hubert, L. M. "Emerging Donors: The Reliability and Validity of the Survey of Women Donors at the University of Notre Dame." Department of Educational Leadership and Policy Analysis, College of Education, University of Missouri–Columbia, 2009.
18. "The 2008 Study of High Net Worth Philanthropy: Issues Driving Charitable Activities Among Affluent Households." Center on Philanthropy at Indiana University, Mar. 2009.
19. Altinkemer, Cheryl. Personal interview. July 20, 2009.
20. Picus, Joy. Personal interview. Aug. 4, 2009.
21. Miles, Barbara. Personal correspondence. Jan. 4, 2010.
22. Collier, C. W. *Wealth in Families.* Cambridge, MA: Harvard University Press, 2006.
23. Remmer, Ellen. Personal interview. Feb. 4, 2010.
24. *The Art and Science of Donor Development Workbook.* Advancement Resources, LLC, 2006.

CHAPTER SEVEN: BRINGING WOMEN TO THE TABLE

1. Women in Philanthropy. [http://www.womeninphilanthropy.com/].
2. Thorne, Dune. Personal interview. Sept. 18, 2009.
3. Bach, D. *Smart Women Finish Rich: 9 Steps to Achieving Financial Security and Funding Your Dreams.* New York: Broadway, 2002.
4. Dempsey, S. "Fidelity Study Finds Women Shaping the Future." [http://www.onphilanthropy.com/site/News2?page=NewsArticle&id=7819]. May 22, 2009.
5. [http://www.news.cornell.edu/chronicle/96/2.15.96/adams.html].
6. Miles, Joyce. Personal correspondence. Dec. 7, 2009.
7. Morris, M. "Purdue Alumni Give to Consumer and Family Sciences to Help Families." [http://news.uns.purdue.edu/html3month/2006/060407.Mullen.gift.html]. Apr. 6, 2006.

8. Grabmeire, J. "Better Grades and Greater Incentives Help Explain Why Women Outpace Men in College Degrees." Ohio State University Research. [http://researchnews.osu.edu/archive/womcolge.htm]. Sept. 19, 2006.

9. Buchmann, C., and DiPrete, T. A. "The Growing Female Advantage in College Completion: The Role of Parental Resources and Academic Achievement." *American Sociological Review*, 2006.

10. DiPrete, T. A., and Buchmann, C. "Gender Specific Trends in the Value of Education and the Emerging Gender Gap in College Completion." *Demography*, 2006.

11. Oppedisano, J. "Leaving Men Behind: Women Go to College in Ever-Greater Numbers." *Women in Management Review*, 2004.

12. "Women in the Professions." Bureau of Labor Statistics. [http://www.bls.gov/opub/ted/2006/dec/wk1/art02.htm]. Dec. 5, 2006.

13. Ibid.

14. Shipman, C., and Kay, K. "Women Will Rule Business." *Time* in partnership with CNN. [http://www.time.com/time/specials/packages/printout/0,29239,1898024_1898023_1898078,00.html]. May 14, 2009.

15. Hesselbein, F., and Collins, J. *Hesselbein on Leadership*. San Francisco: Jossey-Bass, 2002.

16. Helgesen, S. *The Female Advantage*. New York: Broadway Business, 1991.

17. Levesque, C. "Highlights of a Leadership Discussion with Frances Hesselbein." American Society of Association Executives. [http://www.asaecenter.org/files/FileDownloads/Hesselbein_Summary.pdf]. Jan. 28, 2004.

18. Janis, I. L. *Groupthink: Psychological Studies of Policy Decisions and Fiascoes* (2nd ed.) New York: Houghton Mifflin, 1982.

19. Shipman, C., and Kay, K. "Women Will Rule Business." *Time* in partnership with CNN. [http://www.time.com/time/specials/packages/printout/0,29239,1898024_1898023_1898078,00.html]. May 14, 2009.

20. Biskupic, J. "Ginsburg: Court needs another woman." *USA Today*. [http://www.usatoday.com/news/washington/judicial/2009–05–05-ruthginsburg_N.htm]. May 5, 2009.

21. Rooney, Patrick. Personal correspondence. June 1, 2009.

22. Fouke, Dr. Janie. Personal correspondence. Jan. 1, 2010.

23. Peters, T. *Re-Imagine! Business Excellence in a Disruptive Age*. New York: DK Publishing, 2003.

24. Milk, L., and Ryan, E. "2006 Washingtonians of the Year: Anne Mosle." Washingtonian.com., Jan. 31, 2007.

25. McGurn, Linda. Personal interview. July 21, 2009.

26. Lyden, J. "Women Dominate New Hampshire State Senate." *All Things Considered*. [http://www.npr.org/templates/story/story.php?storyId=96799349]. Nov. 9, 2008.

27. West, N. "Women More Likely Than Men to Volunteer." RTI International. [http://www.rti.org/news.cfm?nav=268&objectid=429C1F1D-0B08–428E-A69F74EEB74EA1DB]. June 6, 2006.

28. Minter, M. "Seeking Volunteer Leaders: Tips for Increasing Women's Giving." On Philanthropy. [http://www.onphilanthropy.com/site/News2?page=NewsArticle&id=7737]. Mar. 5, 2009.

29. Nonprofit Governance Index 2007, BoardSource. [http://www.boardsource.org/UserFiles/File/Research/GovIndex-2007.pdf]. 2007.

30. Krotz, J. "Revolution REDUX." *Contribute: The People and Ideas of Giving.* Jan./Feb. 2008.

31. Graybow, M. "Female Directors Improve Financial Results." MSN.money, Oct. 1, 2007.

32. Berkman, J. "Philanthropy from Venus Differs from Philanthropy from Mars." JewishJournal.com. [http://www.jewishjournal.com/philanthropy/article/philanthropy_from_venus_differs_from_philanthropy_from_mars_20081118/]. Nov. 18, 2009.

33. Krotz, J. L. *The Guide to Intelligent Giving: Make a Difference in the World— And in Your Own.* New York: Hearst, 2009.

34. Shaw-Hardy, S., Stevens, C., and Taylor, M. "The Effect of a Global Recession on Women's Giving." [http://www.philwomen.com]. 2009.

Chapter Eight: Women's Philanthropy Programs and Giving Circles

1. Weisberg, Doris. Personal interview. Oct. 3, 2009.

2. Jorgensen, Judy. Personal correspondence. July 30, 2009.

3. Jackson, Patricia. Personal interview. Aug. 26, 2009.

4. Altinkemer, Cheryl. Personal interview. July 20, 2009.

5. McGurn, Linda. Personal interview. July 21, 2009.

6. Gilliams, L. Virginia Tech University Survey of Women's Philanthropy Programs in Higher Education, Aug. 14, 2009.

7. Lovell, Jeanie. Personal correspondence. Oct. 6, 2009.

8. Hubert, Lynn. Personal interview. July 17, 2009.

9. University of California–Los Angeles Women & Philanthropy Web site. [http://women.support.ucla.edu]. Aug. 2009.

10. Freiberg, Kristen. Personal interview. July 9, 2009.

11. "Making Philanthropy Count: How Women Are Changing the World." Women's Philanthropy Institute at the Center on Philanthropy at Indiana University, May 2009.

12. Ibid.

13. Learned, A., and Johnson, L. *Don't Think Pink: What Really Makes Women Buy—and How to Increase Your Share of This Crucial Market.* New York: AMACOM, 2004.

14. Silverman, M., and Sayre, K. "The Female Economy." *Harvard Business Review*, Sept. 2009.

15. Farella, N. Rutgers Survey of Women's Philanthropy Programs in Higher Education, Aug. 5, 2009.

16. Biles, Tracey. Personal correspondence. Aug. 3, 2009.

17. Farella, Rutgers Survey.

18. "Making Philanthropy Count: How Women Are Changing the World." Women's Philanthropy Institute at the Center on Philanthropy at Indiana University, May 2009.

19. Ibid.

20. University of Virginia Web site. [http//campaign.virginia.edu/site]. Sept. 2009.

21. Shaw-Hardy, S. *Women's Giving Circles: Reflections from the Founders.* Women's Philanthropy Institute at the Center on Philanthropy at Indiana University. [http://www.philanthropy.iupui.edu/PhilanthropicServices/WPI/docs/IU_GivingCircle_082809.pdf]. Aug. 2009.

22. Tempel, Eugene. Personal interview. Dec. 18, 2009.

23. Miller, S., and Kelley, T. "Charity Belle: Colleen Willoughby Helps Women Give Money Away." *People*, Nov. 30, 1998.

24. Gladwell, M. *The Tipping Point: How Little Things Can Make a Big Difference.* New York: Back Bay Books, 2002.

25. Shaw-Hardy, S. C. *Creating a Women's Giving Circle.* Women's Philanthropy Institute. [http://www.philanthropy.iupui.edu/Products/product_list.aspx]. 2000.

26. Strup, Linda. Personal interview. Jan. 4, 2010.

27. The Women's Giving Circle of Howard County Web site. [www.womensgivingcircle.org].

28. Moscow Giving Circle Web site. [www.moscowgivingcircle.org].

29. Giving Circles Network Web site. [www.givingcircles.org].

30. The Omaha Venture Group Web site. [www.omahacf.org].

31. Chapman, H. "The Growth of Giving Circles." *The Glass Hammer.* [http://www.theglasshammer.com/news/2009/01/02/the-growth-of-giving-circles/]. Jan. 2, 2009.

32. Eikenberry, Angela. Personal interview. Dec. 15, 2009.

33. Bettger, Sandy. Personal correspondence. Dec. 15, 2009.

CHAPTER NINE: TAUGHT OR CAUGHT: DONOR EDUCATION

1. Krotz, J. "Revolution REDUX." *Contribute: The People and Ideas of Giving.* Jan./Feb. 2008.

2. Women Moving Millions. [http://www.womenmovingmillions.net/].

3. "Merrill Lynch Investment Managers (MLIM) Survey Finds When it Comes to Investing, Gender a Strong Influence on Behavior." Merrill Lynch. [http://www.ml.com/index.asp?id=7695_7696_8149_46028_47486_47543]. April 18, 2005.

4. Burkhart, Lorene. Personal correspondence. Dec. 17, 2009.

5. Ibid.

6. Gaudiani, Claire. Personal correspondence. Dec. 17, 2009.

7. Thorne, Dune. Personal interview. Sept. 18, 2009.

8. Descano, Linda. Personal interview. Jan. 1, 2010.

9. Brainy Quote. [www.brainyquote.com/quotes/quotes/e/eleanorroo393444.html].

10. Gary, T. *Inspired Philanthropy: Your Step-by-Step Guide to Creating a Giving Plan and Leaving a Legacy.* San Francisco: Jossey-Bass, 2008.

11. Ellinger, C. and A. *The Bolder Giving Workbook.* [http://www.boldergiving.org/programs/workbook.php]. Arlington, MA: Bolder Giving, 2010.

12. Rosenberg, C. *Wealthy and Wise.* Boston: Little, Brown, 1994.

13. "Annual Donations Can Raise $27.5 Billion." Newtithing Group. [http://www.charitynavigator.org/index.cfm/bay/content.view/cpid/523]. Oct. 11, 2006.

14. "A Biographical Sketch of Mary Elizabeth Garrett." The Johns Hopkins University School of Medicine. [http://www.medicalarchives.jhmi.edu/garrett/biography.htm]. 2010.

15. "Women—Or the Female Factor." Johns Hopkins Medicine. [http://www.hopkinsmedicine.org/about/history/history6.html]. 2010.

16. Strout, E. "Courting Female Donors." *Chronicle of Higher Education*, July 6, 2007.

17. Miles, Joyce. Personal correspondence. Dec. 7, 2009.

18. Gary, Tracy. Personal interview. Sept. 14, 2009.

19. Stergiou, C. "Kay Sprinkel Grace, America's doyenne of board excellence and mission development." *SOFII*. [http://www.sofii.org/active%20site/Members%20area/GG5KaySprinkelGrace.html]. 2010.

20. Bradshaw, Reene. Personal interview. Sept. 8, 2009.

21. Ghrist, Liz. Personal interview. Aug. 13, 2009.

22. Orvañanos de Rovzar, Marcela. Personal interview. Sept. 14, 2009.

23. Basch, Linda. Personal interview. Sept. 17, 2009.

24. Hall, S. "Six Principles of Women's High-Engagement Philanthropy." Tactical Philanthropy Advisors. [http://tacticalphilanthropy.com/2009/05/six-principles-of-womens-high-engagement-philanthropy]. May 27, 2009.

25. Verhovek, Lisa. Personal interview. July 13, 2009.

Chapter Ten: Bold Women Giving Boldly: New Frontiers of Women's Philanthropy

1. Women Moving Millions. [http://www.womenmovingmillions.net/].

2. Brill, B. "Women in Philanthropy." *Forbes*. [http://www.forbes.com/2009/08/18/brill-women-philanthropy-intelligent-investing-wealth.html]. Aug. 18, 2009.

3. Mieszkowski, K. "Learning and Change—Catherine Muther." *Fast Company*. [http://www.fastcompany.com/magazine/30/muther.html]. Dec. 19, 2007.

4. Shriver, M. *The Shriver Report*. A Study by Maria Shriver and the Center for American Progress. [http://www.awomansnation.com/quotes.php]. Oct. 2009.

5. Talburtt, Peg. Personal interview. Aug. 11, 2009.

6. Minter, Michele. Personal interview. Sept. 17, 2009.

7. Shaw-Hardy, S. *Women's Giving Circles: Reflections from the Founders*. Women's Philanthropy Institute at the Center on Philanthropy at Indiana University. [http://www.philanthropy.iupui.edu/PhilanthropicServices/WPI/docs/IU_GivingCircle_082809.pdf]. Aug. 2009.

8. Malveaux, J. "Black Women and Philanthropy." [http://www.juliannemalveaux.com/downloads/black_women.pdf]. June 2005.

9. Minter, M. "Philanthropy and Impactful Giving." Empowerment Summit for Women, Women's Philanthropy Institute. Oct. 8, 2009.

10. Shaw-Hardy, S. *Women's Giving Circles: Reflections from the Founders.* Women's Philanthropy Institute at the Center on Philanthropy at Indiana University. [http://www.philanthropy.iupui.edu/PhilanthropicServices/WPI/docs/IU_GivingCircle_082809.pdf]. Aug. 2009.

11. Africa, S. "Growth Figures Expose Government's Fake Stimulus, Limits of Relying on Remittances." IBON Foundation. [http://info.ibon.org/ibon_features.php]. Nov. 29, 2009.

12. Osborne, Karen. Personal interview. Aug. 31, 2009.

13. "Expanding the Circle: An African American and Asian Women's Perspective on Giving." A collaboration of the Boston Women's Fund, Haymarket People's Fund and the Women's Theological Center, 2007.

14. Maehara, Paulette. Personal interview. Aug. 11, 2009.

15. Joslyn, M. "A Man's World." *The Chronicle of Philanthropy*, Sept. 17, 2009.

16. Basch, Linda. Personal interview. Sept. 17, 2009.

17. Karimzadeh, M. "Donna's 'Urban Zen': Her Vision for Well-being." WWD.com. [http://www.blingdomofgod.com/urbanzen.pdf]. Apr. 25, 2007.

18. Riddle, K. "Capturing the Moments." Hospice of the Western Reserve. [http://www.hospicewr.org/uploads/pdf/news/A-G/Currents_051806.pdf]. May 18, 2006.

19. Wilson, Trisha. Personal correspondence. Jan. 4, 2010.

20. Rairez, M. "Photos of Dying Children Win Hearts of Many." *Seattle Times*, Sept. 7, 2005.

21. Hall, C. "Dallas Designer Is a 'Rock Star' Overseas: Trisha Wilson Balances Ritzy Career with Healing Efforts in S. Africa." *Dallas Morning News.* [http://www.aegis.com/news/dmn/2006/DM060301.html]. Mar. 5, 2006.

22. Picus, Joy. Personal interview. Aug. 4, 2009.

23. Rockefeller Philanthropy Advisors. [http://rockpa.org/special_programs/muslim-womens-fund/].

24. Sellers, P. "Melinda Gates Goes Public." *Fortune*, Jan. 7, 2008.

25. Dempsey, S. "Fidelity Study Finds Women Shaping the Future." [http://www.onphilanthropy.com/site/News2?page=NewsArticle&id=7819]. May 22, 2009.

26. Remmer, E. "TPI's Remmer Kicks Off Philadelphia Fdn. Women's Philanthropy Network." *Philanthropic Initiative*, Aug. 27, 2008.

27. Ibid.

28. "The Dynamics of Women and Family Philanthropy." *The Transformative Power of Women's Philanthropy.* Council on Foundations, Winter, 2005.

29. Shaw-Hardy, S. *Women's Giving Circles: Reflections from the Founders.* Women's Philanthropy Institute at the Center on Philanthropy at Indiana University. [http://www.philanthropy.iupui.edu/PhilanthropicServices/WPI/docs/IU_GivingCircle_082809.pdf]. Aug. 2009.

30. "Women Unite to Cut Into Hedge Funds' Male Thicket." *Reuters News.* [http://www.100womeninhedgefunds.org/pages/in_the_press.php]. Feb. 6, 2002.

31. Ghandi, M. Thinkexist.com. [http://thinkexist.com/quotation/we_must_become_the_change_we_want_to_see/11442.html].

32. Edwards, M. "Transformative Leadership Employs Spirituality for Social Change." *Chronicle of Philanthropy*, Oct. 1, 2009.
33. Ibid.
34. Maehara, Paulette. Personal interview. Aug. 11, 2009.
35. Grumm, Chris. Personal interview. Aug. 18, 2009.
36. Baretta, Bridget. Personal interview. Jan. 17, 2010.
37. Krotz, Joanna L. Personal interview. May 25, 2009.
38. Roper-Batker, Lee. Personal correspondence. Jan. 4, 2009.
39. Lee, B. "A Woman's Place Is in the White House." *Albany Times Union*, Mar. 3, 2006.
40. Redorbit. [http://www.redorbit.com/news/entertainment/1655838/music_center_of_los_angeles_county_announces_20_million_gift/].
41. Kennedy, J. F. "Poetry and Power." *Atlantic*, Feb. 1964.
42. Grumm, Chris. Personal interview. Aug. 18, 2009.
43. Stepanek, M. "60 Seconds with Philanthropist Sheila Johnson." *Contribute*. [http://www.contributemedia.com/people_details.php?id=203].
44. The Goromonzi Project. [http://www.goromonziproject.org/].
45. Shaw, Janet. Personal correspondence. Jan. 8, 2010.
46. Lampman, J. "Researchers Say Giving Leads to a Healthier, Happier Life." *Christian Science Monitor*, July 25, 2007.

Chapter Eleven: The Age of Women's Philanthropy

1. About.com. Women's History. [http://womenshistory.about.com/od/quotes/a/jane_addams.htm].
2. Solomon, D. "Questions for Ellen Johnson Sirleaf, Madame President." *New York Times Magazine*, Aug. 23, 2009.
3. Shaw-Hardy, S., and Stevens, C. *Women's Giving: A Generational Perspective.* Traverse City, MI: Falconer Group Press, 2008.
4. Hirsch, Liz Levitt. Personal interview. Sept. 29, 2009.
5. Kristof, N., and WuDunn, S. *Half the Sky: Turning Oppression into Opportunity for Women Worldwide.* New York: Knopf, 2009.
6. Weeks, Julie. Personal interview. Sept. 28, 2009.
7. Elkington, John. *Cannibals with Forks: The Triple Bottom Line of 21st Century Business.* Briolola Island, BC, Canada: New Society Publishers, 1998.
8. Orvañanos de Rovzar, Marcela. Personal interview. Sept. 14, 2009.
9. Basch, Linda. Personal interview. Sept. 17, 2009.
10. "Education and Development: Why Is Education Important to Development?" The World Bank. [http://web.worldbank.org/WBSITE/EXTERNAL/TOPICS/EXTEDUCATION/0,,contentMDK:20591648~menuPK:1463858~pagePK:148956~piPK:216618~theSitePK:282386,00.html]. 2009.
11. Belkin, L. "The Power of the Purse." *New York Times Magazine*, Sept. 23, 2009.
12. "Raising Women's Voices for the Health Care We Need." A collaborative initiative of the Avery Institute for Social Change, MergerWatch Project of

Community Catalyst, and the National Women's Health Network. [http://www.raisingwomensvoices.net/storage/pdf_files/RWV-Principles-4.07.08.pdf]. Apr. 7, 2008.

13. Condon, S. "Michelle Obama: Health Care Is a Women's Issue." CBS News Blogs. [http://www.cbsnews.com/blogs/2009/09/18/politics/politicalhot-sheet/entry5320221.shtml]. Sept. 28, 2009.

14. Seattle Children's Hospital. [http://www.seattlechildrens.org/about/history/].

15. Abbott, P., Wallace, C., and Tyler, M. *An Introduction to Sociology: Feminist Perspectives.* New York: Routledge, Taylor & Francis Group, 2005.

16. Ellinger, Anne. Personal interview. Aug. 20, 2009.

17. "Bolder Giving in Extraordinary Times." *FUNdraising Opinions, News & Successes.* [http://fundraisinggoodtimes.wordpress.com/tag/women-in-philanthropy-and-fundraising/]. July 26, 2009.

18. Shriver, M. *The Shriver Report.* A Study by Maria Shriver and the Center for American Progress. [http://www.awomansnation.com/quotes.php]. Oct. 2009.

19. Kawasaki, G. "Hitting the She Spot: How to Market to Women as Consumers and Social Change Agents." Open Forum. [http://www.openforum.com/idea-hub/topics/the-world/article/hitting-the-she-spot-how-to-market-to-women-as-consumers-and-social-change-agents-guy-kawasaki]. June 22, 2009.

20. The Boston Consulting Group. [http://www.bcg.com/media/Press ReleaseDetails.aspx?id=tcm:12–24864]. Sept. 28, 2009.

21. Mesch, Debra. Personal interview. Aug. 27, 2009.

Index

D

211; life experiences relevant to, 65–91, 122–123; new frontiers of, 181–204; new models of, xiv, 28–29; overview of, xiii–xvi, xviii–xix; policy change and, 182–183, 198–199; Prime Time, 74–76; resistance to, xv, 39–40; stories about, 38–39, 42; Traditionalist, 71; transformational aspects of, 205–213; women's earning power and, xiv, 21–22, 211

Women's philanthropy initiatives. *See* Women's philanthropy programs

Women's Philanthropy Institute (WPI), xvi, 13, 36, 70, 140, 148, 177, 195, 209–210

Women's philanthropy movement (modern): diversity in, 183–187; future and trends of, 181–204, 205–213; origins of, 28; role of the media in, 35–38, 41–42; women's motivations and, 43

Women's Philanthropy Network. *See* Women's Philanthropy Institute

Women's philanthropy programs, 133–147; building, 141–147; business plan for, 143; constituent involvement in, 146–147; core advisory group for, 143; defined, 134; educational opportunities in, 138; evaluation of, 143; failure of,

components of, 141–142; goals and purposes of, 134, 135–141, 143; in higher education, 36, 52–54, 133–147; leadership in, 136–138, 143, 145; listening in, 144–145; networking and friendship in, 138–140; philanthropic emphasis of, 135–136; popularity of, 134; regional groups of, 145–146; special goals in, 147; successful, components of, 142–147

Women's philanthropy research. *See* Research, women's philanthropy

Women's Theological Center, 184

Woodward, J., 71

World Bank, 208

World War II, 73

Worthy lifestyle, 69

WuDunn, S., 37, 206

Y

You Just Don't Understand (Tannen), 6

Youth giving circle, 49

Z

Zehner, J., 7

Zimbabwe, 201

Zonta, 123